AN OUTLINE OF
THE BIBLE
BOOK BY BOOK

Benson Y. Landis

BARNES & NOBLE BOOKS

A DIVISION OF HARPER & ROW, PUBLISHERS

New York, Grand Rapids, Philadelphia, San Francisco
St. Louis, London, Singapore, Sydney, Tokyo, Toronto

PREFACE

This book presents an outline and a summary of every book in the King James Bible, with information on authorship, historical background, and literary style.

The purpose is to aid in the various ways that people read and study the Bible. The work is intended for lay readers, students in schools and colleges, any who seek to understand, and all who may find it of interest.

The arrangement, names of books, and the text generally quoted in this book are those of the King James (Authorized) Version, because it is the most widely used Bible in the English-speaking world. More recent translations, however, are clearer in many instances, and sometimes these are noted or quoted for comparison.

This outline, with its selected quotations, is made by a layman who has consulted scholars, drawn on his own reading, and made his own estimates of the interests of readers. Obviously a lay author must sometimes choose among the conclusions of disagreeing scholars, or indicate the range of their opinions. (For example, events in the life of the Apostle Paul have been variously dated.) On a number of controversial points, the different theories have been noted, with the evidence adduced for them.

The book also provides a general description of the contents, composition, and arrangement of the Bible, a relatively simple chronology, a glossary defining many Biblical terms, and other supplements as aids to study.

BENSON Y. LANDIS

TABLE OF CONTENTS

MAPS

NOTE: These are simplified maps prepared especially for this book to show places of Biblical significance. The maps of Jerusalem and the Temple are based on more detailed maps in *Shepherd's Historical Atlas,* 9th edition (New York: Barnes & Noble, Inc., 1964).

THE BIBLE: A GENERAL DESCRIPTION

The Bible is the word of God. It is a record of the unique spiritual experience of a people. It is the most powerful book in the world. It is the most quoted book. It is the best-selling book of all time. It has been called the unread best-seller—but this assertion is only partly true, for the Bible has been read by countless multitudes of people, young and old, rich and poor, mighty and humble alike. Dramatists draw frequently upon it for their themes. The Bible is the basis of great liturgies for worship. It is read both at religious services and at other public meetings. It furnishes texts and ideas for sermons. It is studied in religious schools, such as Sunday schools, and in secular schools and colleges. It has inspired the loftiest moral sentiments and the greatest works of art and literature. People read it for their own devotions. It is a means of missions of the churches. It is printed in newspapers, read on radio and television programs, quoted in conversation and public speaking more often than any other source. It is read by all sorts and conditions of people for all kinds of reasons.

The Bible is admired, loved, and revered. It is praised as a reservoir of infinite wisdom and inspiration. It contains religious and moral teachings to which even the worst transgressors feel obliged to give lip service. Yet, on important matters of belief, both religious leaders and the masses of mankind differ. Also, the Bible is at times called unbelievable and unwholesome. It has been disliked, ignored, despised, and ridiculed. It has been used by men and women for low motives as well as high. Yes, the Bible is many things to the varied peoples of the world.

Contents of the Bible

The Bible is loosely called a book, but actually it is a collection, or library, of books. It contains history, laws, poetry, biography, stories, letters, revelations. One version, called authorized, is associated with the name of King James I of England because he summoned a conference of churchmen in 1604 which proposed the revision; it has been considered the most beautiful writing ever produced in the English language. The Bible is studied as a great work of literature in thousands of colleges. It is consulted as a source of information by archeologists. Today, as in the past, eminent scholars are devoting their lives to the task of interpreting and translating the Bible.

The word Bible is derived from the Greek *biblos*, the name for part of an ancient plant used in making paper books. The Greek word *biblia*, meaning "the books," referred to the Scriptures, the accepted sacred volumes of revealed truth. Then the Greek *biblia* (plural) became the Latin *biblia* (feminine singular), from which came our English word, *Bible*.

Early in the fifth century A.D., Christian Church leaders decided upon the list of books to be included in the Bible. These writings were accepted as inspired and authoritative and became known among scholars as the "canon." Greek and Latin translations of the Old Testament included fourteen disputed books, the Apocrypha. During the sixteenth century the Protestant reformers separated these books from the others and made them an Appendix to the Old Testament. Some Protestant versions thereafter placed the Apocrypha between the Old and New Testaments. Catholic Bibles continued to follow the Latin translation except in the cases of the Third and Fourth Books of Esdras, which were not accepted as authoritative. For the Jews the Bible consisted of 24 books (as the Old Testament) under the title *The Holy Scriptures,* but some books were divided into two volumes during the sixteenth century, making the total 28 books. The modern Protestant Bible has 66 books, to which the Apocrypha may or may not be added. The Roman Catholic Bible, which includes Apocryphal books, has a total of 73 volumes.

Composition and Arrangement of the Bible

The Biblical documents were composed originally in the Hebrew, Aramaic, and Greek languages. Almost all of the Old Testament was written in Hebrew. (Portions of Daniel and Ezra and one verse in Jeremiah [10:11] were in Aramaic.) Jesus probably spoke Aramaic, which was the common language in Palestine when he lived. Thus there is an Aramaic basis for the Gospels, particularly the first three, and for parts of Acts. The rest of the New Testament was written in Greek.

(Note that the word Testament comes from the Latin *testa-*

mentum, which in the Biblical tradition means not "will" but "covenant.")

The Old Testament. The Old Testament (Covenant) was evidence of, and a product of, the spiritual experience of the Jews. Religious faith came first; because of its vitality, its expression in literature was the natural outcome.

The 39 Old Testament books in the Authorized or King James Version are grouped as follows: *The Law,* 5 (Genesis, Exodus, Leviticus, Numbers, Deuteronomy); *Historical Books,* 12 (Joshua, Judges, Ruth, I and II Samuel, I and II Kings, I and II Chronicles, Ezra, Nehemiah, Esther); *Poetical Books,* 5 (Job, Psalms, Proverbs, Ecclesiastes, Song of Solomon); *Prophetical Books,* 17 (*Major,* because long, 5: Isaiah, Jeremiah, Lamentations, Ezekiel, Daniel; *Minor,* because short, 12: Hosea, Joel, Amos, Obadiah, Jonah, Micah, Nahum, Habakkuk, Zephaniah, Haggai, Zechariah, Malachi). (The arrangement of the Hebrew Scriptures is noted on p. 175.)

The New Testament. The New Testament (Covenant) also followed spiritual experience. Jesus lived, taught, and selected disciples who accompanied him on his journeys, were present at his crucifixion, and believed that he had risen from the dead. The influence of Jesus and of his followers so impressed others that there was a gathered group with an identity and integrity of its own before a word of what is now the New Testament was ever put down. The earliest book of the New Testament may have been in the form of a letter from an apostle to a newly organized church, giving advice on significant issues.

All books of the New Testament were probably by Jewish converts, although there is a tradition, accepted by some scholars, that the author of Luke and Acts was a Greek Gentile.

The 27 books in the King James Version are grouped as follows: *Gospels,* 4 (Matthew, Mark, Luke, and John); *History,* 1 (Acts); *Epistles,* 21 (Romans, I and II Corinthians, Galatians, Ephesians, Philippians, Colossians, I and II Thessalonians, I and II Timothy, Titus, Philemon, Hebrews, James, I and II Peter, I, II, and III John, Jude); and *the Apocalypse* (Revelation).

Palestine, Land of the Bible

Biblical Palestine, the setting for most of the writings, had an area of only about ten thousand square miles, somewhat larger than New Jersey or Massachusetts. The land forms the western frontier of the large Syrian Desert, which extends as a plateau eastward to the Euphrates River and the Persian Gulf. The geographic appearance of the area was one of isolation from the rest of the inhabited world. But ancient trade and military routes from the Nile to the Euphrates crossed the country, and thus the people were open to intercourse with, and influence from, other nations.

The largest territory ever under control of Biblical Israel existed from about 1002 to 922 B.C., during the time of Kings David and Solomon. The kingdom then stretched from Kadesh (a city in the north on the Orontes River) southward to the Arabian Desert and westward to the Philistine Mediterranean coast. At that time Palestine may have had a population of about 1,800,000 persons, while the neighboring tribes or groups with an area three times that of Palestine may have had a population of about 3,000,000. (Note that in the days of Jesus the southern part of Palestine, known as Judaea, was under the rule of the Roman Empire. Galilee, in northern Palestine, was ruled by "client kings" allied to Rome.)

At the start of the Christian era, the population may have numbered from 2,000,000 to 2,500,000 persons, half of them in East Palestine. However, by the first century A.D. the Jewish population was already considerably dispersed, so that there were probably as many Jews in other nations as in Palestine. In the year 1945, prior to the establishment of the modern state of Israel, the Jewish population of Palestine was about 565,000; the Christian population, about 135,000 (mostly Christian Arabs); and the Moslem population, about 1,045,000.

PART I: THE OLD TESTAMENT, BOOK BY BOOK

The first five books of the Bible are variously called the books of Moses, the Law, or the Pentateuch (from a Greek word meaning a "five-volumed" document). Some scholars give the name Hexateuch to the first six books (Genesis, Exodus, Leviticus, Numbers, Deuteronomy, and Joshua) on the theory that Joshua is logically part of the same group of writings.

GENESIS

Genesis, meaning "in the beginning," is the first book of the Bible. It narrates the history of Israel from the Creation to the death of Joseph. It contains primitive accounts of the creation of the world and the dispersion of peoples following the Flood, and it tells about the lives of the patriarchs Abraham, Isaac, and Jacob, along with the story of Joseph's career in Egypt. It transmits the traditions of the Hebrew people about their earliest settlements and about the men and women who founded the leading families of the "Chosen People."

The book of Genesis is a witness to the origin and early stages of the religion of the people of Israel. Everywhere there are evidences of the emergence of vital faith. Religious purpose and feeling are earnestly manifested, and the struggles of men and women committed to a belief in one supreme and personal God are recorded.

Jewish tradition accredited Moses as author or compiler of the first five books, and early Christian scholars took the same view. Much later scholarship, however, points to the works as a composite with distinct variations. Moses may have been a contributor, but it appears that the first five or six books were in process of writing and compilation probably before 1000 B.C. and down to 300 B.C., with authors or editors unknown.

Genesis is divided into two parts: that dealing with primeval history of mankind; and that dealing with the lives of the patriarchs. **Primeval History of Mankind (1–11:9).** The final compilers evidently wished to combine early primitive accounts with those about the patriarchs of Israel. The first and well-known verses on the creation of heaven and earth read thus:

In the beginning God created the heaven and the earth.

And the earth was without form, and void; and darkness was upon the face of the deep. And the Spirit of God moved upon the face of the waters.

And God said, Let there be light: and there was light.

And God saw the light, that it was good: and God divided the light from the darkness.

And God called the light Day, and the darkness he called Night. And the evening and the morning were the first day. (1:1–5).

Then God made the firmament and the waters and two great lights, one for the day and the other for the night. "He made the stars also." He created "great whales, and every living creature that moveth." "God created man in his own image, in the image of God created he him; male and female created he them" (1:27). "And God saw every thing that he had made, and, behold, it was very good" (1:31).

ADAM AND EVE. Adam, the first man, and Eve, the first woman, were commanded by God not to eat the fruit of one tree in the garden where he had placed them. But, tempted by the serpent, Eve ate and then gave the fruit to Adam. This episode is referred to as "man's fall." God drove Adam and Eve out of the garden to labor and die on earth and said of man that he "is become as one of us, to know good and evil." (Chapter 3)

CAIN, ABEL, AND SETH. Cain and Abel were born, sons of Adam and Eve. Cain became jealous of Abel and slew him. He then replied to God's question that he did not know where Abel was ("Am I my brother's keeper?"). God banished Cain "to be a fugitive and a vagabond." A third son, Seth, was born to Adam and Eve. (Chapter 4)

NOAH. The descendants of Adam through Seth are listed, down to Noah. In Noah's time the wickedness of man provoked God's wrath and he sent a flood to earth. But Noah "found grace in the eyes of the Lord," who told him to build an ark and enter it with his family and representatives of every living creature. For 150 days the flood raged, so that only Noah and those with him in the ark remained alive to repopulate the earth. (Chapters 6–8)

THE TOWER OF BABEL. After the Flood "the whole earth was of one language." But when men erected a tall tower "to reach unto heaven," God confounded their language and scattered them abroad; therefore the tower was given the name "Babel" (11:1–9).

Accounts of the Patriarchs (11:28–50:26). These accounts begin with Abraham and end with Joseph.

ABRAHAM (11:26–25:10). God called Abraham, commanding him to go to the land of Canaan and promising that out of his issue he would make "a great nation." Abraham obeyed and in Canaan erected altars to God. But later, to escape "a famine in the land," Abraham went to Egypt, where he prospered. On his return he dwelt in Hebron, again building an altar "unto the Lord." Through many trials the faith and character of Abraham were tested. One account tells how almost all of mankind were destroyed when God rained brimstone and fire upon the wicked people of the two cities, Sodom and Gomorrah. Only Abraham's nephew Lot and Lot's two daughters were spared. Afterward "God remembered Abraham," who would therefore become the father of "a multitude of nations." Sarah bore Abraham a son "in his old age," and they named him Isaac. To prove his faith in God, Abraham was willing to offer his son Isaac as a sacrifice, but an angel of the Lord stayed his hand. This episode is interpreted as evidence of the covenant between God and Abraham. It also proves that Abraham's power came to him as a result of his faith in God. Finally, it shows that God did not desire human sacrifices.

Heroic deeds demonstrated the greatness of Abraham as a mature leader of his people. As he approached the end of his long career, he sent a servant to find a wife for Isaac. In this way Rebekah became Isaac's wife. She comforted Isaac, who had lived sad and lonely after his mother Sarah died. Abraham himself had taken another wife, Keturah, who bore him six more sons. Nevertheless, Abraham gave all his possessions to Isaac. Then Abraham "died in a good old age, an old man, and full of years; and was gathered to his people" (25:8).

ISAAC (25:11–26:35). Isaac was the only son of Abraham and Sarah, and he was the one through whom the promise (covenant) of God to Abraham was maintained. However, his father, Abraham, and his son, Jacob, tower above him in the records. In the Biblical story, some of the events associated with Isaac reflect competition of the Hebrews with neighboring tribes for good pasture lands and the danger to women from the activities of these rival tribes. It was evidently a time of strife.

JACOB (Chapters 27–36). Isaac's family life was marred by acute dissension between his twin sons Esau and Jacob. Beginning with Chapter 27, Jacob becomes the main Biblical figure. Lacking both the pure faith of Abraham and the somewhat innocent character of Isaac, his life was one of mighty cross currents. Taking advantage first of Esau's hunger and then of his absence, he acquired the birthright and blessing that rightfully belonged to the elder brother. Then he left his home to serve his uncle Laban in Haran. En route he had a vision of a ladder on which angels were ascending and descending, and of God appearing at the top to renew the convenant.

Jacob married his cousin Rachel, for whom he served fourteen years with his uncle Laban, having been tricked by Laban into first marrying her elder sister Leah. Rachel was barren for a long period while Jacob had children by Leah and by Rachel's and Leah's maids. But God remembered Rachel, and she bore Jacob a son, Joseph. She died giving birth to another son, Benjamin. Jacob's sons were to become progenitors of the twelve tribes of Israel.

The conflict between Jacob and Esau went on for a long time, but eventually the brothers met and were reconciled. Before his meeting with Esau, Jacob wrestled all night with an angel, who changed his name to Israel, meaning "contender with God." Later he built an altar near the city of Shalem.

JOSEPH (Chapters 37–50). Jacob's son Joseph becomes the main character in Chapter 37. His elder brothers, resentful because Jacob "loved Joseph more than all his children," cast him into a pit. He was rescued by traveling merchants, who took him to Egypt and sold him into bondage. There he was pleasing to his master, Potiphar, until Potiphar's wife accused him falsely of trying to seduce her. In prison as a result of this charge, Joseph became trusted and renowned as an interpreter of dreams. He interpreted Pharaoh's dreams to mean that seven years of plenty would be followed by seven years of famine and advised careful storage of food to assure sustenance when crops were small. This plan was carried out, and when the predicted famine arrived, Joseph's brothers were among those who came to Egypt to buy food. Joseph generously forgave them and sent for his father, Israel (Jacob). Israel lived the rest of his life on land that Joseph had given him in the part of Egypt named Goshen. When he felt that he was soon to die, Israel asked to have his body buried in the land of his his people, near the graves of Abraham and Isaac, and Joseph carried out this request. Joseph himself dwelt long in Egypt, but before his death he told his people that God would surely lead them back to the land of Abraham, Isaac, and Jacob.

EXODUS

Exodus, which means "going out," is the second book of the Pentateuch (see p. 5). As noted previously, tradition accredited Moses as the author or compiler, while much later scholarship indicates a compilation by authors unknown. This book is historically important because in it are found the most thorough descriptions that we have of the Mosaic constitution.

Exodus tells of the great awakening of a people through the soul of one man, Moses, who beheld a clear vision of God and was able to articulate that vision in terms of the daily life of his people. Moses brought to the tribes of Israel a degree of unity that they had not theretofore possessed, and he taught them a religion of moral significance. His teachings became a basis for subsequent stirring events in the history of Israel.

This book of Exodus abounds in vivid details about hasty traveling, camp life, and wilderness territory, following the deliverance of the Israelities from Egypt until the time of the stay near Sinai. The quality of the writing suggests an eyewitness source.

The book is divided into two parts: that dealing with the oppression of the Israelites in Egypt, their deliverance, and their travel to Sinai; and that dealing with organization, law-giving, and the Tabernacle at Sinai.

Oppression and Deliverance (Chapters 1–18). "Now there arose up a new king over Egypt, which knew not Joseph" (1:8). The children of Israel had multiplied, and this new Pharaoh feared their strength and numbers. He set taskmasters over them, "made their lives bitter with hard bondage," and ordered their male infants drowned.

MOSES' CALL (Chapters 2–4). One Hebrew mother, however, saved her son by hiding him in the reeds. He was found by Pharaoh's daughter, who adopted him and named him Moses. Despite his upbringing in the Egyptian court, Moses developed a strong loyalty to his own people, and he was forced to flee to Midian because he had killed an Egyptian whom he saw beating a Hebrew. While he was tending the flock of his father-in-law (he had married the daughter of a Midianite priest), an angel appeared to him in a burning bush and the Lord spoke to him from the bush, saying that he had come to deliver the people of Israel and would send Moses to Pharaoh to be a spokesman for them.

ESCAPE FROM EGYPT (Chapters 5–14). God sent nine plagues

9

to Egypt to soften Pharaoh's hard heart, and finally (after a tenth plague killing all the first-born of the Egyptians) the Hebrews were allowed to leave, although Pharaoh later regretted his decision and pursued them. When they came to the Red Sea, "Moses stretched out his hand over the sea; and the Lord caused the sea to go back by a strong east wind all that night, and made the sea dry land, and the waters were divided" so that those fleeing could cross (14:21). But when Pharaoh's chariots in pursuit tried to cross the Red Sea, the waters returned "and the Lord overthrew the Egyptians in the midst of the sea (14:27)." "And the people feared the Lord, and believed the Lord, and his servant Moses" (14:31).

THE WILDERNESS (Chapters 14–18). The way to Sinai was marked by continual complaints and accusations against Moses, as the people were hungry and missed the comforts of Egypt. But God sent manna from heaven for food, turned the bitter water sweet, and gave the Hebrews victory in their skirmish with the people of Amalek, who occupied the desert region south of Canaan.

Organization, Law-giving, and the Tabernacle (Chapters 19–40). The Israelites came in their journey to the desert near the Mount of Sinai. From the mountain God spoke to Moses, saying that if the people would obey his voice and keep his covenant they would become "an holy nation." Then God called Moses to the top of Mount Sinai, where he gave him the Ten Commandments and the Book of the Covenant.

THE TEN COMMANDMENTS (Chapter 20). The Decalogue, as the Ten Commandments are also called, is given in another version in Deuteronomy (5:6–21). The version in Exodus (20:1–17), in brief form, follows:

1. Thou shalt have no other gods before me.
2. Thou shalt not make unto thee any graven image.
3. Thou shalt not take the name of the Lord thy God in vain.
4. Remember the sabbath day, to keep it holy.
5. Honour thy father and thy mother.
6. Thou shalt not kill.
7. Thou shalt not commit adultery.
8. Thou shalt not steal.
9. Thou shalt not bear false witness against thy neighbour.
10. Thou shalt not covet . . . any thing that is thy neighbour's.

THE BOOK OF THE COVENANT (Chapters 21–23). This is a series of detailed and specific laws concerning murder, theft, damages, trespass, borrowing, fornication, witchcraft, bestiality, idolatry, treatment of strangers, servants, and widows, usury, slander, agriculture (land to lie fallow the seventh year), and observance of the Sabbath.

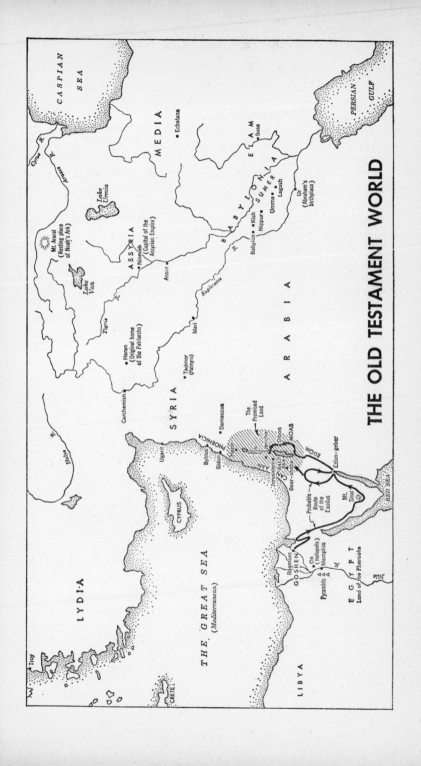

THE OLD TESTAMENT WORLD

THE TABERNACLE AT SINAI (Chapters 24–40). Moses told the people of the laws, and they promised to obey them. God called him up to the mountain again and gave him directions for the construction of the Tabernacle * and the Ark,* and also tables of stone on which the Commandments were written. However, when he returned with the tables he discovered that in his absence the people had resumed the practice of idolatry and were worshipping a golden calf. Furious, he broke the tables and ordered three thousand of the idolaters slain. But then he felt compassion for his people and prayed God to forgive them.

Again Moses was called to the mountain top, where God renewed the covenant and replaced the tables. The Tabernacle was then built and the Ark placed inside it. Aaron, brother of Moses, and his sons were consecrated to be priests. And "the cloud of the Lord was upon the tabernacle by day, and fire was on it by night, in the sight of all the house of Israel, throughout all their journeys" (40:38).

LEVITICUS

Leviticus, the third book of the Bible, as well as of the Pentateuch (see p. 5), consists of ritual laws. The name comes from the tribe of Levi, to which the hereditary priests belonged. The book is evidently a composite of previously widely separated materials.

This treatise supplements the laws in Exodus (see p. 10), including instructions for the building of the Tabernacle and the beginning of religious services there, and is thus one section of the long legalistic accounts that appear in the first six books of the Bible. The fact that the earlier portions of Leviticus are much more simple than the later ones is evidence of the integration in the book of diverse materials. The first part tells much about the early rural life of the people and is thus a valuable source of ancient agricultural laws, afterward modified by city dwellers. In the later sections there is information concerning the strict organization of the people's religious practices. The Holiness Code (or "Holiness to Jehovah") takes high moral ground.

The text itself is proof of the antiquity of the document or of the sources that may have preceded it, but the material probably reached its present form as the result of a long process from 800 to 300 B.C.

* See Glossary.

The laws described in Leviticus are often referred to in the book of Ezekiel (see p. 69). The book of Hebrews in the New Testament (see p. 154) makes several specific references to Leviticus, and much more of this Old Testament book underlies or is implicit in that book.

Leviticus may be divided into four parts: three deal mainly with sacrifice, the priesthood, and cleanliness and atonement, while the fourth consists of miscellaneous teachings which include the Holiness Code.

Laws relating to Sacrifice in General (Chapters 1–7). These are briefly summarized near the end of this section: "This is the law of the burnt offering, of the meat offering, and of the sin offering, and of the trespass offering, and of the consecrations, and of the sacrifice of the peace offerings; Which the Lord commanded Moses in mount Sinai, in the day that he commanded the children of Israel to offer their oblations unto the Lord, in the wilderness of Sinai" (7:37–38).

Consecration of the Priesthood (Chapters 8–10). "The Lord spake unto Moses," telling him to consecrate Aaron and his sons to the priesthood. When Moses and Aaron came before the people to bless them, "the glory of the Lord appeared unto all the people." Two of the sons of Aaron, Nadab and Abihu, "offered strange fire before the Lord, which he commanded them not. And there went out fire from the Lord, and devoured them, and they died before the Lord" (10:1,2). The remaining sons of Aaron, Eleazar and Ithamar, carried on as faithful priests.

Laws concerning Clean and Unclean Beasts, Personal Cleanliness, and the Day of Atonement (Chapters 11–16). Here are listed the animals whose flesh may and may not be eaten, laws for the purification of women after childbirth, and hygienic regulations. There was also established a "day of atonement": "And this shall be a statute for ever unto you: that in the seventh month, on the tenth day of the month, ye shall afflict your souls, and do no work at all, whether it be one of your own country, or a stranger that sojourneth among you: For on that day shall the priest make an atonement for you, to cleanse you, that ye may be clean from all your sins before the Lord" (16:29–30).

Miscellaneous Laws for Israel (Chapters 17–27). These include the Holiness Code (Chapters 17–26) and laws in a supplementary chapter (27) on vows and tithes. This section is usually considered to have been written after the Exile. It gives regulations for personal conduct, as well as for national religious observances. Laws with respect to marriage, chastity, respect for parents, and justice to neighbors are stated. The seventh day is established as a "sabbath of rest." The Passover, commemorating the escape from Egypt,

is set on the "fourteenth day of the first month at even . . . And
on the fifteenth day of the same month is the feast of unleavened
bread unto the Lord: seven days ye must eat unleavened bread"
(23:5,6). Other annual holidays are set, including a harvest festival,
or formal thanksgiving, for the crops (Chapter 23). Every seventh
year is declared a sabbath of rest for the land, when the fields
should lie fallow, and every fiftieth year is to be a year of jubilee
celebrated by the freeing of slaves, the return of alienated lands,
and the cessation of sowing and reaping (25:1–17). Rules are laid
down for humane treatment of the poor and of servants (25:35–
55). A tithe is established—one tenth of the produce of the land,
flocks, and herds "shall be holy unto the Lord" (27:30–33).

NUMBERS

*Numbers, the fourth book of the Bible, so named because of
the two numberings of the people described therein, consists of both
laws and historical narratives. It is the fourth of the books traditionally ascribed to Moses (see p. 5). It tells the experiences of
the Hebrews from their second year in the wilderness to the arrival
on the borders of Moab close to the Promised Land.*

The outstanding feature of this book is its portrayal of Moses, the
leader who was both statesman and prophet. His patience, fidelity,
and strength as he led his people during the long, trying years of
the Exodus all add up to a picture of noble grandeur.

The book records two censuses taken by the leaders of Israel.
(The numbering of people is often cited by political scientists as
one of the oldest functions of government.) In both, the aim was
primarily to list the names of men "twenty years of age and upward" who could go to war for the nation.

The text was probably the result of a long process of compilation and writing between 1000 and 300 B.C. It may be divided into
four sections: (1) the first census and other ordinances at the
beginning of the journey; (2) the travel from Sinai to Moab; (3)
events of the first ten months of the fortieth year in the wilderness;
and (4) the second census and other preparations to enter Canaan.

**A Census, Marriage Laws, the Consecration of Nazarites and
Levites (1:1–10:10).** The Lord spoke to Moses in the wilderness of
Sinai, saying: "Take ye the sum of all the congregation of the
children of Israel, after their families, by the house of their fathers,
with the number of their names. . ." (1:2). In the first month of

the second year following the Exodus, Moses and Aaron assembled all the people, and they were numbered by the names of the tribes. The total number of males over twenty was found to be 603,550. (The Levites were exempted from this count but were appointed separately as persons destined for Tabernacle service.) Other ordinances included laws relating to marital purity, special instructions for the observance of the Passover, and the provision for the consecration of Nazarites (who set themselves apart for a period of dedication to the Lord).

A formula for blessing the people was given by God to Moses and Aaron:

The Lord bless thee, and keep thee:
The Lord make his face shine upon thee, and be gracious unto thee:
The Lord lift up his countenance upon thee, and give thee peace.
   (6:24–26)

The Journey from Sinai to Moab (10:11–19:22). Events in this period of thirty-eight years included many vicissitudes and the promulgation of numerous laws. As the people neared Canaan, the Lord spoke to Moses, commanding him to send out men to "search the land" which God had promised to the children of Israel. The people murmured on hearing the scouts' reports of the strong forces within Canaan. Some wished to return to Egypt, and Moses was called upon to quell several rebellions. After calm had been restored, the Lord spoke to Aaron, telling him the duties of priests and other Levites.

Events of the First Ten Months of the Fortieth Year (Chapters 20–24). The Hebrews moved to the steppes of Moab, east of the river Jordan. Aaron died on Mount Hor, and his son Eleazar succeeded him as high priest. The rulers of the tribe of Edom would not permit the travelers to pass through their territory, and the Moabites, too, were afraid because the newcomers were so numerous. The King of Moab attempted to bribe the magician Balaam to curse the Hebrews, but Balaam instead was led by several miracles (including a rebuke from his ass) to bless them. Balaam then foretold the happiness of the people of Israel: "How goodly are thy tents, O Jacob, and thy tabernacles, O Israel!" (24:5).

Events of the Last Two Months of the Fortieth Year (Chapters 25–36). The men of Israel, now camped near Moab, began to have Moabite women as prostitutes, and God sent a plague to punish them. After the plague another census was taken, and 601,730 males twenty years old and upward were reported. Moses was allowed by God to see the promised land of Canaan but told that he would die without entering it because of an act of disobedience. Joshua was designated as his successor.

A war of extermination against the tribe of Midian was reported to have been successful, but the destruction was apparently not complete because the Midianites later invaded Israel (Judges, Chapters 6–8). Moses allotted land east of the Jordan to Reuben, Gad, and Manasseh on condition that they aid in conquering land west of the river for the other tribes. The borders of Canaan, as they existed when the Israelites appear to have taken possession of the land, were defined, and tribal leaders were appointed to assist Joshua.

DEUTERONOMY

Deuteronomy, the fifth book of the Bible, is the last book of the Pentateuch, traditionally ascribed to Moses (see p. 5). The name means "second law" and refers to the repetition by Moses of God's commandments. Deuteronomy stands apart from the other four (or five) of the first group of books, being made up almost entirely of addresses delivered by Moses, directed not to priests or leaders but to the whole people.

The text makes no claim that Moses was the author or compiler, although much of the material is attributed to him. The book appears to have been first compiled around the year 650 B.C. (The early prophets—e.g., Isaiah and Amos—reveal no knowledge of it.) It was probably put into its present form between 650 and 300 B.C.

Although the literary quality of the book is generally good, it lacks unity. Chapters 5–26 and 28 appear to have been the original nucleus to which material at the beginning and the end was added.

Deuteronomy combines summaries of codes of law with a prophetic strain of teaching. Because Moses was traditionally associated with the formulation of the law, it was probably only normal procedure for a compiler who knew of later prophets to link prophecy also to him.

The high religious value of Deuteronomy is indicated by the following emphases: the unity, supremacy, and goodness of God; the total regulation of the life of the people in accordance with the principle of loyalty to God; and the organization of worship at one sanctuary.

The book appears to have been one of the most influential works of the Old Testament. Jeremiah (see p. 63) was a student of it, and it was also used by the writers of history who compiled Judges, Samuel, and Kings (see pp. 20, 24, and 29).

Deuteronomy may be divided into five parts: (1) a résumé of events in the wilderness; (2) an address by Moses repeating the Ten Commandments and giving other laws; (3) a speech by Moses on writing down the law; (4) Moses' farewell speech and his charge to Joshua; and (5) Moses' last days and death.

A Résumé of events in the Wilderness (Chapters 1–4). Moses reviewed the forty years of wandering, recalling God's promise to the people of Israel that he would give them the land of Canaan; noting God's anger because of their incredulity and disobedience; and exhorting them to obedience.

The Decalogue and Other Laws (Chapter 5–26). Moses recalled the covenant of God at Horeb (Mount Sinai) and the Ten Commandments (compare this version with that found in Exodus 20).

Thou shalt have none other gods before me.
Thou shalt not make thee any graven image.
Thou shalt not take the name of the Lord thy God in vain.
Keep the sabbath day to sanctify it.
Honour thy father and thy mother.
Thou shalt not kill.
Neither shalt thou commit adultery.
Neither shalt thou steal.
Neither shalt thou bear false witness against thy neighbour.
Neither shalt thou desire thy neighbour's wife . . . or any thing that is thy neighbour's. (5:7–21, in abbreviated form.)

Moses counseled the people to hear God and keep his commandments. He warned them to destroy everything connected with idolatry and to kill anyone who enticed them to the worship of other gods. He gave numerous laws covering diet, religious observances, treatment of the poor and of servants, judicial procedures, relations with other peoples, marital rights, and other matters of daily life and conduct. Some of these laws show highly developed ethical standards. Every seventh year the creditor was to release the poor debtor. The gleanings of the field were to be left for the stranger, the fatherless, and the widow. Oppression of servants was forbidden (the Hebrews were reminded that they themselves had once been servants in the land of Egypt). Whipping of criminals was restricted to forty stripes, and offenders were to be punished only for their own wrongdoing, not for that of their relatives.

The people were told that God would send another prophet to succeed Moses and were instructed on how to distinguish false prophets from true ones (18:15–22).

Written Law (Chapters 27–28). Moses commanded that the law be written and preserved upon stones and that a stone altar be built for sacrifices to God. He promised that obedience to God would be followed by blessings.

Moses' Farewell Speech and His Charge to Joshua (29:1–31:13). Moses repeated his exhortation to obedience. He presented the people to the Lord, saying that God would not spare the wicked but that he would be merciful to the penitent. The commandment of God was not in heaven or beyond the sea, he went on, but was in their own hearts, telling them: "I have set before you life and death, blessing and cursing: therefore choose life. . ." (30:11–20).

The people, Moses concluded, should love the Lord their God, obey his voice, and cleave unto him, "for he is thy life, and the length of thy days: that thou mayest dwell in the land which the Lord sware unto thy fathers. . ." (30:20).

"Be strong and of a good courage," Moses said to his successor, Joshua, "for thou must go with this people unto the land which the Lord hath sworn unto their fathers to give them; and thou shalt cause them to inherit it" (31:7). He commanded the priests to teach the law—to read it in public every seven years so that all the people would learn and obey it (31:10–13).

Moses' Last Days and Death (31:14–34:12). God told Moses that he must soon die, instructed him to present himself with Joshua in the Tabernacle, and there gave him the words of a last song: "I will publish the name of the Lord: ascribe ye greatness unto our God. He is the Rock, his work is perfect: for all his ways are judgment: a God of truth and without iniquity, just and right is he" (32:3–4). After this song and a final blessing to Israel, Moses was sent by God up to Mount Nebo, where he might see the promised land of Canaan before his death. "So Moses the servant of the Lord died there in the land of Moab, according to the word of the Lord" (34:5). And Joshua, a man "full of the spirit of wisdom," succeeded him.

JOSHUA

Joshua is the last of the first six books of the Bible, called the Hexateuch (see p. 5). It is named for the successor of Moses, who led the Israelites into Canaan, and it contains the only systematic Biblical account of the Hebrew conquest of that land. It also includes valuable source material on the geography of ancient Palestine.

Like the five preceding books, Joshua was probably part of a long process of writing and editing between 1000 and 350 B.C. There is some Deuteronomic material, including specific information on priestly activities. The composition is not well unified, indicating a piecing together from diverse sources. Although Joshua is well portrayed as a leader, it seems probable that the people at the time of their battles in Canaan were not integrated under one military head and that Joshua's role was built upon by later legends.

A reading of Joshua may lead one to conclude that the conquest of Canaan was complete. But a close examination reveals that qualifications must be made. The Hebrew gains did not carry into some of the more important areas of the country. Joshua's victories, while of great significance, probably resulted in the acquisition only of what might be called a good bridgehead on the Plain of Jericho and a good section of land in the center of the mountains. But these were strategic outposts, from which at later times cities not secured by Joshua came into the Israelites' hands.

Joshua may be considered in three sections: the conquest of Canaan; the division of the conquered land; and Joshua's last speech and death.

Conquest of Canaan (Chapters 1–12). After the death of Moses, God spoke to Joshua, saying, "As I was with Moses, so I will be with thee: I will not fail thee, nor forsake thee . . . unto this people shalt thou divide for an inheritance the land, which I sware unto their fathers to give them" (1:5,6).

Joshua informed the people of the impending struggle and sent out spies, who brought back favorable reports. Then Joshua moved his forces to the Jordan River and passed over with all the people, as the priests carrying the Ark of the Covenant "stood firm on dry ground in the midst of Jordan" (3:9–17).

Other miracles followed. The walls of the besieged city of Jericho fell flat at the sound of trumpets blown by the priests and the people's shouts, and the Israelites "utterly destroyed all that was in the city. . ." (6:1–21). In order to facilitate one of Joshua's victories, it is recorded, the sun and moon stood still at the word of Joshua to the Lord "until the people had avenged themselves upon their enemies" (10:12–13).

At first God allowed the city of Ai to withstand the Hebrews successfully because of Achan's sin in appropriating for himself some of the spoils of Jericho. But after the Hebrews had killed Achan and his family, they took the city by ambush. The King of Ai and many other kings were captured; territory was conquered both east and west of the Jordan. "So Joshua took the whole land, according to all that the Lord said unto Moses. . ." (11:23).

Division of the Land (Chapters 13–22). The tribes were assigned new lands by lot (except for those tribes previously allocated territory by Moses [see p. 16]). There was some dissatisfaction and contention, but in the end a settlement pleasing to all was made by Joshua's deputies. Certain cities were assigned to the Levites (see p. 14); other cities were designated cities of refuge where "the slayer that killeth any person unawares and unwittingly" might escape the vengeance of the dead man's relatives.

Joshua's Last Speech and His Death (Chapters 23–24). After a long interval of peace, Joshua called the people and said: "I am old and stricken in age . . . ye have seen all that the Lord your God hath done unto all these nations because of you; for the Lord your God is he that hath fought for you" (23:2,3). He cited the benefits of obedience to God, the perils of disobedience, and God's promises. He renewed the covenant between God and the people. "And it came to pass after these things, that Joshua the son of Nun, the servant of the Lord, died, being an hundred and ten years old" (24:29).

JUDGES

The book of Judges is the seventh of the Bible and is also the first of a group of historical books that follows the Hexateuch (see p. 5). It is so named because it deals with the activities of a number of "judges" of Israel, individuals who were in practical terms rulers of the people during the period between their entry into Canaan and the establishment of the monarchy.

Authorship must be regarded as uncertain. The book has been credited to Samuel, one of the great leaders of Israel (see p. 24), and he may have written a portion. The Song of Deborah (Chapter 5) was apparently written shortly after the events described. It seems probable that the work except for the last five chapters was completed prior to the exile in Babylon about 598–538 B.C.

The book contains valuable historical detail on the period starting from the death of Joshua and going through the Hebrews' gradual conquest of Palestine until just before their establishment of a monarchy. However, the reports are fragmentary and many important episodes receive brief treatment. On the other hand, although the book gives only a cursory view, it does indicate a general direction of stirring events. It also provides insights into the governing processes, abilities, and characters of the judges, or elders. In addition, the writers show real knowledge of the geography of Palestine.

Judges tells us about the numerous, varied, and rather loosely organized tribes; the contentions among these tribes; the problems of relations with conquered Canaanites; the long struggles with neighboring Philistines and Ammonites; and the crudities of early national life. Also of significance is information found in Judges about the development of Judaism. For there emerged from the more primitive forms of the Hebrew religion, and from its clash with Canaanite Baal-worship, the beginning of conditions which eventually had to be condemned by the great prophets.

Judges falls into three divisions which have no close connections with one another: the introduction, the main narrative of historical events, and two appendixes added at some later date.

Introduction (1:1–2:5). This part includes a summary of the conquest of various parts of Canaan. It was evidently put in to form a transition between the book of Joshua and subsequent events.

The Main Narrative (2:6–16:31). This part relates history from the death of Joshua to that of Samson. The opening sentences are a repetition from Joshua 24:28–31. The author then continues with a statement on the spiritual significance of the events described. After the death of Joshua the Israelites "forsook the Lord God of their fathers . . . and followed other gods, of the gods of the people that were round about them. . . And the anger of the Lord was hot against Israel, and he delivered them into the hands of spoilers. . ." (2:12,14).

Many tribes were left to "prove" Israel, among them the Philistines and the Moabites. "Nevertheless the Lord raised up judges, which delivered them out of the hand of those that spoiled them" (2:16). The accounts of these leaders are arranged in a somewhat unsystematic fashion, which does not clearly indicate whether some of the judges ruled consecutively or contemporaneously.

OTHNIEL (3:7–11). Othniel, the first of the judges, delivered his people from a king of Mesopotamia, "And the land had rest forty years."

EHUD (3:12–30). The people "did evil again in the sight of the Lord" and had to serve the King of Moab eighteen years. Then Ehud, under the pretext of delivering a message from God, assassinated the tyrant, afterward leading the Israelites to victory in battle against the Moabites.

DEBORAH (Chapters 4–5). Deborah, a prophetess and judge, who has been compared to Joan of Arc, directed and inspired the campaign led by Barak against the forces of Sisera, a Canaanite general. Deborah's and Barak's song of thanksgiving for their victory is among the most beautiful examples of Hebrew poetry: "The kings came and fought . . . they took no gain of money. They fought from heaven; the stars in their courses fought against Sisera. The river of Kishon swept them away . . . O my soul, thou hast trodden down strength" (5:19–21).

GIDEON (Chapters 6–8). Gideon, the son of a farmer, is por- trayed as a man of valor, military skill, and faith in God. As a result of his great victories over the Midianites, he was offered a crown by the people of central Israel, the first evidence of a trend toward monarchy. Gideon declined the offer, but he probably lived a life equivalent to that of a king. He maintained a large establishment, including a harem and many children, thus departing from the earlier simplicity of Hebrew life.

ABIMELECH (Chapter 9). Abimelech, a son of Gideon, killed all but one of his half-brothers, and attempted to start a monarchy in Israel after being made "king" by the Shechemites. But after a reign of three years, his subjects revolted, as his wise half-brother Jotham had predicted, and he was killed while besieging the city of Thebez.

TOLA (10:1–2). Tola was probably a local hero who became a judge after Abimelech's death. Of his career as a judge little is said.

JAIR (10:3–5). Jair was the judge who arose after Tola. He "had thirty sons that rode on thirty ass colts, and they had thirty cities . . . in the land of Gilead."

JEPHTHAH (10:6–12:7). Jephthah judged Israel six years after a turbulent career during which he subdued the Ammonites and then tragically sacrificed his only daughter to keep an ill-considered vow.

IBZAN (12:8–10). Ibzan ruled for seven years after Jephthah. He is reported to have had thirty sons and thirty daughters.

ELON (12:11–12). Elon succeeded Ibzan and judged Israel for ten years.

ABDON (12:13–15). Abdon had "forty sons and thirty nephews, that rode on threescore and ten ass colts. . . ." He judged for eight years.

SAMSON (Chapters 13–16). Samson is said to have judged for twenty years, although he is portrayed as a somewhat solitary epic hero, rather than as a ruler. He is described in a series of unique stories, which perhaps should be understood as representing early incidents in the long struggle of the Israelites with the Philistines.

In his youth Samson married a Philistine woman, quarreled with her tribe because of his marriage, and killed a thousand of his enemies with the jawbone of an ass. After this feat he judged Israel for twenty years.

Then he was enticed by another Philistine woman, Delilah, who weakened him by having his hair cut while he slept (as a Nazarite [see p. 14] he was under a vow to remain unshaven). He was then captured, blinded, and imprisoned by the Philistines. But in prison his hair began to grow again; and when the Philistines brought him to the temple of their god to make sport of him, he prayed God to renew his strength so that he might be avenged. Then, grasping the pillars of the temple, he "bowed himself with all his might," and the temple fell, killing Samson together with his enemies. "So the dead which he slew at his death were more than they which he slew in his life" (16:30).

Appendixes (Chapters 17–21). These chapters tell, first, of the conquest of the city of Laish by the Hebrew tribe of Danites, who renamed the City Dan and set up in it a graven image made by the Ephraimite Micah; and, second, of the shameful abuse of a Levite's concubine by Benjamites of Gibeah, her resulting death, and the subsequent war of vengeance by the rest of Israel that nearly resulted in the extermination of the tribe of Benjamin. The book concludes: "In those days there was no king in Israel: every man did that which was right in his own eyes" (21:25).

RUTH

The book of Ruth, the eighth in the Bible, tells a story of the days of the judges (see p. 20) and is hence regarded as one of the historical narratives. It concerns the family of a man of Bethlehem who was forced by famine to migrate to Moab and whose Moabite daughter-in-law became an ancestress of King David.

One of the objects of the book was evidently to give the Davidic ancestral line. Because this line began with a foreign woman, the book is often considered, like Jonah (see p. 81) in purpose, as a parable demonstrating the wide reach of God's love and mercy. The events described must have taken place more than a hundred years before the reign of David, but the story was probably composed much later than his era. The genealogical table, while incomplete, gives valuable historical data.

The book may be divided into three portions beginning with the sojourn in Moab and ending with Ruth's marriage to Boaz and the listing of their descendants down to David.

Sojourn in Moab (1:1–5). During the days of the judges' rule, Elimelech and Naomi, with their two sons, went to Moab to escape a famine in their native Bethlehem. The sons, Mahlon and Chilion, married women of Moab, Orpah and Ruth. All of the men died.

Ruth's Choice (1:6–22). Naomi, hearing that there was again bread in her native land, decided to return to Bethlehem, and her two daughters-in-law wished to go with her. Naomi told them to go back to their own families. Orpah agreed, but Ruth said to Naomi: "Intreat me not to leave thee, or to return from following after thee . . . thy people shall be my people, and thy God my God" (1:16).

Ruth's Marriage to Boaz (Chapters 2–4). In Bethlehem Ruth gleaned in the fields of Boaz, a kinsman of Elimelech "a mighty man of wealth," and found favor in his eyes. Recognizing her kinship and its customary rights, Boaz protected her by marriage, and from this union King David was descended.

I SAMUEL

I Samuel, the ninth book in the Bible and third of the series of historical books that follow the Hexateuch, records events leading toward the establishment of the kingdom of Israel and subsequent events during the reign of Saul, the first king. The book is named for Samuel, the great judge and leader who figures prominently in it. The period of Samuel and Saul was about 1050–1002 B.C.

I Samuel and II Samuel (see p. 27) were originally part of one book which also contained I and II Kings (see pp. 29 and 33). That book was a compilation from varied original sources which may have included some of the material in Samuel. However, I Samuel was probably not put into its final form until after the division of the kingdom of Israel into two nations—Israel and Judah—about 922 B.C. (see p. 31). Despite the fact that the book consists of annals which are sometimes repetitious and at other times contradictory, it is of great historical value and interest.

The book has two parts: one tells about the life and work of Samuel until he retired as a judge; the other deals with the reign of Saul until his death in battle.

The Life and Work of Samuel (Chapters 1–12). As judge, prophet, priest, and kingmaker, Samuel was a link between the old heroes, starting with Moses, and the new ones, going on to the great prophets.

SAMUEL'S CHILDHOOD AND CALL. Samuel, the child of Elkanah and Hannah, was presented to the Lord by his mother, who, during a long barren period, had prayed for a son. Upon the birth of Samuel, Hannah sang a song of thanksgiving (2:1–10) comparable to Mary's Magnificat (see p. 107). She left the baby at the temple of Shiloh to be brought up by the priest Eli. Afterward she "made him a little coat, and brought it to him from year to year, when she came up with her husband to offer the yearly sacrifice" (2:19).

Eli had wicked sons who "knew not the Lord." "A man of God" pronounced judgment on them to Eli. Then God called young Samuel, who had grown "in favour both with the Lord, and also with men," and revealed to him the forthcoming end of Eli's house. The boy told Eli, who said, "It is the Lord: let him do what seemeth him good." "And all Israel from Dan even to Beer-sheba knew that Samuel was established to be a prophet of the Lord." (Chapters 2–3.)

SAMUEL'S SUCCESSION AS JUDGE. The Philistines defeated Israel in battle and captured the Ark of the Covenant.* Eli's two sons, Hophni and Phinehas, were slain. When Eli heard the bad news he fell backward, broke his neck, and died, after having been a judge and priest for forty years. Following many vicissitudes, the Ark was returned to Israel and placed in Kirjath-jearim. (4:1–7:2.)

Samuel called on the people to "put away the strange gods . . . and prepare your hearts unto the Lord, and serve him only: and he will deliver you out of the hand of the Philistines." Then, under Samuel's leadership, the Philistines were defeated in battle. "And Samuel judged Israel all the days of his life." (Chapter 7.)

SAMUEL'S ANOINTING OF SAUL. In his old age Samuel made his sons judges, but they "turned aside after lucre, and took bribes, and perverted judgment." Consequently, all the elders of Israel came to Samuel asking for "a king to judge us like all the nations." Samuel, after praying to God, warned them that a king would have great power over them and would rule arbitrarily. But the people "refused to obey the voice of Samuel" and said that they would have a king. (Chapter 8.)

Saul, "a choice young man, and a goodly," seeking his father's lost asses, heard of Samuel's reputation as a seer and came to ask

* See Glossary.

his guidance. God had meanwhile revealed to Samuel that the man who came should be anointed king. When Saul arrived, Samuel honored him at a feast, told him that he was to be king, and anointed him with oil. (9:1–10:8.)

However, upon leaving Samuel, Saul's heart was changed by God. He began to prophesy, but he did not announce his selection as king. Then Samuel called the people together at Mizpeh to choose a king by lot. Saul was chosen again, but "when they sought him, he could not be found." God disclosed his hiding place, and they led him forth and publicly proclaimed him king. (10:9–27.)

After Saul had won a great victory over the Ammonites, the kingdom was renewed in a ceremony at Gilgal. (Chapter 11.)

SAMUEL'S FAREWELL. Samuel delivered a farewell address, defending his integrity, calling upon the people to obey God, and rebuking them for their ingratitude. As a sign that they had been wrong to demand a king, he called on the Lord to send thunder and rain that day, which was harvest time, and the Lord did so. Then Samuel comforted the people by telling of God's mercy. (Chapter 12.)

The Reign of Saul. Saul's reign lasted twenty years, during which the monarchy was consolidated, battles were fought with the Philistines and other tribes, and the tormented King's own tragedy was enacted.

INTRODUCTION OF DAVID. How Saul's successor David came into the Hebrew court is the subject of somewhat conflicting stories that indicate compilation of the book from various sources.

There was further war with the Philistines, during which Saul disobeyed the word of God by offering a sacrifice himself instead of waiting for Samuel to do it. In the same war Samuel called on Saul to exterminate Amalek; again Saul disobeyed. As a result Samuel saw no more of Saul, and "the Lord repented that he had made Saul king over Israel." (Chapters 13–15.)

Samuel was then sent by God to Bethlehem, where he anointed a ruddy shepherd boy named David, the youngest son of Jesse and great-grandson of Ruth and Boaz (see p. 23), as future king of Israel. Saul, though unaware that his successor had been chosen, was troubled by an evil spirit. David, whose talent as a musician had become known at the court, was sent for to comfort the King by playing his harp. Saul became fond of the boy and made him his armor-bearer. (Chapter 16.)

Another account tells how Goliath, a giant Philistine, challenged the Hebrews to pick someone to meet him in single combat. David, who had been sent by his father to take food to his brothers in Saul's army, begged the King to let him accept the challenge. He put five smooth stones into a shepherd's bag, and, armed with his sling, he slew Goliath. The Philistines fled, and Saul rewarded the boy by taking him into his court. The friendship of David and Jonathan, a son of Saul, became one of the most moving stories in all Hebrew literature. (17:1–18:4.)

CONFLICT BETWEEN DAVID AND SAUL. David advanced to a high position in the court and the army. Saul, becoming jealous because of David's military victories and popularity ("Saul hath slain his thousands, and David his ten thousands"), sought to kill him but failed. (Later Saul also sought unsuccessfully to kill Jonathan because he continued his friendship with David.) Aided by Saul's daughter Michal, whom he had just married, David escaped and went into exile. (Chapters 18–20.)

He became the leader of a band that, despite the constant necessity to dodge the King's forces, engaged in separate guerrilla warfare with the Philistines and won victories. Twice David had the opportunity to kill Saul but spared him. The second time Saul confessed that he had sinned and asked David to return to him, but David apparently did not trust him. (Chapters 21–26.)

Then for a time David lived in the territory of the Philistines and joined their army. Before a decisive battle between the Hebrews and the Philistines, Saul consulted the witch of Endor. The witch raised up the form of Samuel, who had meanwhile died; and the ghost foretold that God would give the kingdom to David. Saul, who had not eaten all day, fainted and was restored with food. (Chapters 27–28.)

The Philistines, distrusting David's loyalty, sent him away before the battle, fought at Gilboa. There the Philistines were victorious, Saul's three sons were killed, and Saul committed suicide by falling on his sword. (Chapters 29–31.)

II SAMUEL

II Samuel, the tenth book of the Bible, concerns the reign of David, who became King of Judah and, later, King of all Israel. It was probably compiled some time after his reign, which lasted from about 1002 to 962 B.C. Samuel may have prepared early portions of the book, but authorship of the final version is not known. (See discussion of I Samuel, p. 24.)

The book begins after the battle (see above) in which Saul and his sons died and continues the story of David until his old age.

Attainment of the Monarchy (Chapters 1–10). When David received the news of the deaths of Saul and Jonathan, he lamented: "The beauty of Israel is slain upon the high places: how are the mighty fallen!" (Chapter 1.)

Then David was directed by God to go up to Hebron, where he was made King of Judah. But Abner, one of Saul's captains, appointed a surviving son of Saul named Ish-bosheth king over certain other tribes, and he was called King of Israel. Then came war between the "house of Saul and the house of David," ending with the assassination of Ish-bosheth and David's anointment as king over Israel. The beginning of David's reign was marked by victories over the Philistines and the bringing of the Ark (see p. 25) to Jerusalem, which became his capital. David performed other brave deeds, and the prophet Nathan foretold the permanence of his house. (Chapters 2–10.)

DAVID AND BATH-SHEBA (Chapters 11–12). However, David's favor with God was cut short by a great sin. He fell in love with a woman named Bath-sheba whom from his roof he saw bathing and made her his mistress, although she was married to Uriah, a Hittite serving in the Hebrew army. When he learned that Bath-sheba was to have his child, David ordered Uriah sent to "the forefront of the hottest battle." The order was carried out, and Uriah was killed. (Chapter 11.)

God then sent the prophet Nathan to tell David the story of a rich man with many flocks and herds and a poor man with "one little ewe lamb, which he had bought and nourished up." Having a dinner guest, the rich man instead of taking one of his own flock, killed the poor man's lamb for meat. David was very angry at this reported injustice and said that the offender deserved to die. Nathan's reply was crushing: "Thou art the man." As punishment for their sin the baby son born to David and Bath-sheba died, causing the King great grief. But soon another son, Solomon, was born. (Chapter 12.)

DAVID AND ABSALOM (Chapters 13–19). Absalom, David's unruly and treacherous son, was another cause of much anguish to the King. He led a conspiracy and rebellion against David, forcing him to flee from Jerusalem. After long conflict and much intrigue, Absalom was slain by one of David's commanders, Joab, despite the King's order to "Deal gently for my sake with the young man, even with Absalom." When the King received the news he mourned, "O my son Absalom, my son, my son Absalom! would God I had died for thee, O Absalom, my son, my son!" (18:33). The people, who had been rejoicing over the military victory, turned to mourning when they heard how the King grieved for his foolish son.

Later Events in David's Reign (Chapters 20–24). David surrounded himself with a number of strong officers, who aided him in keeping order and in dealing with further rebellion, although they sometimes fought among themselves. For example, the rebellion of Sheba, was suppressed by Joab after Joab had killed Amasa, whom David had appointed to replace him as commander. (Chapter 20.)

Other chapters tell of a famine that was ended by the hanging of seven of Saul's sons (Chapter 21); a song of thanksgiving by David upon being delivered from his enemies (Chapter 22), which appears in another version as Psalm 18; a list of David's mighty men (Chapter 23); the taking of a census, which angered God so that he offered David his choice of three punishments, and the King's choice of pestilence as the least of the evils (when David confessed his sin, interceded for the people, and built an altar, the plague was ended) (Chapter 24).

I KINGS

I Kings, the eleventh book of the Bible and one of the historical group, tells of the death of King David (see I and II Samuel above); the reign of Solomon; the division of the kingdom after Solomon's death; and part of the history of the separate kingdoms of Israel and Judah. (The division between I and II Kings is altogether arbitrary.) The book is of unknown authorship and is drawn from many sources. As noted earlier, it was once part of a larger work that included I and II Samuel and II Kings.

Kings I and II both show effects of the Deuteronomic influence. Probably the authors used Deuteronomy (see p. 16) as a model because it was the commanding book for a long period. Here are recorded the strivings of those who sought the worship of the one true God and the total regulation of life in accordance with loyalty to him. This is history in a pragmatic sense, or a historical account with an instructive message. The kings are assessed not by their material achievements but by their moral purpose "in the sight of the Lord." The book was probably written about 600 B.C. or later.

Though the account is informal throughout, the authors have given an interesting working outline of the history of a people during a significant period—the peak of their prosperity and the beginning of its decline. The book includes the well-known and stirring stories about the prophet Elijah, which, although they may be legendary, add to the human interest of the historical narrative.

I Kings is divided into two parts: the first covering the period from the death of David through the reign of Solomon and the division of the kingdom after Solomon's death (about 962 to 922 B.C.); and the second giving parallel accounts of the two kingdoms, Israel and Judah.

The Succession and Reign of Solomon (Chapters 1–11). Solomon's reign lasted for about forty years, and was outwardly one of peace and prosperity, although there were undercurrents of dissatisfaction.

DAVID'S DEATH. When David was "stricken in years," Adonijah, the King's eldest surviving son, "exalted himself, saying, I will be king." Nathan, the prophet (see p. 28), hearing of the plan, asked Bath-sheba to intercede with the King on behalf of her son Solomon, who was supported by a powerful faction. Bath-sheba claimed that David had previously promised to make Solomon his successor, and the King agreed that Solomon should rule at once. Accordingly Zadok, the priest,* anointed him about 962 B.C. After final instructions to Solomon to "keep the charge of the Lord thy God . . . David slept with his fathers, and was buried in the city of David." (1:1–2:10.)

CONSOLIDATION OF THE NEW REGIME. Adonijah, who had been pardoned by Solomon, made a request for Abishag, one of David's concubines. Since the harem of a king descended to his successor, Solomon considered the request treasonable and had Abonijah slain. Abiathar,* the priest who had supported Abonijah's claim to the throne, was deposed; and two other adherents of Abonijah— Joab and Shimei—were killed, the latter for disobeying an order confining him to Jerusalem. (2:11–46.)

SOLOMON'S POWER AND WISDOM. Solomon made an alliance with Egypt and married Pharaoh's daughter. One night the Lord appeared to him in a dream, saying: "Ask what I shall give thee." Solomon requested "an understanding heart to judge thy people, that I may discern between good and bad," and the gift was granted. God also told Solomon that he would give him what he had not asked—riches, honor, and long days. The King appointed princes and officers, and he extended his dominion over a large area until "Judah and Israel were many, as the sand which is by the sea in multitude, eating, and drinking, and making merry." (Chapters 3–4.)

BUILDING OF THE TEMPLE. The order went out from Solomon to build the Temple that God had promised. It was a long building constructed out of cedars from Lebanon with walls of stone, flooring of fir or cypress, and doors of olive wood, and it was richly

* Zadok and Abiathar were apparently joint high priests.

decorated with brass and gold. The people were joyful when the Temple was dedicated in an impressive ceremony with a solemn prayer and blessing by the King. Solomon carried out other extensive building projects, and he made regular sacrifices to God. (Chapters 5–9.)

THE QUEEN OF SHEBA'S VISIT. The Queen of Sheba (an Arabian), arrived in Jerusalem from her country in the southeast on a state visit to see with her own eyes whether the reports concerning Solomon were true. After viewing the King's riches and having a long conversation with him, she told him: "Thy wisdom and prosperity exceedeth the fame which I heard." The two monarchs then exchanged elaborate gifts. (Chapter 10.)

CONDITIONS AT SOLOMON'S DEATH. Despite his wisdom, "King Solomon loved many strange [foreign] women, together with the daughter of Pharaoh. . ."; and his numerous wives and concubines led him toward idolatry. Because of this the Lord was angry and stirred up adversaries to Solomon. Among them was Jeroboam, one of Solomon's chief civil servants. Jeroboam escaped Solomon's attempt to kill him for his attempted rebellion and fled to Egypt. Dissension continued until the death of Solomon. "And Solomon slept with his fathers, and was buried in the city of David his father: and Rehoboam his son reigned in his stead." (Chapter 11.)

DIVISION OF THE KINGDOM. Rehoboam rejected wise old men's counsel and consulted instead with his own cohorts, who advised him to increase the already heavy burden of taxation. The ten northern tribes thereupon revolted and chose as their king Jeroboam, who had returned from Egypt upon learning of Solomon's death. The two southern tribes, Benjamin and Judah, remained loyal to the House of David and formed the kingdom of Judah, including Jerusalem and other large cities.

Parallel Account of Israel and Judah (Chapters 12–22). The kings whose reigns are described in I Kings, with approximate dates of accession are:

JUDAH, SOUTH		ISRAEL, NORTH	
Year	*King*	*Year*	*King*
922	Rehoboam	922	Jeroboam I
915	Abijam	901	Nadab
913	Asa	900	Baasha
873	Jehosaphat	877	Elah
849	Jehoram	876	Zimri
		876	Omri
		869	Ahab
		850	Ahaziah
		849	Joram

The parallel narrative is continued in II Kings (see p. 33).

AHAB (16:29–22:40). Ahab, who ruled from 869 to 850 B.C., was probably Israel's ablest ruler in this period, despite his proverbial wickedness. He made an alliance with Phoenicia, and he sought to co-operate with the King of Judah in an attempt to heal the schism between the two nations. For a time it seemed that this attempt would succeed. Although it did not, Israel and Judah formed close bonds. The contemporary Southern ruler, Jehosaphat, also adopted a friendly policy and aided Israel in the disastrous battle against Syria in which Ahab was killed.

ELIJAH (Chapters 17–19, 21:17–29). Interwoven with these events is the story of Elijah, undoubtedly the most influential prophet of the Northern Kingdom. Elijah combined moral insight with practical knowledge of events. His word was clear and unequivocal: Jehovah was the sole God of Israel. He thus anticipated the moral monotheism taught in the following century by Isaiah, Hosea, Amos, and Micah.

Elijah appeared before Ahab to denounce the Baal-worship introduced by Ahab's notorious foreign wife Jezebel. He predicted drought, which came. For the further instruction of Ahab he brought about a contest between himself and the prophets of Baal, which ended with his own sacrifice being consumed by fire from the Lord while that of the Baalites remained untouched. Elijah ordered the false prophets slain. Then a great rain came, ending the drought. (Chapters 17–18.)

In exile because of Jezebel's wrath at the slaying of her prophets, Elijah, utterly discouraged, prayed to die. But an angel brought him food and drink, and God told him to go up on a mountain. "And, behold . . . a great and strong wind rent the mountains . . . but the Lord was not in the wind: and after the wind an earthquake; but the Lord was not in the earthquake: And after the earthquake a fire; but the Lord was not in the fire: and after the fire a still small voice." God told Elijah to anoint Hazael king of Syria, Jehu king of Israel, and Elisha as prophet to succeed himself. (Chapter 19.)

Another story tells how Ahab coveted the vineyard of Naboth, who refused to sell it to him. Jezebel then falsely accused Naboth of blasphemy and had him killed, so that her husband could take the property. Elijah appeared before Ahab again and predicted that because of his wickedness his House would be completely destroyed. (21:17–29.)

The career of Elisha, appointed to succeed Elijah, is reported in II Kings (see p. 34).

II KINGS

II Kings, the twelfth book of the Bible and one of the historical group, continues the narrative begun in I Kings (see p. 29) of the separate kingdoms of Israel and Judah. It gives brief accounts of the problems and achievements of many monarchs from about 842 to 562 B.C. Authorship is unknown; like the preceding books it was compiled from a number of sources.

The nature of the book is the same as that of I Kings—brief pragmatic history, in the Deuteronomic tradition, which subordinates affairs of state to religious development. It stresses belief in one God, stern opposition to Baal-worship (an incessant temptation to the Hebrews from the neighboring peoples who practiced it), and the regulation of all of life in accordance with religious principles. It also includes a number of stories about the prophet Elisha, successor to Elijah (see p. 32).

The two parts of II Kings are: a continuation of the parallel accounts of the kingdoms of Judah and Israel until the destruction of the kingdom of Israel; and the subsequent history of the kingdom of Judah to the fall of Jerusalem and the Babylonian captivity.

Parallel Accounts of Israel and Judah. The kings during this period whose reigns are described in II Kings, with approximate dates of accession are:

JUDAH, SOUTH		ISRAEL, NORTH	
Year	*Ruler*	*Year*	*Ruler*
842	Ahaziah	842	Jehu
842	Athaliah	815	Jehoahaz
837	Jehoash (Joash)	801	Jehoash
800	Amaziah	786	Jereboam II
783	Uzziah (Azariah)	746	Zechariah
750	Jotham	745	Shallum
735	Ahaz	745	Menahem
715–687	Hezekiah	738	Pekahiah
		737	Pekah
		732	Hoshea

THE END OF THE NORTHERN KINGDOM. Beginning with Menahem, the kings of Israel came under the domination of Assyria. In about 722 B.C. the Assyrians captured Samaria, the capital, and deported many Israelites to parts of their empire. Those who remained in Palestine were formed into a province of Assyria and

33

intermixed with other peoples imported by the Assyrians. Thus the ten Northern tribes disappeared from history.

THE REIGN OF HEZEKIAH IN JUDAH. In the Southern Kingdom only Hezekiah, who ruled from about 715 to 687 B.C., is given nearly full approval by the authors of this section of II Kings for his administration in the light of God's teaching. Hezekiah began his reign with steps toward religious purification. He made Jerusalem the national center of worship, abolishing local altars which had been used for idolatry (18:1–6). He was interested in education, as indicated by a note in Proverbs (see p. 52) stating that portions of that work were transcribed by "men of Hezekiah king of Judah" (25:1). He was responsive to the message of the prophet Isaiah (see p. 58), and is credited with a passage of Isaiah (38:10–20), a song of thanksgiving for his recovery from a critical illness.

Hezekiah also proved himself to be, on the whole, an able civil and military administrator. He fortified Jerusalem elaborately and constructed a water system for that city. He carried on a campaign against the Philistines, driving them back to the Gaza strip in the southwestern section of Palestine. However, he encountered great difficulties in dealing with the rulers of Babylon and Assyria. His lavish entertainment of, and foolish display of his treasures to, the King of Babylon drew a rebuke from the prophet Isaiah, who predicted the Babylonian captivity (20:12–19).

At another time Hezekiah was forced to pay tribute to Assyria (18:13–16). But then a military campaign led by Sennacherib, king of Assyria, against Judah failed when "the angel of the Lord went out, and smote in the camp of the Assyrians an hundred fourscore and five thousand: and when they arose early in the morning, behold, they were all dead corpses." Upon returning to Nineveh, Sennacherib was assassinated by his own sons, and the threat to Judah was temporarily ended. Hezekiah lived out his reign without further molestation from foreign powers. (18:17–19:37.)

ELISHA. The outstanding figure in the Northern Kingdom during this period was the prophet Elisha. Elijah (see p. 32) had been instructed by God to anoint Elisha as his successor. Elisha prayed that a double portion of Elijah's spirit might be upon him, and in token of the granting of this prayer, Elijah's mantle fell upon him after Elijah himself had been carried into heaven by a whirlwind. With this mantle Elisha smote the waters of the Jordan River so that they divided, proving to the people that he was indeed Elijah's successor. Elisha is also reported to have performed other miracles, such as purifying a spring by casting salt into it, making ditches fill up with water to supply the armies allied against Moab, restoring a dead child to life, and curing the leprosy of a Syrian captain who had heard of him from his wife's little Hebrew maid. In contrast to these healing miracles, there is a stark story of how children who mocked the prophet were eaten by bears when he cursed them. (Chapters 2–5.)

Elisha was sent to anoint Jehu, who ruled Israel from about 842 to 815 B.C., after killing his predecessor Joram and Jezebel, who was then queen mother, thus fulfilling Elijah's prophecy (see p. 32). (Chapter 9.)

The last miracle associated with Elisha took place after his death, when a dead man was restored to life by touching the prophet's bones (13:20–21).

The End of the Southern Kingdom (Chapters 21–25). The conclusion of II Kings covers the period from the end of Hezekiah's reign (see p. 34) to the fall of Judah and the Hebrew exile to Babylon. This is compact history; at times only a few verses sum up momentous events. The rulers described during the period, with approximate dates of accession, are:

KINGDOM OF JUDAH

Year	Ruler
687	Manasseh
642	Amon
640	Josiah
609	Jehoahaz
609	Jehoiakim
598	Jehoiachin
598	Zedekiah

JOSIAH. The good reign of Josiah occurred in this period, beginning about 640 B.C. Like Hezekiah before him, Josiah destroyed idolatry and achieved centralization of worship at Jerusalem. In the course of repairing the Temple, a book of law was found which became the basis for the important Deuteronomic Biblical writing. Josiah, dismayed at being reminded by this book how the people had disobeyed God's commandments, called them together, had the entire book read to them, and "made a covenant before the Lord, to walk after the Lord, and . . . to perform the words of this covenant that were written in this book. And all the people stood to the covenant." Josiah's reform was brought to an end when he was killed in a battle with Egypt. (22:1–23:30.)

CONQUEST OF JUDAH BY BABYLON (23:31–25:30). Josiah's son Jehoahaz was imprisoned by the Egyptian Pharaoh, who placed on the throne another son of Josiah, Jehoiakim. Jehoiakim fell under the dominance of Babylon as a result of that power's victory over Egypt. During the reign of his son Jehoiachin, Nebuchadnezzar, king of Babylon, captured Jerusalem and took the King, together with many of his people, into Babylon as prisoners. Jehoiachin's uncle, Zedekiah, was then enthroned by Babylon. In about 588 B.C. as a consequence of Zedekiah's attempted revolt, he, too, was deposed; Jerusalem was destroyed; and a second deportation to Babylon was carried out. A Hebrew governor, Gedaliah, was appointed over the people that remained in Palestine. But he was killed in a revolt led by Ishmael, a member of the royal family, and the remnant of the people fled to Egypt in terror. Some years later, in about 562 B.C., Jehoiachin was released from prison by the new Babylonian king and given an allowance for the rest of his life.

I CHRONICLES

I and II Chronicles, the thirteenth and fourteenth books of the Bible, recapitulate previous books; but they concentrate on events in the Southern Kingdom, developments related to Temple worship, and genealogies.

The Chronicles were apparently at one time parts of a work that included Ezra and Nehemiah (see pp. 39 and 41). The writing was probably put into its final form after 350 B.C., following the return of a group of Hebrews from the Babylonian exile. The authors are unknown but are thought to have been Levites who wished to portray a golden age of the past as a lesson and inspiration to the people of their own time. Hence they omitted stories of crude life and internecine warfare such as those found in the book of Judges.

I Chronicles is usually divided into two sections: genealogies from Adam to King David and the period of King David.

Genealogies (Chapters 1–9). These trace the ancestry of the tribes and name their allotted dwelling places. Chapter 6 gives in 81 verses the descendants of Levi through Aaron, emphasizing their religious consecration.

Period of King David (Chapters 11–29). These chapters, especially 22–26, stress the importance of the Temple and worship therein. They tell how David made preparations for the building, saying that it "must be exceeding magnifical, of fame and of glory throughout all countries" (22:5). David, himself forbidden by God to build the Temple because of his many acts of war, gave detailed instructions for it to his young son Solomon. (The name Solomon means "man of peace.")

After planning the organization of Temple worship, David assembled all the leaders of his country and told them that Solomon was God's choice to succeed him. He exhorted them: "Now therefore in the sight of all Israel the congregation of the Lord, and in the audience of our God, keep and seek for all the commandments of the Lord your God: that ye may possess this good land, and leave it for an inheritance for your children after you for ever" (28:8). To Solomon he said that the Lord had chosen him to build the sanctuary and added: "Be strong and do it" (28:10).

He also charged Solomon: "Know thou the God of thy father, and serve him with a perfect heart and with a willing mind: for the Lord searcheth all hearts, and understandeth all the imaginations of the thoughts: if thou seek him, he will be found of thee; but if thou forsake him, he will cast thee off for ever" (28:9). David then said a prayer, thanking God for his many gifts and asking that Solomon might keep God's commandments and build the Temple. "And all the congregation blessed the Lord God of their fathers, and bowed down their heads, and worshipped the Lord, and the king" (29:20).

II CHRONICLES

As noted in the previous summary (see p. 36), I and II Chronicles, the thirteenth and fourteenth books of the Bible, are histories that supplement other books. They are by an unknown, probably Levitical, author or authors and were written in their present form about 350 B.C. or later.

The books of Chronicles, together with Ezra and Nehemiah (see pp. 39 and 41), were probably once a single work. Their value lies largely in their additions to earlier sources, their attention to the Temple, and their focus on the Southern Kingdom.

II Chronicles is arranged in two parts: the reign of King Solomon and the subsequent history of the Southern Kingdom until the Babylonian captivity.

The Reign of King Solomon (Chapters 1–9). In these chapters the Temple is the center of interest. The story is repeated from I Kings of how Solomon asked God for wisdom and knowledge and God granted these gifts, adding riches and honor (1:7–12). Solomon then assembled material for building the Temple. He

"began to build the house of the Lord at Jerusalem in mount
Moriah, where the Lord appeared unto David his father. . ."
(3:1). The holy house contained many decorations and treasures,
most important of which was the Ark * symbolizing the covenant
between God and the people, which was carried to the Temple by
a solemn procession. Solomon then said a prayer, consecrating the
Temple and asking God to hear the people and forgive their sins
when they repented. He concluded:

Now therefore arise, O Lord God, into thy resting place, thou and
the ark of thy strength: let thy priests, O Lord God, be clothed with
salvation, and let thy saints rejoice in goodness.

O Lord God, turn not away the face of thine anointed: remember
the mercies of David thy servant. (6:41–42.)

The History of the Kingdom of Judah (Chapters 10–36). This
narrative duplicates much of II Kings but virtually ignores the
history of the Northern Kingdom except for its relations with
Judah. (The last two verses of Chapter 36 belong logically to the
book of Ezra.)

The account begins with the story of how Solomon's son
Rehoboam, upon succeeding to the monarchy, refused the wise old
men's counsel and thus brought about the revolt of the ten northern
tribes (see p. 31). Rehoboam's grandson Asa destroyed idolatry
and strengthened the kingdom of Judah. Asa's son Jehosophat
reigned well, sending out many Levites to teach the law and seeking reconciliation with the Northern Kingdom. On the other hand,
the reign of Jehosophat's son Jehoram was noted for its wickedness,
as was that of Jehoram's son Ahaziah.

Joash was the only one of Ahaziah's children saved from a
massacre carried out by the queen mother, Athaliah, who seized
the throne upon her son's death. After six years of Athaliah's rule,
another revolt, led by the priest Jehoiada, killed Athaliah and placed
Joash on the throne. Under the influence of Jehoiada, Joash ruled
well for a while, but after the priest's death, he fell into idolatry.

The next good reign was that of Hezekiah, in the following
century. Hezekiah restored religion and cleansed the house of God.
With Hezekiah's wicked son Manasseh, the power of Babylon began
to be felt, and Manasseh himself was taken to Babylon as a captive.
However, Manasseh later repented and was then restored to his
kingdom. (This story is not mentioned in II Kings.)

Manasseh's grandson Josiah gave Judah another good reign,

* See Glossary.

destroying idolatry, repairing the Temple, and renewing the covenant between God and people.

As related in II Kings, Josiah's son Jehoahaz was deposed by the Egyptian Pharaoh, who made his brother (Jehoiakim) king. In turn Jehoiakim was carried into exile by Nebuchadnezzar, king of Babylon, and his son (Jehoiachin) succeeded him. He too was taken prisoner by Nebuchadnezzar, who made his uncle (Zedekiah) king. Zedekiah refused to listen to the prophet Jeremiah (see p. 63) and was evil in other ways, as were his people. After a reign of eleven years, Zedekiah attempted to revolt against Babylon, but to punish him and the people for their transgressions God allowed Nebuchadnezzar to destroy Jerusalem and carry its inhabitants into captivity.

EZRA

Ezra, the fifteenth book of the Bible, is a historical narrative closely linked with Nehemiah (p. 41) and with I and II Chronicles (see pp. 36 and 37). The four are thought to have been part of a single work of unknown authorship, written about 350 B.C. or later. This book is named for the priest Ezra because he is its chief figure.

Probably the historical Ezra's diaries or memoirs are the basis of the author's work. Some passages appear to be exact quotations from a record kept by the priest. For example, Ezra 7:27–28, 8:1–32, and Chapter 9 are all written in the first person. Other passages mention Ezra in the third person; possibly these sections are summaries from the same source.

All that is known of Ezra is the information found in the books of Ezra and Nehemiah. From these sources we learn that his mission was to revive Temple worship at Jerusalem and to establish strict observance of the Mosaic law. He was one of the most important figures in Palestine after the return of a group of Jews from the Babylonian exile. The exact date when Ezra arrived at Jerusalem is not known. The years 458, 428, and 398 B.C. have been suggested by various scholars. He is credited with winning wide acceptance of the older national religious ideal, together with a new emphasis upon adherence to the law, and is therefore sometimes called the father of Judaism. As part of his campaign to remove outside influences, he achieved the drastic reform of forcing Jews who had married foreign women to divorce them.

The book falls into three parts: the return of Zerubbabel and his co-workers and the start on rebuilding the Temple; the completion of the Temple; and the return of Ezra and his reforms.

The Return of Zerubbabel and His Work on the Temple, c. 538–536 B.C. (Chapters 1–4). In the first year after his capture of Babylon, Cyrus, king of Persia, permitted the return of the exiled Jews to Jerusalem. Cyrus also brought out treasures that Nebuchadnezzar had taken as booty and gave them to "Sheshbazzar, the prince of Judah" (not further identified) to carry back to Jerusalem.

Zerubbabel, a prince of Judah and leader of the exiled Jews, is mentioned in Chapter 2 as head of a large group that returned to Palestine. In the book of Zechariah (see p. 89) he is credited with being the rebuilder of the city. Ezra (Chapter 3) tells how he and other leaders of the group set up an altar and laid the foundation for the new Temple. However, the reconstruction was hindered by "adversaries" (Samaritans living in territory formerly occupied by Israel), and, after some controversy, Artaxerxes, then king of Persia, ordered the work stopped.

The Completion of the Temple (Chapters 5–6). But Zerubbabel and Jeshua (a priest) "rose up" and resumed work on the Temple during the reign of Darius of Persia. Darius, hearing of their activity, discovered the old decree of Cyrus authorizing the rebuilding and thereupon issued a decree of his own that the work was not to be hindered.

And the elders of the Jews builded, and they prospered through the prophesying of Haggai the prophet and Zechariah the son of Iddo. And they builded, and finished it, according to the commandment of the God of Israel. . .

And the children of Israel, the priests, and the Levites, and the rest of the children of the captivity, kept the dedication of the house of God with joy, . . .

And kept the feast of unleavened bread seven days with joy: for the Lord had made them joyful, and turned the heart of the king of Assyria * unto them, to strengthen their hands in the work of the house of God, the God of Israel. (6:14,16,22.)

Return of Ezra and His Reforms (Chapters 7–10). Ezra, "a ready scribe in the law of Moses, which the Lord God of Israel had given," was authorized by Artaxerxes to return to Jerusalem, with any Jews who wished to accompany him, and there to teach and enforce that law. Those who accompanied Ezra are listed in

---

* Interpreted as loose usage or an error in transcribing; the king of Persia is obviously meant.

Chapter 8. Before departing he proclaimed a fast "that we might afflict ourselves before our God, to seek of him a right way for us, and for our little ones, and for all our substance" (8:21). Upon arriving in Jerusalem, Ezra was dismayed to learn that some of the Jews had been intermarrying with neighboring peoples. He mourned and prayed to God for guidance. Finally, as a result of his exhortations, all the "strange wives" were divorced. (The names of those who had taken foreign wives are listed in Chapter 10.)

NEHEMIAH

Nehemiah, the sixteenth book in the Bible, continues the history recorded in I and II Chronicles and in Ezra (see pp. 36, 37, and 39), and is believed to have been compiled by the author or authors of these books. Nehemiah, the political leader for whom the book is named, shares with Ezra, the priest, the credit for the reconstruction of Jerusalem and the revival of Judaism after the Babylonian exile.

All that is known of Nehemiah is contained in the book which bears his name because he is its principal figure. Undoubtedly, some of his own writing was incorporated by the compiler or editor of the book. It was probably composed about 300 B.C. However, the events described in it took place much earlier. Nehemiah was appointed governor of Judah about 445 B.C., and Jerusalem was walled and fortified at about the same time. It is hence uncertain whether Nehemiah preceded or followed Ezra (see p. 39).

When in exile, Nehemiah became a cupbearer of Artaxerxes, king of Persia, who, understanding his sorrow for the needs of his people, entrusted him with the office of governor. He is renowned for his achievement of building the walls of Jerusalem and for his reforms to establish strict observance of the Mosaic law and the sanctity of Temple worship. Like Ezra, he opposed intermarriage of the Jews with other peoples.

The book is arranged in three sections (the first and third being rendered in the first person) covering the following topics: the building and dedication of the wall; Ezra's reading of the law to the people and a list of leaders who signed a new covenant; and redistribution of the population and various reforms of Nehemiah.

Building and Dedication of the Wall of Jerusalem (Chapters 1–7). Nehemiah, in exile, was informed that the people in Jerusalem were afflicted and that the wall of the city was broken down. He wept and prayed to God for help. Later, when he brought a cup of wine to Artaxerxes, the King asked him why he was so sad. Nehemiah replied that it was because of the condition of his people in Judah. The King then gave him permission to go to aid in rebuilding Jerusalem.

When he arrived in Jerusalem he found skeptics. Sanballat the Horonite and others laughed in scorn when he mentioned building the wall. The work was begun, however, after Nehemiah said: "The God of heaven, he will prosper us; therefore we his servants will arise and build. . . ." (2:19,20.)

Sanballat and his colleagues continued to scoff and threatened Nehemiah and his workers. But Nehemiah continued the task, praying to God and at the same time setting guards. Though "the people had a mind to work" (4:6), some of them were oppressed by their debts and complained to Nehemiah, who persuaded the creditors to restore their property. In spite of subsequent intrigue and treachery the wall was finished.

Ezra's Reading of the Law (Chapters 8–10). These chapters, which indicate a mixing up at some stage of the Ezra and Nehemiah narratives, tell how the people gathered daily to hear Ezra read the law. "Ezra the scribe stood upon a pulpit of wood, which they had made for the purpose. . . So they read in the book in the law of God distinctly, and gave the sense, and caused them to understand the reading" (8:4,8). After hearing the law, "the children of Israel were assembled with fasting, and with sackclothes, and earth upon them"; and they "separated themselves from all strangers, and stood and confessed their sins, and the iniquities of their fathers" (9:1,2). Then the Levites said:

Stand up and bless the Lord your God for ever and ever: and blessed be thy glorious name, which is exalted above all blessing and praise.

Thou, even thou, art Lord alone; thou hast made heaven, the heaven of heavens, with all their host, the earth, and all things that are therein, the seas, and all that is therein, and thou preservest them all; and the host of heaven worshippeth thee. (9:5,6.)

After further confessing God's manifest goodness and their own wickedness, the people made a covenant, which a number of the leaders signed, promising to observe the law and not to let their children intermarry with foreigners.

Population Distribution and Nehemiah's Reforms (Chapters 11–13). It was decided that the rulers and every tenth man chosen by lot would dwell in Jerusalem, the rest in other cities (Chapter

11). The priests who came with Zerubbabel and their succession are listed in Chapter 12.

Chapter 13 lists various reforms of Nehemiah. These were apparently carried out during Nehemiah's second leave of absence to attend to the affairs of Jerusalem (13:6). The people of Israel were separated from "the mixed multitude." The officers of the Temple were commanded to reform. "Why is the house of God forsaken?" Nehemiah asked. Soon all the people were bringing their tithes into the treasuries; and Nehemiah "made treasurers over the treasuries," including a priest, a scribe, and a Levite. Seeing that people were "treading wine presses . . . and bringing in sheaves, and lading asses," as well as buying and selling food, on the Sabbath, he commanded them to cleanse themselves and "to sanctify the sabbath day." Again he inveighed against mixed marriages, reminding the people that such alliances had caused even Solomon to sin.

ESTHER

Esther, the seventeenth book of the Bible and the last in order of the historical works, is a narrative that has been called a historical novel. The book was evidently prepared for reading in Jewish homes during the celebration of Purim, and it attained great popularity among the Jews. It is named for its principal character, a Jewish woman who became the queen of Xerxes, king of Persia, and whose name was thereupon changed from the Hebrew Hadassah to the Persian Esther.

The author is unknown. The book has sometimes been credited to a group of teachers, successors of "the men of Hezekiah" (see p. 34). The writer or writers had some knowledge of the life of Xerxes and of Persian customs. The date of composition is uncertain but is generally thought to have been after 150 B.C., a time when Jewish patriotism had been inflamed by Hellenistic oppression.

The purpose of the book is obviously to explain, from history, the origin and object of the festival of Purim. Although the entire historical character of the book has been questioned, there may have been sufficient evidence of a succession of events to account for the inclusion of the festival in the Jews' sacred calendar. According to this story, it celebrates their deliverance, with the aid of Esther, from Haman's plot to destroy them.

The fact that the name of God is not mentioned in the book caused long discussion among the Church fathers over whether it should be included in the Bible. However, the omission may have been intentional, to avoid irreverence, since the holiday was probably heathen in origin and was more secular than religious in tone.

The sequence of the story is as follows:

Ahasuerus (the Hebrew form of Xerxes), king of Persia, was holding a feast in Susa, the site of one of his palaces. On the seventh day of the celebration the King sent for Vashti, the Queen, to appear "to shew the people and the princes her beauty." But the Queen refused to come. The King was "very wroth, and his anger burned in him." He consulted his wise men, who advised that Vashti "come no more before king Ahasuerus." (Chapter 1.)

Several years later Ahasuerus decided to seek another queen. A Jew named Mordecai (a descendant of the Babylonian exiles) brought to the King his young kinswoman named "Hadasseh, that is, Esther." The King loved her above all others brought to him. (He did not know that she was a Jewess, for Mordecai had advised her to conceal her identify.) He "set the royal crown upon her head, and made her queen instead of Vashti." Shortly afterward, Mordecai learned of a plot to kill the King and told Esther, who informed Ahasuerus, and the would-be murderers were hanged. (Chapter 2.)

Now enters Haman, who became the King's favorite. Mordecai, a faithful Jew, would not bow down to Haman, as court protocol required. Then Haman urged Ahasuerus to destroy all the Jews on the grounds that they had strange laws of their own and would not obey the King's laws. The King agreed, and the order went out. Mordecai informed Esther, beseeching her to intercede and warning her of the consequences if she did not. Esther agreed to go to the King. (Chapters 3–4.)

The King listened to Esther's plea at a banquet, to which she had invited him and Haman. Understanding why Haman had plotted against the Jews and remembering how Mordecai had saved his life, Ahasuerus then ordered Haman hanged on the gallows that Haman had prepared for Mordecai. (Chapters 5–7.)

Now Mordecai received honors. However, the King could not revoke his previous decree against the Jews. (The "laws of the Persians and the Medes" were proverbially unalterable.) Instead he permitted the Jews not only to defend themselves but also to take vengeance upon those who came to destroy them. Accordingly, "the Jews smote all their enemies with the stroke of the sword, and slaughter, and destruction, and did what they would unto those that hated them" (9:5). To celebrate this victory a time was set for "feasting and joy" and "of sending portions one to another, and gifts to the poor." This was called Purim. The last chapter tells how Mordecai attained wealth and honor and in his high position sought the welfare and peace of his people.

JOB

Job, the eighteenth book of the Bible, is the first of five poetical books. Whether it is also historical is a matter of controversy between one school of thought holding that it was written as a poetic exploration of faith and another maintaining that it is largely historical. A middle view is that it is an inspired poem based on actual occurrences. The book is named for the character whose life and words are recorded. Its central theme is an ancient problem: Why does a righteous man have to suffer.

Job was not an Israelite but a resident of the land of Uz, which may have been in the northeast of Palestine. That there was a person named Job is noted in Ezekiel 14:14, where he is mentioned with Daniel and Noah. He was evidently a man of means and of the deepest piety. He is represented as living in the early period of the patriarchs. However, nothing definite can be said about author or date of composition. Some scholars believe that the main part of the book was written during the fourth century B.C. The author makes no references to historical events. He was evidently familiar with the geography of East Palestine and also had some knowledge of animals found in Egypt but not in Palestine, the crocodile and the hippopotamus.

The meaning of the book has been the subject of vigorous debate, for it plumbs the depths of human experience. It was widely thought and preached among the ancient Hebrews that suffering and outrageous fortune were the punishment for sinful living. But experience showed that righteous persons were at times forced to undergo unspeakable trials, while those openly wicked often seemed to go free and even to flourish. Thus a serious difficulty presented itself to the person interested in the religious life.

There are five divisions to the book: (1) a prologue in prose; (2) a discussion in poetry between Job and his friends; (3) the speeches of Elihu, in poetry; (4) God's reply to Job, in poetry; and (5) an epilogue in prose. Many scholars believe that the prologue and epilogue were written either before or after the main portion of the book; some also believe that the speech of Elihu was a later interpolation.

Prologue (Chapters 1–2). This tells of the great piety and prosperity of Job. "There was a man in the land of Uz, whose name was Job, and that man was perfect and upright, and one that feared God, and eschewed evil. . . . His substance also was seven thousand sheep, and three thousand camels, and five hundred yoke of oxen, and five hundred she asses, and a very great household; so that this man was the greatest of all men of the east" (1:1,3).

There came a day when Satan said to God: "Doth Job fear God for nought? Hast thou not made an hedge about him. . . ? thou hast blessed the work of his hands, and his substance is increased in the land. But put forth thine hand now, and touch all that he hath, and he will curse thee to thy face. And the Lord said unto Satan, Behold all that he hath is in thy power; only upon himself put not forth thine hand." (1:9–12.) Then occurred a series of misfortunes: Job's oxen were stolen, his sheep and servants were destroyed by lightning; his camels were taken by Chaldeans; his house was blown down and his children killed in a hurricane. But Job, in the midst of his mourning, fell down and worshipped God, saying, "The Lord gave, and the Lord hath taken away; blessed be the name of the Lord" (1:21).

Satan again obtained God's permission to tempt Job, on the condition only that he spare his life. So Satan "smote Job with sore boils from the sole of his foot unto his crown . . . and he sat down among the ashes." Job's wife asked him, "Dost thou still retain thine integrity? curse God, and die." But Job reproved her, saying that she spoke as a foolish woman. "What? shall we receive good at the hand of God, and shall we not receive evil?" Three of Job's friends, Eliphaz, Bildad, and Zophar, hearing of his condition, came "to mourn with him and to comfort him." They wept to see him and in their grief sat with him for seven days and nights without speaking.

Discussion between Job and His Friends (Chapters 3–31). After this interval Job spoke in eloquent language, cursing the day of his birth. "Let the day perish wherein I was born, and the night in which it was said, There is a man child conceived. Let that day be darkness; let not God regard it from above, neither let the light shine upon it. . . . Lo, let that night be solitary, let no joyful voice come therein." (3:3–4,7.)

This speech of Job's gave his three friends opportunity to say to him, in the language of traditional religion, that his affliction must be the result of previous sin. In turn Eliphaz, Bildad, and Zophar spoke, and Job replied to each (Chapters 4–14; 15–21; 22–31).

In these addresses, the friends pressed their points of view upon Job with increasing intensity, urging him to submit himself to the justice of God. Job replied with depth of conviction, reiterating his righteousness in the face of their arguments: "Till I die I will not remove mine integrity from me" (27:5).

When especially hard-pressed, Job acknowledged God's omnipotence and wisdom but questioned his justice. "He destroyeth the perfect and the wicked. If the scourge slay suddenly, he will laugh at the trial of the innocent" (9:22–23). An oft-quoted statement, the meaning of which scholars have debated, is 13:15, which the King James Version translates: "Though he slay me, yet will I trust in him: but I will maintain mine own ways before him"; and the Revised Standard Version * translates: "Behold, he will slay me; I have no hope; yet I will defend my ways to his face." Another famous verse, 19:25, "For I know that my redeemer liveth, and that he shall stand at the latter day upon the earth," has been interpreted by some as a prophecy of the coming of Christ, by others as Job's expression of confidence in his ultimate reconciliation with God. Job finally turned from answering his friends' insinuations to a direct challenge to God: "My desire is, that the Almighty would answer me . . . I would declare unto him the number of my steps; as a prince would I go near unto him" (31:35,37).

The Speeches of Elihu (Chapters 32–37). Elihu was a young observer who had heard the discussion between Job and his friends, and who intervened at its conclusion to assert his own opinion. After apologizing for presuming to dispute with the older men, Elihu criticized the positions both of Job and of his three friends. He contended that God sent affliction to prove or to purge the sufferer, and he urged Job to cease his rebellion because "God is great, and we know him not" (36:26). Job made no reply.

God's Answer (38:1–42:6). At last God spoke to Job out of a whirlwind, in response not to his questions but to his plea for a meeting between them. He made no reference to Job's specific case, nor did he give an explanation for misfortune. He did not say that Job was guilty of hidden sin or crime. He did ask Job, "Who am I?" and "What art thou?" In a series of portrayals from the world of nature, God's glory and magnificence passed before Job. God thus resolved the great dilemmas of the book by changing the attitude of Job's heart from bitterness to wonder and awe.

This word from God was sufficient for Job. He confessed humbly:

---

* This and subsequent quotations from the Revised Standard Version (RSV) are copyright (1946, 1952) by Division of Christian Education of the National Council of the Churches of Christ in the United States of America.

"I know that thou canst do every thing, and that no thought can be withholden from thee. . . . I have heard of thee by the hearing of the ear: but now mine eye seeth thee. Wherefore I abhor myself, and repent in dust and ashes." (42:2,5–6.)

Epilogue (42:7–17). God spoke to Eliphaz: "My wrath is kindled against thee, and against thy two friends: for ye have not spoken of me the thing that is right, as my servant Job hath." "Also the Lord gave Job twice as much as he had before. . . . So the Lord blessed the latter end of Job more than his beginning. . . After this lived Job an hundred and forty years, and saw his sons, and his sons' sons, even four generations. So Job died, being old and full of days."

PSALMS

Psalms, the nineteenth book of the Bible, is the second of the poetical books. It has been called a treasury of prayer, praise, and adoration and a Bible in miniature. It is a compilation of 150 poems (psalms, from the Greek psallein, *to play upon a stringed instrument). Psalms have been used as hymns by Jews since several centuries B.C. and in portions of Christendom since early centuries A.D.*

The text of the Jewish Bible mentions the following persons as authors or sponsors: Moses, one; Solomon, two; Asaph, twelve; Heman, one; Ethan, one; the sons of Korah, ten; David, seventy-three. The value of these titles has been variously estimated. In most instances they are probably not decisive evidence of authorship or of the date of writing or arrangement. Many of the psalms are preceded by ascription, often to David, who probably sponsored a collection.

When the book of Psalms is used for public worship it is called a Psalter. Certain psalms are also frequently used in private worship —for example, 6, 23, 32, 38, 51, 102, 130, and 143. Several psalms are found in other books of the Bible, such as, for example, I Samuel 2:1–10; Isaiah 38:12–20; and Habakkuk 3.

The themes of the 150 psalms vary widely. There are prayers; praises; lamentations; reflections on God's providence, his moral government of the world, and the wonders of his creation; expressions of joy, faith, and resignation; renditions of personal circumstances; national, historical, and royal poems; teachings of religion and morality. The religious emphases of the psalms are generally similar to those of the prophetical books. They give modern readers a vivid awareness of the spiritual life of the devout among the ancient Hebrews.

The book of Psalms may be considered in five sections, each of which concludes with a short doxology: Psalms 1–41, Psalms 42–72; Psalms 73–89; Psalms 90–102; and Psalms 107–150.

Psalms 1–41. Of this first group only 1,2,10, and 33 are without titles. The remaining thirty-seven are ascribed to David. The first psalm begins:

Blessed is the man that walketh not in the counsel of the ungodly, nor standeth in the way of sinners, nor sitteth in the seat of the scornful.

But his delight is in the law of the Lord; and in his law doth he meditate day and night.

And he shall be like a tree planted by the rivers of water, that bringeth forth his fruit in his season. . . (1:1–3.)

Psalm 6 opens as follows:

O Lord, rebuke me not in thine anger, neither chasten me in thy hot displeasure.

Have mercy upon me, O Lord; for I am weak: O Lord, heal me; for my bones are vexed.

Possibly no psalm has been more widely read and quoted than the 23rd:

The Lord is my shepherd; I shall not want.

He maketh me to lie down in green pastures: he leadeth me beside the still waters.

He restoreth my soul: he leadeth me in the paths of righteousness for his name's sake.

Yea, though I walk through the valley of the shadow of death, I will fear no evil: for thou art with me; thy rod and thy staff they comfort me.

Thou preparest a table before me in the presence of mine enemies: thou anointest my head with oil; my cup runneth over.

Surely goodness and mercy shall follow me all the days of my life: and I will dwell in the house of the Lord forever.

A portion of the 24th reads:

The earth is the Lord's and the fulness thereof; the world, and they that dwell therein.

For he hath founded it upon the seas, and established it upon the floods.

Who shall ascend into the hill of the Lord? or who shall stand in his holy place?

He that hath clean hands, and a pure heart; who hath not lifted up his soul unto vanity, nor sworn deceitfully. (24:1-4.)

Psalms 42-72. Of these psalms only four (43,66,67, and 71) are not ascribed. Eighteen (51-65 and 68-70) are ascribed to David; seven (42 and 44-49) to the sons of Korah; one (50) to Asaph; and one (72) to Solomon.

Psalm 42 is an ardent prayer:

As the hart panteth after the water brooks, so panteth my soul after thee, O God.

My soul thirsteth for God, for the living God: when shall I come and appear before God? (42:1-2.)

Confession is emphasized in Psalm 51:

Have mercy upon me, O God, according to thy loving-kindness: according unto the multitude of thy tender mercies blot out my transgressions.

Wash me thoroughly from mine iniquity, and cleanse me from my sin.

For I acknowledge my transgressions: and my sin is ever before me.

Against thee, thee only, have I sinned, and done this evil in thy sight: that thou mightest be justified when thou speakest, and be clear when thou judgest. . . .

Purge me with hyssop, and I shall be clean: wash me and I shall be whiter than snow. (51:1-4,7.)

The living Word is expressed in Psalm 62:

Truly my soul waiteth upon God: from him cometh my salvation.

He only is my rock and my salvation; he is my defence; I shall not be greatly moved. (62:1-2.)

Psalms 73-89. Of these, eleven (73-83) are ascribed to Asaph; three (84-85 and 87) to the sons of Korah; one (86) to David; one (88) to both the sons of Korah and to Heman; and one (89) to Ethan.

Portions of Psalm 84 are used in public worship:

> How lovely is thy dwelling place,
>   O Lord of hosts!
> My soul longs, yea, faints
>   for the courts of the Lord;
> My heart and flesh sing for joy
>   to the living God. . . .
> Blessed are those who dwell in thy house,
>   ever singing thy praise! (RSV 84:1,2,4.)

Psalms 90–106. Of these, one (90) is ascribed to Moses; two (101 and 103) to David; all others are anonymous.

An exhortation to praise is found in Psalm 100, often used at thanksgiving services:

Make a joyful noise unto the Lord, all ye lands.
Serve the Lord with gladness: come before his presence with singing.
Know ye that the Lord he is God: it is he that hath made us, and not we ourselves; we are his people, and the sheep of his pasture.
Enter into his gates with thanksgiving, and into his courts with praise: be thankful unto him and bless his name.
For the Lord is good; his mercy is everlasting; and his truth endureth to all generations. (100:1–5.)

Psalms 107–150. Of these, fifteen (108–110, 122, 124, 131, 133, and 138–145) are ascribed to David; one (127) is ascribed to Solomon; the remainder are unascribed. Psalms 120–134 are called "songs of degrees" or "songs of ascents," supposedly because they were sung by those going up to Jerusalem on pilgrimages. In this section are a number of widely quoted psalms.

In Psalm 107, verse 15 reads: "Oh that men would praise the Lord for his goodness, and for his wonderful works to the children of men!"

Another psalm often used is 121, which in the Scottish metrical version of the psalms reads:

I to the hills will lift mine eyes,
    From whence doth come mine aid.
My safety cometh from the Lord,
    Who heaven and earth hath made.
Thy foot he'll not let slide, nor will
    He slumber that thee keeps.
Behold, he that keeps Israel,
    He slumbers not, nor sleeps. (121:1–4.)

The last psalm, 150, is rendered thus in the same version:

Praise ye the Lord. God's praise within
    His sanctuary raise;
And to him in the firmament
    Of his power give ye praise. (150:1.)

There has been much discussion about the meaning of the word "Selah," which occurs some seventy times in the book of Psalms. Speculations range from the conclusion that it was simply a call for pause; that it marked a division; or that it was a signal for a fresh outburst of vigor in singing.

PROVERBS

Proverbs, the twentieth book of the Bible, is the third of the poetical group. It has also been classified, together with Job and Ecclesiastes in the Old Testament and Ecclesiasticus and the Wisdom of Solomon in the Apocrypha, as "wisdom" literature. It is a collection of maxims, or wise sayings, which is arranged in no special order, although usually proverbs in the same general area are placed together. Authors and dates of the several parts are uncertain. The book was traditionally credited to Solomon, but most scholars now regard it as having been in process from about 500 to 150 B.C.

Despite the arguments of modern scholars against authorship or compilation of the book by Solomon, there may be good reason for assigning some proverbs to him. Solomon had contacts with the royal house of Egypt, and there were sages in that country who wrote from a very early date. While granting this possibility, it seems sure that the major parts of Proverbs were composed much later than the reign of Solomon and some passages appear to have been added after the Babylonian exile. (Solomon began to reign about 962 B.C., and Jews began to return from the Exile about 538–536 B.C.)

The book is arranged in seven sections: (1) an introduction; (2) "the proverbs of Solomon"; (3) an anthology of short selections; (4) a second collection of "the proverbs of Solomon"; (5) "the words of Agur"; (6) "the words of King Lemuel"; and (7) a discourse on the good wife. The first nine chapters appear to have been written by a compiler after he had brought the other parts together. Probably Chapters 10–22 form the oldest section and the one most reliably associated with Solomon.

Introduction with Sayings on the Excellence of Wisdom (Chapters 1–9). The opening verses (1:1–6) give the objectives of the book, among them being "to know wisdom and instruction; to perceive the words of understanding." The first proverb is: "The fear of the Lord is the beginning of knowledge: but fools despise wisdom and instruction."

A notable reading personifying wisdom is:

Wisdom crieth without; she uttereth her voice in the streets:
She crieth in the chief place of concourse, in the opening of the gates: in the city she uttereth her words, saying,

How long, ye simple ones, will ye love simplicity? and the scorners delight in their scorning, and fools hate knowledge?

Turn you at my reproof: behold, I will pour out my spirit unto you, I will make known my words unto you. . . .

. . . whoso hearkeneth unto me shall dwell safely and shall be quiet from fear of evil. (1:20–23, 33.)

Another well-known verse reads:

Wisdom is the principal thing; therefore get wisdom: and with all thy getting get understanding. (4:7.)

Wisdom in its ideal aspects is treated in Chapter 8, which includes the following passage:

I was set up from everlasting, from the beginning, or ever the earth was.

When there were no depths, I was brought forth; when there were no fountains abounding with water.

Before the mountains were settled, before the hills was I brought forth . . .

Then I was by him, as one brought up with him: and I was daily his delight, rejoicing always before him . . .

Blessed is the man that heareth me, watching daily at my gates, waiting at the posts of my doors.

For whoso findeth me findeth life, and shall obtain favor of the Lord. (8:23–25,30,34–35.)

The Proverbs of Solomon (10:1–22:16). Here are what have been called "sundry observations of virtues, and their contrary vices," covering the field of practical morality. For example:

Wise men lay up knowledge: but the mouth of the foolish is near destruction. (10:14.)

He that walketh in his uprightness feareth the Lord: but he that is perverse in his ways despiseth him. (14:2.)

He that oppresseth the poor reproacheth his Maker: but he that honoureth him hath mercy on the poor. (14:31.)

Righteousness exalteth a nation: but sin is a reproach to any people. (14:34.)

Short Selections (22:17–24:34). These have the same emphasis as the preceding writings but are not in the same form.

Here occurs a well-known passage describing a drunkard:

Who hath woe? who hath sorrow? who hath contentions? who hath babbling? who hath wounds without cause? who hath redness of eyes?

They that tarry long at the wine; they that go to seek mixed wine. (23:29–30.)

On the rewards of wisdom:

A wise man is strong; yea, a man of knowledge increaseth strength.
(24:5.)

On love of fellow man:

Rejoice not when thine enemy falleth, and let not thine heart be glad
when he stumbleth. (24:17.)

**Another Collection of "The Proverbs of Solomon" (Chapters
25–29).** These are of the same general nature as those in the second
section. They are said in the text to have been copied by "the men
of Hezekiah, king of Judah." A famous example is:

If thine enemy be hungry, give him bread to eat; and if he be thirsty,
give him water to drink:
For thou shalt heap coals of fire upon his head, and the Lord shall
reward thee. (25:21–22.)

"The Words of Agur" (Chapter 30). This is a brief collection of
sayings. It comprises a confession of ignorance before God, followed by various instructions. Selections follow:

Every word of God is pure: he is a shield unto them that put their
trust in him.
Add thou not unto his words, lest he reprove thee, and thou be
found a liar. (30:5–6.)
Remove far from me vanity and lies: give me neither poverty nor
riches; feed me with food convenient for me:
Lest I be full, and deny thee, and say, Who is the Lord? or lest
I be poor, and steal, and take the name of my God in vain. (30:8–9.)

"The Words of King Lemuel" (31:1–9). Lemuel is not identified
in the text. This brief portion is a lesson in chastity and temperance:

It is not for kings . . . to drink wine; nor for princes strong drink:
Lest they drink, and forget the law, and pervert the judgment of any
of the afflicted. (31:4–5.)

A Discourse in Praise of the Good Wife (31:10–31). This poem
is an acrostic in Hebrew.

Who can find a virtuous woman? for her price is far above rubies.
The heart of her husband doth safely trust in her, so that he shall have
no need of spoil.
She will do him good and not evil all the days of her life. . . .

She stretcheth out her hand to the poor; yea, she reacheth forth her hands to the needy. . . .

She openeth her mouth with wisdom; and in her tongue is the law of kindness. (31:10–12, 20, 26.)

ECCLESIASTES

Ecclesiastes, the twenty-first book of the Bible, is grouped with the poetical works and also with the wisdom literature. It considers life with deep skepticism and pessimism but closes with a preachment (thought by some scholars to be a later addition) to remember the Creator and keep his commandments. The title means preacher or orator (Hebrew, Koheleth; *Greek,* Ekklēsiastēs*), but the tone of discussion is more frequently that of a critical philosopher.*

The book is unique both in style and in organization. As a consideration of the vanity of purely human wishes, it has been called the greatest collection of pessimism in literature. Its inclusion in the Bible is thought to be partly due to the fact that it was attributed to Solomon, or regarded as put into the mouth of Solomon by another author or other authors. But it does not seem probable that it could have been written in the tenth century B.C., when Solomon lived. The date of final composition is placed between 300 and 200 B.C. The unsystematic arrangement argues for several authors, editors, and compilers.

Illustrating the varied emphasis in the book are these declarations on wisdom. In 1:13 it is said: "I gave my heart to seek and search out by wisdom concerning all things that are done under heaven: this sore travail hath God given to the sons of men to be exercised therewith." A different accent is found in 2:13: "I saw that wisdom excelleth folly, as far as the light excelleth darkness."

All things here below are vain, says the Preacher. Then follows a consideration on human life which is plainly pessimistic. But mingled with this view is one that the things of life are from God, and therefore man should live Godward. In 3:14 this is put:

I know that, whatsoever God doeth, it shall be for ever; nothing can be put to it, nor any thing taken from it: and God doeth it, that men should fear before him.

Chapter by chapter the book proceeds in its disillusioned reflections.

"Vanity of vanities, saith the Preacher, vanity of vanities; all is vanity" (1:2). This conclusion is illustrated in all kinds of human activity—pleasure-seeking, building, planting, gathering possessions and wealth. (Chapters 1–2.)

"To everything there is a season, and a time to every purpose under the heaven." But how can man find this proper season or escape from the endless circle? His strivings seem of no avail. (3:1–15.)

The fate of man is like that of the beasts of the fields ("All go unto one place; all are of the dust, and all turn to dust again"). Hence man can only enjoy the present. (3:16–22.)

The wickedness of oppression with no relief, the evils of isolation, the vanity of political life—are all depicted in Chapter 4.

Some vexations of present life may be avoided with prudence and care. Riches bring much trouble but are blessings when God gives opportunity to enjoy them. (Chapter 5.)

However, God often denies opportunity to enjoy wealth, and no matter how man toils he cannot attain his objective because he cannot "contend with him that is mightier than he." (Chapter 6.)

Man may alleviate his distress by avoiding frivolity and by becoming prudent and resigned. He should not brood but seek wisdom, which is his best guide. One of the greatest trials in life is an evil woman "whose heart is snares and nets, and her hands as bands." (Chapter 7.)

Care in all matters affecting the king and those in authority is recommended. Nevertheless, the memory of the righteous and wise is often short-lived, while the wicked are honored. Man's efforts to grasp God's purposes are fruitless; all life is subject to time and chance; death quickly comes. Therefore, man must extract what pleasure he can from the life that he has. There follows a collection of proverbs on wisdom and the results of folly. (Chapters 8–10.)

The rewards of charity or benevolence are stressed. "Cast thy bread upon the waters: for thou shalt find it after many days." Rejoice in youth; walk in the ways of your heart; but remember that "for all these things God will bring thee into judgment." (Chapter 11.)

Let us hear the conclusion of the whole matter: Fear God, and keep his commandments: for this is the whole duty of man. (12:13.)

THE SONG OF SOLOMON

The Song of Solomon, also known as the Song of Songs, is the twenty-second book of the Bible and one of the poetical works. It is a poem of human love, containing lyrics of varied lengths, some fragmentary.

This has been called the most obscure book in the Bible. It has also been designated as secular rather than religious. It appears to have been included in the Bible largely because of its association with Solomon and because it was thought to be an allegory : by Jews, of the love between God and Israel; by Christians, of the love between Christ and his Church. It is usually dated after the Babylonian exile, which ended in 538 B.C.

Some readers find it difficult to assign high religious value to a poem on erotic love. Others hold that pure and faithful love between one man and one woman is of all things human most like the relation between a loving God and man. They thus defend the poem as an inspiring treatment of a great teaching.

The book has been called a drama. Its style is one of beauty and splendor, and it includes lovely descriptions of nature and rural life.

A summary of the story is as follows. (This is one of several interpretations that have been made.) A beautiful girl from the rural community of Shulam (Shunem, in Judah) was discovered by a king on his travels and taken to Jerusalem. There she lived in the royal palace, where the "daughters of Jerusalem" (defined as the harem) were singing the praises of Solomon. The King endeavored to win the affection of the Shulammite girl, but she was faithful to the memory of love of a shepherd who finally appeared. The magnanimous King permitted the shepherd to return with his beloved to his mountain home.

The shepherd who was the successful lover is given the beautiful lines in the final chapter:

Set me as a seal upon thine heart, as a seal upon thine arm: for love is strong as death; jealousy is cruel as the grave: the coals thereof are coals of fire, which hath a most vehement flame.

Many waters cannot quench love, neither can the floods drown it: if a man would give all the substance of his house for love, it would be utterly condemned. (8:6–7.)

ISAIAH

Isaiah, the twenty-third book of the Bible, is also the first of five prophetical books regarded as major works because of their length. It receives its name from the great prophet Isaiah, who was active in Judah from about 738 to 700 B.C. Isaiah is regarded as undoubted author of the first part of the book, Chapters 1–39, although, as is the case with other Biblical books, there were probably some additions by later compilers. This first section differs markedly from the second, Chapters 40–66, authorship of which is in dispute. Most modern scholars ascribe Chapters 40–55 to an unknown prophet, "II Isaiah," or "Deutero-Isaiah," who preached and wrote at the time when the Babylonian exile was coming to an end, about the middle of the sixth century B.C. The second part of the book is further divided by some scholars, who ascribe Chapters 55–66 to a postexilic prophet, "III Isaiah," or "Trito-Isaiah."

Isaiah is exalted in style and contains beautiful poetry. It is especially significant because of the idea of God that it presents: God is the friend, the "Holy One," of Israel, but this relationship is conditioned by his plan for Israel as his servant and teacher in the whole world. The book is frequently quoted in The New Testament.

Isaiah: Chapters 1–39 ("I Isaiah")

Chapters 1–39 refer to conditions in large part related to Assyria.

Isaiah was an aristocrat and statesman of Jerusalem in a crucial era of Judah's history. He was the son of Amoz, a man otherwise unknown (not to be confused with the prophet Amos). He received his call to prophesy toward the end of King Uzziah's (Azariah's) reign and prophesied during the rules of Jotham, Ahaz, and Hezekiah—a period of about forty years. He was married and had two sons. It is not known when or how he died; there is a tradition that he suffered martyrdom, but this is considered doubtful by scholars.

Isaiah was a leader and prophet who sought political, as well as religious, reform. He opposed the steady aim of Egypt to make Palestine her satellite so as to ward off the rising power of Assyria, which in 721 B.C. overwhelmed Israel, the Northern Kingdom. Isaiah's neutralist position was considered unpatriotic, because Judah also opposed Assyria and sought an alliance with Egypt against her. Although this great prophet achieved most effective results during the reign of King Hezekiah, who came to power in Judah about 715 B.C., even Hezekiah provoked him by his foolish conduct of foreign relations (see p. 34). When his advice was rejected, Isaiah wrote that he saw God's hand in the approaching downfall of Judah.

This first part of Isaiah is divided into six sections: (1) a collection of oracles addressed to Judah; (2) prophecies regarding foreign nations; (3) a prophecy of Judah's restoration after defeat; (4) prophecies relating to Assyria's aggression; (5) prophecies relating to Israel and Edom; and (6) history.

Oracles to Judah and Israel (Chapters 1–12). Isaiah's call to prophesy is recorded in unforgettable language that had a great impact upon subsequent Judaeo-Christian religious experience.

In the year that king Uzziah died I saw also the Lord sitting upon a throne, high and lifted up, and his train filled the temple.

Above it stood the seraphims; each one had six wings . . . And one cried unto another, and said, Holy, holy, holy, is the Lord of hosts: the whole earth is full of his glory . . . Then said I, Woe is me! . . . I am a man of unclean lips, and I dwell in the midst of a people of unclean lips . . .

Then flew one of the seraphims unto me, having a live coal in his hand . . . And he laid it upon my mouth, and said, Lo, this hath touched thy lips; and thine iniquity is taken away, nd thy sin purged.

Also I heard the voice of the Lord, saying, Whom shall I send, and who will go for us? Then said I, Here am I; send me. (6:1–8).

Having accepted this charge, Isaiah proceeded to rebuke and to warn his people:

To what purpose is the multitude of your sacrifices unto me? saith the Lord . . .

Wash you, make you clean; put away the evil of your doings from before my eyes; cease to do evil;

Learn to do well; seek judgment, relieve the oppressed, judge the fatherless, plead for the widow.

Come now, and let us reason together, saith the Lord: though your sins be as scarlet, they shall be as white as snow; though they be red like crimson, they shall be as wool.

If ye be willing and obedient, ye shall eat the good of the land:

But if ye refuse and rebel, ye shall be devoured with the sword . . .
(1:11, 16–20.)

The prophet then warned of terrible days coming for Judah and Israel as a consequence of, and judgment for, their disregard of God's word. But he foresaw great joy following affliction:

The people that walked in darkness have seen a great light: they that dwell in the land of the shadow of death, upon them hath the light shined. . . .

For unto us a child is born, unto us a son is given: and the government shall be upon his shoulder: and his name shall be called Wonderful, Counsellor, The mighty God, The everlasting Father, The Prince of Peace. (9:2,6.)

After this message of hope, associated by Jews with the expected Messiah and by Christians with Christ, the book continues with prophecies of judgment. Assyria is called the rod of God's anger (the instrument for his judgment of Judah and Israel). But Assyria herself will be punished in due course for her pride and arrogance, and a remnant of Israel shall be saved. Then a peaceable kingdom shall come from descendants of Jesse (the father of David).

Prophecies regarding Foreign Nations (Chapters 13–23). Other nations were also involved in the general political ferment, and Isaiah prophesied concerning them. He predicted the destruction of Babylon by the Medes; the devastation of Moab and of Syria; the conquest of Egypt and Ethiopia by Assyria; the invasion of Judah by Elam and Kir; and the overthrow and later recovery of Tyre. Chapter 14 again foretells the downfall of the oppressors and God's merciful restoration of Israel.

Prophecy of Restoration after Defeat (Chapters 24–27). These chapters foretell the desolation of Judah, followed by a return of a remnant of the faithful: "Lo, this is our God; we have waited for him, and he will save us . . ." (25:9).

Prophecies relating to Assyria's Aggression (Chapters 28–33). These are direct utterances on the political situation in Isaiah's own time, when Judah was attempting to stave off the Assyrian threat. Isaiah warned of the folly of confidence in alliances and in arms:

Woe to them that go down to Egypt for help; and stay on horses, and trust in chariots, because they are many; and in horsemen because they are very strong; but they look not unto the Holy One of Israel, neither seek the Lord! . . .

Now the Egyptians are men, and not God; and their horses flesh, and not spirit. When the Lord shall stretch out his hand, both he that helpeth shall fall, and he that is holpen shall fall down, and they shall all fail together. (31:1,3.)

Isaiah upbraided the people, "Which say to the seers, See not; and to the prophets, Prophesy not unto us right things, speak unto us smooth things. . . ," and who ignored the word of God: "In returning and rest shall ye be saved; in quietness and in confidence shall be your strength" (30:10, 15). Nevertheless, "As birds flying, so will the Lord of hosts defend Jerusalem . . . Then shall the Assyrian fall . . ." (31:5,8).

Prophecy relating to Israel and Edom (Chapters 34–35). Edom, a long-time enemy of Israel, was to come under the vengeance of the Lord. This prophecy is followed by another poem about Zion's redemption.

History (Chapters 36–39). This material is taken largely from II Kings 18–20. It includes an account of the invasion of Judah by Sennacherib, king of Assyria. King Hezekiah of Judah, in his distress, asked Isaiah to pray for the people. Isaiah comforted the King, saying that God would defend Jerusalem. Isaiah then records the story of how Sennacherib's forces were stricken by a plague and the city was saved (see p. 34). In Chapter 39 the Babylonian captivity is predicted.

Isaiah: Chapters 40–66 ("II and III Isaiah")

Chapters 40–66 refer to conditions mainly related to Babylon (or Chaldea) and the exile there. As noted previously, they are hence regarded by many scholars as the work of a prophet, or prophets, who lived two centuries after Isaiah.

This beautiful poetic prophecy may be divided into three parts: first, a promise of God's mercy and redemption through release from captivity; second, the prophecy of the servant of God; third, prophecies concerning restoration after the Exile.

Mercy and Redemption (Chapters 40–48). The writer emphasizes the certainty of release, proclaiming the power and the love of God.

Comfort ye; comfort ye my people, saith your God. . . .

Behold, the Lord God will come with strong hand, and his arm shall rule for him: behold, his reward is with him, and his work before him.

He shall feed his flock like a shepherd: he shall gather the lambs with his arm, and carry them in his bosom, and shall gently lead those that are with young. . . .

Hast thou not known? hast thou not heard, that the everlasting God, the Lord, the Creator of the ends of the earth, fainteth not, neither is weary? there is no searching of his understanding.

He giveth power to the faint; and to them that have no might he increaseth strength. . . .

. . . they that wait upon the Lord shall renew their strength; they shall mount up with wings as eagles; they shall run and not be weary; and they shall walk, and not faint. (40:1, 10, 11, 28, 29, 31.)

God has shown his merciful providence; the people should praise, trust, and obey him. Reliance on idols is vain ("shall I fall down to the stock of a tree?"). God will move Cyrus (king of Persia) to open the way for the return to Jerusalem.

The Servant of God (Chapters 49–55). These chapters, which prophesy God's spiritual salvation of Israel and, therewith, of all mankind, are among the most beloved and often quoted in the Bible. The identity of the Suffering Servant through whom salvation was to be accomplished has long been questioned and debated. Some scholars have thought him to be Jeremiah or another prophet; others, the Messiah; others, a personification of Israel. Christians have found here more than in any other Old Testament passage a portrayal of Christ.

He is despised and rejected of men; a man of sorrows, and acquainted with grief: and we hid as it were our faces from him; he was despised, and we esteemed him not.

Surely he hath borne our griefs, and carried our sorrows: yet we did esteem him stricken, smitten of God, and afflicted.

But he was wounded for our transgressions, he was bruised for our iniquities: the chastisement of our peace was upon him; and with his stripes we are healed. (53:3–5.)

The prophet joyfully proclaims the message of salvation:

How beautiful upon the mountains are the feet of him that bringeth good tidings, that publisheth peace; that bringeth good tidings of good, that publisheth salvation; that saith unto Zion, Thy God reigneth! (52:7.)

He calls to faith and repentance:

Ho, every one that thirsteth, come ye to the waters, and he that hath no money; come ye, buy, and eat; yea, come, buy wine and milk without money and without price. . . .

Seek ye the Lord while he may be found, call ye upon him while he is near:

Let the wicked forsake his way, and the unrighteous man his thoughts: and let him return unto the Lord, and he will have mercy upon him; and to our God, for he will abundantly pardon . . .

For as the rain cometh down, and the snow from heaven, and returneth not thither, but watereth the earth, and maketh it bring forth and bud, that it may give seed to the sower, and bread to the eater:

So shall my word be that goeth forth out of my mouth: it shall not return unto me void, but it shall accomplish that which I please, and it shall prosper in the thing whereto I sent it.

For ye shall go out with joy, and be led forth with peace. . . (55:1, 6–7, 10–12.)

Restoration after the Exile (Chapters 56–66). These chapters, thought by some scholars to have been written by a third prophet (see p. 58), speak of God's promise to reward those true to the law and of punishment for those who disregard the law. The glory of redeemed Zion is portrayed.

For behold, I create new heavens and a new earth. . . They shall not hurt nor destroy in all my holy mountain saith the Lord. (65:17, 25.)

JEREMIAH

Jeremiah is the second in the group of major prophetical works and the twenty-fourth book of the Bible. It is named for the prophet Jeremiah. The time in which Jeremiah lived was one of conflict, political breakup, and maneuver among the great powers surrounding Palestine—Egypt, Assyria, and Babylon (Chaldea). One result of this struggle for power was that in 598 B.C. the Chaldeans invaded Judah and captured Jerusalem. In this book a sensitive and deeply feeling man deplores his nation's sinful tendencies and her oncoming doom.

The book includes a combination of materials describing historical events and the prophet's own experience and teaching. There were probably three main compilations on which the present text is based. All three contain some material which must have been inserted much later than the era in which Jeremiah prophesied (beginning about 626 B.C.). Possibly the book in its present form was prepared in the fourth century B.C., with other additions being made even later.

Jeremiah was the son of a Benjamite priest who lived in Anathoth, a town a few miles north of Jerusalem. Though Jeremiah worked mainly in Jerusalem, he seems to have kept his ties to his native village, where he loved and observed carefully the natural ways of bird and beast and plant life.

He was a lonely man. He sought no public authority and he believed that his vocation as a prophet precluded marriage and family bonds. His unpopularity and difficulties with his own people began early and continued throughout his life, as he called for spiritual reform when they were hard-pressed and threatened by surrounding foreign powers. For about forty years he labored to this end, probably feeling some reward only during the reign of the good King

Josiah (640–609 B.C.; see p. 35). But he was dubious even of Josiah's reliance on centralization of worship at Jerusalem, feeling that true reform must come from within.

During the political upheaval that preceded the Babylonian conquest, Jeremiah was flogged and imprisoned. Yet he persisted in speaking out, compelled by his double loyalty to his people and his God. After the destruction of Jerusalem, he lived for a while in Mizpah; he was then taken to Egypt, and there is no further historical record of him.

Jeremiah the person thus appears before the world as an unhappy pessimist. But through his realization of great disasters present and his vision of future calamities beyond, he left to the world a picture of triumph when he prophesied a new covenant. This covenant was to be written upon men's hearts, and Jeremiah has been called "the poet of the heart." He wrote, in a lyrical style that students of Hebrew call exquisite, concerning a new personal relation among men and between man and God.

The book is divided by some scholars into five parts; (1) prophecies concerning Judah; (2) biographical writings; (3) a narrative telling of the work and suffering of Jeremiah at the time of the Babylonian invasion; (4) prophecies against foreign nations; and (5) a historical appendix.

Prophecies concerning Judah (Chapters 1–25). These chapters, written mainly in the first person, begin with an account of how as a young man Jeremiah received his call to prophesy, in the thirteenth year of King Josiah's reign.

Then the word of the Lord came unto me, saying . . . before thou camest forth out of the womb I sanctified thee, and I ordained thee a prophet unto the nations.

Then said I, Ah, Lord God! behold, I cannot speak: for I am a child.

But the Lord said unto me, Say not, I am a child: for thou shall go to all that I shall send thee, and whatsoever I command thee thou shalt speak.

Be not afraid of their faces: for I am with thee to deliver thee, saith the Lord.

Then the Lord put forth his hand, and touched my mouth. And the Lord saith unto me, Behold, I have put my words in thy mouth.

See, I have this day set thee over the nations and over the kingdoms, to root out, and to pull down, and to destroy, and to throw down, to build, and to plant. (1:4–10.)

Jeremiah then prophesied that invasion and conquest would come as a result of Judah's sins. He exhorted the people to repent and to trust in God as their only salvation.

In this part occur lines called the "chaos vision," portraying the impact of a spiritual experience in terms of cosmic destruction.

I beheld the earth, and, lo, it was without form, and void; and the heavens, and they had no light.
I beheld the mountains, and, lo, they trembled, and all the hills moved lightly.
I beheld, and, lo, there was no man, and all the birds of the heavens were fled.
I beheld, and, lo, the fruitful place was a wilderness, and all the cities thereof were broken down at the presence of the Lord, and by his fierce anger. (4:23–26.)

Chapter 7 tells of how Jeremiah daringly stood within the very gates of the Temple to attack those who placed external reforms before true repentance.

Trust ye not in lying words, saying, The temple of the Lord, The temple of the Lord, The temple of the Lord . . .
Will ye steal, murder, and commit adultery, and swear falsely, and burn incense unto Baal, and walk after other gods whom ye know not;
And come and stand before me in this house, which is called by my name, and say, We are delivered to do all these abominations? (7:4, 9–10.)

Biographical Writings (Chapters 26–36). These chapters are thought to be based upon the memoirs of Jeremiah's secretary, Baruch, who worked the prophet's words and acts into a historical narrative.

Chapter 26 recapitulates the "Temple sermon," telling how Jeremiah was arrested and nearly lost his life because of his warning that, if the people did not reform, God "will make this house like Shiloh,* and . . . this city a curse to all the nations of the earth" (26:6).

During the reign of Zedekiah (which began about 598 B.C.; see p. 36), Jeremiah declared that it was futile to revolt against Babylon or to hope that Babylonian domination would soon cease (Chapters 27–28).

However, in the gloomy days of siege Jeremiah prophesied that the people of Judah and Israel would regain their land. As a sign of his faith that "houses and fields and vineyards shall be possessed again in this land" he himself bought a field and put the record of purchase in a safe place. (Chapters 30–33.)

---

* The site of a temple previously destroyed, probably in conflict with the Philistines.

It was at this time that Jeremiah's prophetic message reached its dramatic climax in the idea that God would make a new covenant with Israel and Judah.

. . . I will put my law in their inward parts, and write it in their hearts; and will be their God, and they shall be my people.

And they shall teach no more . . . saying, Know the Lord: for they shall all know me, from the least of them unto the greatest of them, saith the Lord: for I will forgive their iniquity, and I will remember their sin no more. (31:33–34.)

Subsequent passages tell how Jeremiah rebuked the people for failing to keep their promise that they would free the slaves when the siege was temporarily lifted (Chapter 34): and how he praised the tribe of the Rechabites for faithfulness to their rule of abstinence (Chapter 35).

Chapter 36 records that Jeremiah asked Baruch to write out his prophecies and to read them in the Temple. King Jehoiakim ordered the book roll burned, whereupon Jeremiah told Baruch to write the account again, "and there were added besides unto them many like words." These events took place toward the end of Jehoiakim's reign, about 598 B.C.

Narrative of Jeremiah's Experiences at the Time of the Fall of Jerusalem (Chapters 37–45). This account, written in the third person, tells of the work and suffering of Jeremiah during the siege, and after the fall, of Jerusalem (about 586 B.C.). During the reign of King Zedekiah (about 598–588 B.C.), the prophet was imprisoned on false charges of deserting to the Babylonians. After Jerusalem was captured, he was set free by Babylonian officers. Later, he was forced by Johanan, leader of the group that fled to Egypt (see p. 36), to accompany them. Jeremiah, who had told the people that it was God's will for them to remain in their own land and submit to Babylon, prophesied that those who sought refuge in Egypt would be destroyed there. But he comforted the dismayed Baruch with the words: "The Lord saith thus; Behold, that which I have built will I break down, and that which I have planted I will pluck up, even this whole land" (45:4).

Prophecies against Foreign Nations (Chapters 46–51). These chapters, set apart from the preceding text, foretell the destruction of Egypt, Babylon, and other nations and the redemption of Israel.

Historical Appendix (Chapter 52). This chapter, evidently taken in large part from II Kings 24:18–25 (see p. 33), tells of the conquest of Judah, the Babylonian captivity, and the later release of Jehoiachin.

LAMENTATIONS

Lamentations, the twenty-fifth book of the Bible, consists of five poems. It is placed among the major prophetical works even though it is only five chapters in length, probably because of a tradition now regarded as doubtful that it was written by the major prophet Jeremiah (see p. 63). Most scholars believe that authorship is unknown, and some think that there were several authors. The first four poems are acrostic in form.

The poems in this book bewail the general desolation during and after the siege of Jerusalem by the Babylonians (Chaldeans), about 596 B.C. (see p. 35). However, there is opinion to the effect that the present form of the writing should be dated somewhat later than the events described, which are not necessarily all related to the fall of Jerusalem. (Chapter 5, for example, might refer to any one of a number of crucial periods in Palestine's history.)

The general progression of the book is from expression of grief, to recollection of God's love as ground for hope, exhortation to repentance and confession, and, finally, fervent prayer for deliverance from tribulation.

The first poem (Chapter 1) depicts Jerusalem's misery resulting from her sin, portrays her bemoaning her afflictions, and, in the final verse, asks for vengeance on her enemies.

How doth the city sit solitary, that was full of people! how is she become as a widow! she that was great among the nations, and princess among the provinces, how is she become tributary!

She weepeth sore in the night, and her tears are on her cheeks: among all her lovers she hath none to comfort her: all her friends have dealt treacherously with her, they are become her enemies.
(1:1–2.)

The second poem (Chapter 2) makes hardly any mention of sin, and does not ask for vengeance. The calamity is great; the prospect is gloomy; let the people turn to God and beseech his aid. "Arise . . . pour out thine heart like water before the face of the Lord: lift up thy hands toward him for the life of thy young children, that faint for hunger in the top of every street" (2:19).

The third poem (Chapter 3) differs greatly in style and seems to be a collection of four psalms. Parts of the poem resemble Psalm 88 in lamenting great personal affliction.

In the first of these psalms (Verses 1–24) are these sentences:

It is of the Lord's mercies that we are not consumed, because his compassions fail not.
They are new every morning: great is thy faithfulness.
The Lord is my portion, saith my soul; therefore will I hope in him. (3:22–24.)

The second short psalm (Verses 25–39) includes the following:

The Lord is good unto them that wait for him, to the soul that seeketh him.
It is good that a man should both hope and quietly wait for the salvation of the Lord. . . .
For he doth not afflict willingly nor grieve the children of men. (3:25–26, 33.)

The third psalm (Verses 40–51) opens thus:

Let us search and try our ways, and turn again to the Lord.
Let us lift up our heart with our hands unto God in the heavens.

The fourth psalm (Verses 52–66) includes the following:

O Lord, thou hast pleaded the causes of my soul; thou hast redeemed my life.
O Lord, thou hast seen my wrong: judge thou my cause. (3:58–59.)

The writer concludes by saying that he knows that God has seen the vengeance of enemies against Jerusalem and asks for recompense.

Chapter 4 is much like Chapter 2 in style, but it emphasizes sin as the cause of affliction. Priests and prophets, too, have sinned "that have shed the blood of the just in the midst of her."

The fifth poem (Chapter 5) is a fervent prayer. The final verses read:

Thou, O Lord, remainest for ever; thy throne from generation to generation.
Wherefore dost thou forget us for ever, and forsake us so long time?
Turn thou us unto thee, O Lord, and we shall be turned; renew our days as of old.
But thou hast utterly rejected us; thou art very wroth against us.

EZEKIEL

Ezekiel, the twenty-sixth book of the Bible, is one of the major prophetical works. In addition to being a prophet, Ezekiel was a priest, a mystic, and a writer of elaborate design—a rare combination of talents. He wrote with fervor and passion concerning the needs of his people in a time of social crisis. He placed a new emphasis upon the individual's responsibility to God for his own deeds. His plans for religious organization to develop an independent ecclesiastical power within the state contributed greatly to the recovery and growth of Judaism after the Exile; for this he has been called "father of Judaism."

Ezekiel belonged to the aristocracy of Jerusalem. He began his career at some time after King Jehoiakim's revolt against Nebuchadnezzar (c. 602–598 B.C.). Like his older contemporary Jeremiah, he prophesied both before and after the destruction of Jerusalem by Babylon (c. 588 B.C.). He was carried into Babylonian exile with many other Judeans, probably between 598 and 583 B.C. While there he added to his written works, addressing them to his fellow exiles. However, it cannot be stated with certainty when the writings were composed. Probably at some time after the Exile one of the prophet's followers edited them. It is also probable that other compilers made some additions at later dates.

In his emphasis on worship, Ezekiel foreshadowed the teachings of the priest Ezra (see p. 39). The prophet's life and work are regarded as comparable in influence to Jeremiah's and Isaiah's (see pp. 63 and 58). He has also been called the most individualistic of the prophets.

The book is so neatly divided into two parts that some scholars have concluded that they were once two books: Chapters 1–24 on the invasion and fall of Jerusalem; Chapters 25–48 on the restoration of Jerusalem as the center of a nation and of a religious organization. The book may be further divided as follows: (1) the prophet's call and his prophecies concerning Jerusalem; (2) elaboration of the same theme centering on the threatened exile; (3) further rebuke for numerous sins; (4) prophecies against other nations; (5) prophecies of the restoration of the people of Israel to their own land; and (6) prophecies of the ideal restored city, centering on the Temple.

Call and Prophecies concerning Jerusalem (Chapters 1–11). Ezekiel records his commission and instruction:

As the appearance of the bow that is in the cloud in the day of rain, so was the appearance of the brightness round about. This was the appearance of the likeness of the glory of the Lord. And when I saw it. I fell upon my face, and I heard a voice of one that spake.

And he said unto me, Son of man, stand upon thy feet, and I will speak unto thee.

And the spirit entered into me when he spake unto me, and set me upon my feet, that I heard him that spake unto me.

And he said unto me, Son of man, I send thee to the children of Israel, to a rebellious nation that hath rebelled against me: they and their fathers have transgressed against me, even unto this very day.

For they are impudent children and stiffhearted. I do send thee unto them; and thou shalt say to them, Thus saith the Lord God.

And they, whether they will hear or whether they will forbear, (for they are a rebellious house,) yet shall know that there hath been a prophet among them. (1:28–2:5.)

By dramatic symbols Ezekiel portrayed the oncoming fall of Jerusalem because of her people's idolatry, and he said that the glory of God would go "from the midst of the city."

Prophecies of Exile (Chapters 12–19). As a portent of the approaching exile, Ezekiel publicly moved from one house to another. He denounced false and lying prophets, priests, and people for their flagrant departures from the right way, and he predicted judgment for their sins. An unusual allegory of Jerusalem "the harlot" is found in Chapter 16.

However, in this section also occurs Ezekiel's well-known proclamation of individual responsibility and personal judgment:

. . . The son shall not bear the iniquity of the father, neither shall the father bear the iniquity of the son: the righteousness of the righteous shall be upon him, and the wickedness of the wicked shall be upon him. . . .

Again, when the wicked man turneth away from his wickedness that he hath committed, and doeth that which is lawful and right, he shall save his soul alive. (18:20,27.)

Further Rebuke (Chapters 20–24). The prophet foretold Jerusalem's destruction by the symbol of a boiling pot.

. . . the word of the Lord came unto me, saying . . . utter a parable unto the rebellious house, and say unto them, Thus saith the Lord God; Set on a pot, set it on, and also pour water into it:

Gather the pieces thereof into it, even every good piece, the thigh and the shoulder; fill it with the choice bones.

Take the choice of the flock, and burn also the bones under it, and make it boil well, and let them seethe the bones of it therein.

Wherefore thus saith the Lord God; Woe to the bloody city, to the pot whose scum is therein, and whose scum is not gone out of it! . . .
(24:1,3–6.)

Prophecies against other Nations (Chapters 25–32). Under condemnation for their great transgressions were Amon, Moab, Edom, the Philistines, Tyre, Sidon, and Egypt. Egypt received six distinct discourses and a funeral dirge.

Prophecies of Restoration of Israel (Chapters 33–39). This section begins with a recapitulation of Ezekiel's call to prophesy and his instructions from God. The prophet then told how in exile he heard the news of the Jerusalem's fall. He went on to reprove the bad shepherds of Israel: "Woe be to the shepherds . . . that do feed themselves! should not the shepherds feed the flocks?" (34:2). But God has promised himself to save the flock: "Behold, I even I, will both search my sheep, and seek them out" (34:11). Ezekiel had a vision of the coming of a good Shepherd, whom he called David, and of a covenant of peace between God and Israel.

And they shall no more be a prey to the heathen, neither shall the beast of the land devour them; but they shall dwell safely, and none shall make them afraid. . . .
And ye my flock, the flock of my pasture, are men, and I am your God, saith the Lord God. (34:28,31.)

Ezekiel then declared forthcoming doom for Edom (Mount Seir) and the renewal and blessing of Israel. The revival of Israel was prophesied both directly and allegorically. The prophet told that God had set him in a valley full of bones and told him to prophesy to the bones the word of the Lord. So Ezekiel prophesied, and the bones came together. Then God told him to "say to the wind, Thus saith the Lord God; Come from the four winds, O breath, and breathe upon these slain, that they may live." Ezekiel did as he was told, and the bones "lived, and stood up upon their feet, an exceeding great army." (Chapter 37.)

This section concludes with a symbolic rebuke to enemies of God, called Gog and Magog, and with a plain prediction of Israel's renewal and ultimate victory.

Then shall they know that I am the Lord their God, which caused them to be led into captivity among the heathen: but I have gathered them unto their own land . . .
Neither will I hide my face any more from them: for I have poured out my spirit upon the house of Israel, saith the Lord God. (39:28–29.)

The Restored Israel (Chapters 40–48). Renewal of the people on their own land was portrayed by Ezekiel as an ideal theocratic community. He gave elaborate details for the plan of the new Temple and priestly regulations. He had a vision of the return of the glory of God to the Temple, "and his voice was like a noise of many waters: and the earth shined with his glory" (43:2). The final chapter includes a plan for fair and just division of the land among the tribes.

DANIEL

Daniel is the twenty-seventh book of the Bible and the last of the major prophetical works. It consists of narratives telling of the trials and triumphs of Daniel as a captive in Babylon and of prophetical descriptions of Daniel's visions. The latter are called "apocalyptic" in Biblical terms; they portray beyond the dark historic present the glorious final triumph of the forces of God.

According to the book, Daniel was taken into exile, along with many others, during the reign of King Jehoiakim (609–598 B.C.) of Judah, at the time when Nebuchadnezzar was king of Babylon. As the book comes down to us it is written partly in Hebrew, partly in Aramaic, the common language in Palestine after the Exile. This fact adds to the difficulty of determining the author and date of the book. Although it was traditionally credited to Daniel (a legendary hero referred to in Ezekiel), later scholarship indicates an author who may have written in the name of Daniel in a time of grave national crisis during the second century B.C.

Palestine was part of the Persian territory conquered by Alexander the Great in the fourth century B.C. and divided among four of his generals after his death. In 198 B.C., as a result of war between descendants of these Hellenistic rulers, the land passed from the comparatively mild rule of the Egyptian Ptolemies to the oppressive rule of the Syrian Seleucids. During the following years the Jews were subjected to brutal persecution and attempted Hellenization, culminating in 168 B.C. in the desecration of their Temple. They then rose in revolt, led by the Maccabees, and eventually succeeded in gaining a large measure of self-government. It was at this time that the book of Daniel may have been written, in esoteric language, intended to conceal the author's real meaning from the oppressors, while making it clear to the faithful Jews.

The central teaching of the book is the power of God. God is spoken of as great and even dreadful. He is, however, one who keeps his covenant and is merciful to those who love him and obey his commandments. Angels are spoken of as direct messengers of God, and there are references to a belief in a life beyond death. Teachings that apply to Israel alone are given, but there are also passages indicating the kingdom of God to be a universal and spiritual one. There are statements on the coming of the Son of Man, who was to rule this everlasting Kingdom.

Jesus referred to Daniel, according both to Matthew 24:15 (see p. 93) and to other passages of the Gospels. Parts of Revelation (see p. 168) are based on Daniel's vision.

The book is divided into two sections of about equal length: the first section about Daniel, seer and interpreter of dreams; the second, describing his visions.

Portrait of Daniel (Chapters 1–6). The Jews taken from Judah to Babylon included four children among those chosen because of their high birth and exceptional intelligence to serve in the King's palace. Their names were Daniel, Hananiah, Mishael, and Azariah. Faithful to Jewish dietary laws, they refused to eat any of the Babylonian food except pulse (peas and beans). At the end of a test period they were more robust than the children who had eaten the King's meat: "God gave them knowledge and skill in all learning and wisdom: and Daniel had understanding in all visions and dreams" (1:17). They received the King's favor, and he came to rely on their advice. (Chapter 1.)

King Nebuchadnezzar sought the meaning of a forgotten dream by consulting magicians, astrologers, and sorcerers. When they failed, the King ordered them executed, along with Daniel and his fellows, who were now included among them. After prayer Daniel received a vision of the dream and was able to interpret it to the King as foretelling the rise and fall of kingdoms ending with the everlasting kingdom of God. Daniel was then given great gifts and placed "over all the wise men of Babylon." He asked that his friends, Shadrach, Meshach, and Abednego, be appointed to administer the province of Babylon. (Chapter 2.)

THE FIERY FURNACE. Like other high officials, Shadrach, Meshach, and Abednego were commanded by the King to bow down before an idol. When they refused, explaining that the Jews did not worship Babylonian gods, the King said that he would cast them into a fiery furnace. They replied in one of the great passages of the Bible:

If it be so, our God whom we serve is able to deliver us from the burning fiery furnace, and he will deliver us out of thine hand, O king.

But if not, be it known unto thee, O king, that we will not serve thy gods, nor worship the golden image which thou hast set up. (3:17–18.)

They were thereupon cast into the fire but emerged unhurt, accompanied by another, ". . . and the form of the fourth is like the Son of God.* " (Chapter 3.)

THE KING'S PUNISHMENT. Again the King dreamed and Daniel interpreted. He prophesied that the King would be punished with insanity because of his pride. After the predicted interval of madness had ended, the King repented and praised and honored the "King of heaven." Here (4:3) Daniel says of God: "His kingdom is an everlasting kingdom, and his dominion is from generation to generation." (Chapter 4.)

THE HANDWRITING ON THE WALL. Belshazzar, Nebuchadnezzar's successor, held an "impious feast," using for wine cups vessels previously pillaged from the Temple at Jerusalem. During the feast a man's fingers appeared and wrote a message on the wall, which no one present could interpret. Daniel was brought in, and he said that the writing meant the imminent end of the kingdom. One line in the message, according to Daniel, was: "Thou art weighed in the balances, and art found wanting." That same night Belshazzar was slain and Darius the Mede (king of Persia) took the kingdom. (Chapter 5.)

THE LIONS' DEN. Daniel was at first given a high position under King Darius, but his jealous fellow officials plotted against him to enact a royal statute that for a thirty-day period there should be no petitions except to the King. Daniel, making his customary prayers to God, was taken into custody, and, as punishment, cast into a den of lions. (Though the King had wished to release him, he was bound, like Ahasuerus [see p. 43] by unalterable law.) But God sent an angel to shut the lions' mouths, and Daniel was not hurt "because he believed in his God." (Chapter 6.)

A Series of Visions (Chapters 7–12). These accounts were probably intended to portray events of the author's own historic period, which he believed would culminate in the overthrow of tyrants and the establishment of God's kingdom.

VISION OF THE FOUR BEASTS. The subject matter here is much the same as that of Nebuchadnezzar's dream about the four kingdoms recounted in Chapter 1. The fourth beast, for example, is called "the fourth kingdom upon earth, which shall be diverse from all kingdoms, and shall devour the whole earth, and shall tread it down, and break it in pieces" (7:23). This is interpreted by some scholars as referring to the Seleucid rule. But, after judgment on

* The RSV translates, "a son of the gods."

the last king, "the kingdom and dominion, and the greatness of the kingdom under the whole heaven, shall be given to the people of the saints of the most High, whose kingdom is an everlasting kingdom, and all dominions shall serve and obey him." (Chapter 7.)

VISION OF THE RAM AND THE GOAT. This is regarded by some scholars as a reference to conflict between the Greek and Persian empires and the oppression of the Jews under Antiochus IV (Epiphanes), who came to the throne of Syria about 175 B.C. (Chapter 8.)

PROPHECY OF RESTORATION. Daniel prayed for his people, confessing their common sins, and begging for mercy. Seeking the meaning of Jeremiah's prophecy of seventy years of desolation for Jerusalem, he was told by the angel Gabriel of suffering for "seventy weeks" (interpreted as seven times seventy years, or 490 years) and also of the restoration under "the Messiah the Prince." (Chapter 9.)

FINAL VISION. After a period of mourning and fasting, Daniel beheld a glorious vision concerning the "latter days." The wars between the king of the north (Syria) and the king of the south (Egypt) are depicted. Following the victory of the king of the north, there would be a time of oppression and suffering. But at last the angel Michael would stand up to deliver Daniel's people. Many "that sleep in the dust of the earth shall awake, some to everlasting life, and some to shame and everlasting contempt. And they that be wise shall shine as the brightness of the firmament; and they that turn many to righteousness as the stars for ever and ever" (12:2–3). (Chapters 10–12.)

HOSEA

Hosea is the twenty-eighth book of the Bible and the first of the group of minor prophetical books, so called because they are relatively brief. The prophet Hosea probably spent his public life between 750 and 730 B.C. He lived in the Northern Kingdom (Israel) and was a contemporary of Amos (see p. 78), whose work he seems to have known. These prophets came just before Isaiah (see p. 58), who lived in the Southern Kingdom. Hosea prophesied during the time of political unrest and religious backsliding that preceded the Assyrian conquest of Israel.

Of the author of the book little is known, except that he was evidently a prominent citizen, much interested in public affairs. Because he seems to have had intimate knowledge of the problems and corruptions of the priesthood, it is thought that he may have been a priest before becoming a prophet. From his writing one may judge that he was a man of courage, deep feeling, and keen understanding of spiritual teachings. His poetry of originality and passion indicates a highly sensitive nature. (It appears that Jeremiah [see p. 63], who, like Hosea, spoke with deep emotion from unhappy personal circumstances, may have known Hosea's work, although probably not in its final Biblical form.)

Hosea's prophetic witness is written in terms of his own sad domestic experience. (Some scholars maintain that this is merely an allegory, but most agree that it has the ring of truth.) He married a woman named Gomer, who was unfaithful. After bearing three children, she left Hosea and became a slave concubine to a man of means who could give her a life of luxury. However, Hosea's love for her persisted. He sought her out and secured her return to him. Hosea, manifestly feeling under God's guidance, was led to see in his own steadfast feelings toward the unfaithful wife an illustration of God's unfailing love toward idolatrous Israel. In his own forgiveness of Gomer he envisioned God's willingness to forgive and restore Israel.

The arrangement of the writing is in two parts: first, an allegory telling of Hosea's marriage and, second, a series of denunciations of Israel, concluding with an assurance of God's mercy.

Hosea's Marriage (Chapters 1–3). The story of the prophet's tragic experience, as summarized above, is told in this section. Hosea's compassionate yearning for his erring wife is poetically expressed in terms of God's feeling for Israel:

> "Therefore, behold, I will allure her,
> and bring her into the wilderness
> and speak tenderly to her. . . .
> And there she shall answer as in the days of her youth,
> as at the time when she came out of the land of Egypt.
> "And in that day, says the Lord, you will call me, 'My husband,' and no longer will you call me, 'My Baal.' For I will remove the names of the Baals from her mouth . . . And I will betroth you to me for ever . . ." (RSV 2:14,15,16,19.)

Denunciation and Mercy (Chapters 4–14). This section contains a series of vivid denunciations of Israel, the theme of which is given in 4:1: "There is no truth, nor mercy, nor knowledge of God in the land." These reproaches, however, are accompanied by God's pleadings to the people to turn away from their sins and idolatries. Chapter 11, in its metaphor of God's fatherly love for a wayward child, suggests that Hosea may have suffered from the acts of rebellious children as well as those of an unfaithful wife.

His message is a blend of denunciation and hope. He ranged widely in his rebukes, including princes, priests, and common people. Yet he preached the mercy of God as wide enough for the redemption of Israel and her restoration to a place of favor. He emphasized that God's law for Israel was essentially a moral rather than a ceremonial one. The word *mercy* often used in Hosea is regarded as having a meaning closer to that of love than any other word used in the Old Testament. Hosea's 6:6, "For I desired mercy * and not sacrifice," is mentioned with approval by Jesus in Matthew 9:13 and 12:7.

JOEL

Joel, the twenty-ninth book of the Bible and the second among the minor prophetical works, is a short book, consisting of only three chapters. Of the author nothing definite is known except that he was the son of one Pethuel. His career was probably carried on in Judah, and especially in Jerusalem, at some time after the Babylonian exile ended, perhaps between 350 and 200 B.C. His writing reveals him to be a man of moral insight and force. The text is in poetic form.

The arrangement is one of three discourses. In the first two (1:2–2:17) the prophet himself addresses the people on the occasion of a locust plague. The first chapter, after describing the disaster, calls upon the people to take notice of God's warning and judgment. The second chapter begins with a colorful description of large numbers of locusts ("They shall run like mighty men; they shall climb the wall like men of war . . ."). The people are advised to repent, "And rend your heart, and not your garments, and turn unto the Lord your God. . . ." The third discourse (2:18–3:21) represents God speaking and promising that the suffering people will yet be blessed. The prophet emphasizes the judgment of God but concludes with predictions of the redemption of Jerusalem, the Spirit of God being poured out to the people, the fertility of the land, and the Lord dwelling on Mount Zion: ". . . then shall

---

* In the RSV Hosea 6:6 is translated, "For I desire steadfast love and not sacrifice." In Matthew both 9:13 and 12:7, however, the RSV reads, "I desire mercy and not sacrifice."

Jerusalem be holy, and there shall no strangers pass through her any more." (Joel 3, like Zechariah 14 (see p. 89), reveals thought similar to that of Hosea (see p. 75) in its concepts of the restoration.)

There is much speculation that there may have been two authors of the book: that the portrayer of events of natural calamity in the style of the first two chapters could hardly have produced the apocalyptic vision of the third.

AMOS

Amos, the thirtieth book of the Bible, is probably the first prophetical book to have been written. Amos' witness was made during the reign of King Jereboam II (786–746 B.C.) of Israel, the Northern Kingdom. He lived somewhat earlier than Isaiah (see p. 58) and was a contemporary of Hosea (see p. 75). He was probably active after the year 763 B.C., at a time when Israel, though threatened by foreign powers, had become prosperous. Wealth and luxury had been followed by national complacence and moral laxity.

Amos was a Judean from Tekoa, a village south of Bethlehem. He was a shepherd who marketed wool and was also a grower of sycamore trees. He lived in the midst of a semi-wilderness and was well acquainted with the creatures of the woods. Yet he traveled to Samaria and Bethel, cities of northern Palestine, and observed social conditions there. In fact, he did most of his preaching to the people of the Northern Kingdom.

This austere herdsman-prophet opened a new era in prophecy— he wrote for the world a message of ethical theory and teaching. Having absorbed the laws and traditions that had come down from the days of Moses to his own time, he proclaimed that repeating the commandments was not enough; their central meaning must be applied in practical terms.

He sternly confronted the evils of society and offered a drastic remedy: The spirit of God must be transfused into the social order. He said that the essence of the law was not sacrifice but justice, and he condemned religious observances by people who were leading unrighteous lives. In his view, there could be no purity of worship without purity of life.

In making his plea for social justice, Amos emphasized the transcendence of God and his rule of all nations and all history.

God would not come primarily to help Israel in her conflict with her enemies but to judge all those, including Israel, who had ignored his moral will. Amos thus gave to mankind lasting thoughts on the relation of the individual to society in the sight of God.

The book of Amos is simply arranged in four sections: (1) an indictment of Israel and other peoples for their sins against humanity; (2) broad denunciations of Israel's sins; (3) five visions of judgment; and (4) hopeful oracles. Most of the text is in poetic form.

Indictment of Israel and Other Peoples (Chapters 1–2). The prophet's general message of doom is followed by specific denunciations of Damascus, Philistia, Phoenicia, Edom, Ammon, Moab, Judah, and finally Israel. These utterances are oracles, that is, God's answers with respect to the issues of the times.

His condemnation of Israel is the more severe because of her special relationship with God, who had taught her the holy laws now broken:

. . . I brought you up from the land of Egypt, and led you forty years through the wilderness . . . And I raised up your sons for prophets, and your young men for Nazarites *. . . . But ye gave the Nazarites wine to drink; and commanded the prophets, saying, Prophesy not. (2:10–12.)

Denunciations of Israel's Sins (Chapters 3–6). In this section the prophet attacks the empty formalism of worship and the luxury of the wealthy contrasted with the dire needs of the poor. He points out the futility of national pride and hope under such conditions. The heart of his message is summed up in his declaration of God's word: "I hate, I despise your feast days, and I will not smell in your solemn assemblies. . . . But let judgment run down as waters, and righteousness as a mighty stream" (5:21,24).†

The people have been punished for their transgressions by drought, blight, pestilence, and earthquake, and worse judgments were to come.

Five Visions of Judgment (7:1–9:7). The first vision is one of locusts damaging the land. The second is one of a devouring fire. The third is one of God standing beside a wall with a plumb line for judging Israel. The series of visions is here interrupted by an account of the conflict between Amaziah, priest of Bethel, and

* See p. 15.
† The Revised Standard Version translates this declaration as follows: "I hate, I despise your feasts, and I take no delight in your solemn assemblies. . . . But let justice roll down like waters, and justice like an ever-flowing stream."

Amos. To Amaziah's charge of conspiracy against the King, because of his threatening prophecies, Amos replied that though he was "no prophet, nor a prophet's son," he had been called by the Lord to prophesy to Israel, and he concluded with a graphic pronouncement of doom that specifically included Amaziah. The fourth vision is one of a basket of summer fruit, indicating the approaching end of Israel.* This passage is followed by short oracles against those who "buy the poor for silver, and the needy for a pair of shoes." In Chapter 9 is described the fifth vision, one of God destroying a sanctuary and the worshippers. This account is followed immediately by plain words about the forthcoming complete destruction of Israel. Then come a hymn of praise and more brief oracles.

Hopeful Oracles (9:8–15). These declarations regarding the future restoration of Israel differ sharply in tone from the five visions of judgment. Some scholars believe that Amos added them at a later date; others believe that they were added by another writer after the Exile. They tell of the people rebuilding, repairing, and planting in their once more fertile land, from which they would never again be uprooted.

OBADIAH

Obadiah, the thirty-first book of the Bible, is the shortest of the prophetical books, having only twenty-one verses. It is placed fourth among the works of the minor prophets. The name Obadiah was a common one (meaning "servant of the Lord"), and it is not known who wrote the brief contents. The book was probably written in the first half of the fifth century B.C. It is in poetic form.

The prophet thundered fiercely against Edom, a neighboring tribe long hostile to the Hebrews, saying that God had sent a messenger to stir up a widespread rising against her. (The occasion was apparently an invasion of the land by Arab tribes.) Edom's ruin was to be accomplished by the treachery of her former allies. This punishment was God's judgment for Edom's unbrotherly conduct toward Judah at the time of dire calamity, the sack of Jerusalem by Babylon.†

---

* The prophet employs a pun, the words for "end" and "summer fruit," being similar.

† The resemblance between verses 1–9 of Obadiah and Jeremiah 49:7–22 makes it evident that both passages had a common source or that one bor-

The judgment of God was to come to all nations, and Edom would share in the destruction. But the house of Jacob, Judah restored and reunited with the other Hebrew tribes, would exterminate Edom. All the ancient territory of the Hebrews would be returned to them. "And saviours shall come up on mount Zion . . . and the kingdom shall be the Lord's."

JONAH

Jonah, the thirty-second book of the Bible, is placed fourth among the minor prophetical works. It has only four chapters. The book is identified with "Jonah, the son of Amittai," an Israelite prophet who lived during the reign of Jereboam II (786–746 B.C.) and who predicted the restoration of "the coast of Israel from the entering of Hamath unto the sea of the plain . . ." (II Kings 14:25). However, authorship and date are difficult to determine. Some scholars believe that the book was written after the Exile, much later than the original Jonah's dates. The book is in the form of a story, considered by many to be a parable or allegory.

The central teaching is that God is the God of all peoples; that he is merciful; that his love extends to Ninevites, to pagan sailors, and even to the beasts of the field. The Assyrians, whose capital was Nineveh, had invaded and conquered Israel (see p. 33) in 722 B.C. This and other circumstances have led to the theory that the writer of Jonah was criticizing the narrow nationalistic tendencies of the postexilic period and reminding the people that God's love and mercy went beyond their borders and included their enemies.

Chapter 2 is in poetic form, and the entire book has been called a poem teaching a moral lesson. The content of the book is homogeneous in style except for 2:2–9, a psalm believed by some scholars to be a later interpolation. The story is as follows.

In Chapter 1 the prophet is given a command by God: "Arise, go to Nineveh, that great city, and cry against it; for their wickedness is come up before me" (1:2). But Jonah, wishing to avoid obedience to the command, went in the opposite direction, to Joppa (the modern Jaffa) on the Mediterranean. There he found a ship going to Tarshish (possibly Tartessus, an ancient city of

---

rowed from the other. The threats expressed against Edom in Obadiah are also similar to those in Ezekiel 25:12–14 and Chapter 35; in Psalms 137; in Lamentations 4:21–22; and in Isaiah 34:5–6 and 63:1–6.

Spain). "So he paid the fare thereof, and went down into it, to go with them unto Tarshish from the presence of the Lord" (1:3). While he was on the ship a storm arose at sea, endangering the vessel. The members of the crew asked themselves whether their peril could have been caused by the anger of a passenger's god. In order to identify the offender, "they cast lots and the lot fell upon Jonah" (1:7). Jonah said: "Take me up, and cast me forth into the sea; so shall the sea be calm unto you: for I know that for my sake this great tempest is upon you" (1:12). "Nevertheless the men rowed hard" to bring the ship to land, "but they could not: for the sea wrought, and was tempestuous against them." (1:13). In desperation they threw Jonah into the sea. "Now the Lord had prepared a great fish to swallow up Jonah. And Jonah was in the belly of the fish three days and three nights" (1:17).

Chapter 2 quotes the prayer of Jonah "out of the fish's belly." Some of the descriptions in this chapter (for example, the waves encompassing Jonah and the weeds wrapped about his head) are inappropriate for one surrounded by the flesh of a sea monster. As noted earlier, this prayer may have been a later addition to the book. When Jonah remembered that "Salvation is of the Lord" (2:9), he was delivered out of the fish's belly. This episode is thought by some scholars to be an allegory of the exile in Babylon, from which God delivered the Jews.

Chapter 3 tells of God's renewed commission to Jonah: "Arise, go unto Nineveh, that great city, and preach unto it the preaching that I give thee" (3:2). Reluctantly obeying, Jonah predicted the fall of sinful Nineveh in forty days. But when the people of the city fasted and put on sackcloth as a symbol of repentance, God spared them.

In Chapter 4 Jonah is pictured as grieving and indeed angry because of God's mercy to Nineveh. He told God that he had fled to Tarshish because he had known that just such a thing would happen. "Then said the Lord, Doest thou well to be angry?" (4:4).

Still sulking, Jonah went to the outskirts of the city and sat down to rest. God made a gourd come over him for shade. But the next morning God sent a worm to destroy the gourd, so that Jonah was left exposed to the hot sun. Jonah felt pity and anger because of the gourd's death.

Then said the Lord, Thou hast had pity on the gourd, for the which thou hast not laboured, neither madest it grow; which came up in a night, and perished in a night.

And should not I spare Nineveh, that great city, wherein are more than sixscore thousand persons that cannot discern between their right hand and their left hand; and also much cattle? (4:10–11.)

MICAH

Micah, the thirty-third book of the Bible, is placed sixth among the minor prophetical works. The prophet Micah was a contemporary of Isaiah in Judah, the Southern Kingdom, during the reign of King Hezekiah (see p. 34). He was active probably between 715 and 700 B.C., prophesying, in the strain of Amos and Hosea, of God's judgment to come for the nation's sins.

The problem of dating the book is difficult because of doubts concerning its unity. It seems clear only that Micah wrote Chapters 1–3, but even these may have been compiled some time after he lived. The later chapters may have been written in large part by others and may not have been put into their present form until the latter part of the fifth century B.C. or even afterward.

Of the personal life of Micah little is known. He lived in the farming district of Shephelah, between the highland of Judah and the Mediterranean. There he observed the depressed condition of those who worked the land and was much affected by it. The book of Micah is unique in that, except for a passing mention in Isaiah, it is the only book in the Bible that discusses the social injustice in rural Judah. Like Amos, Micah saw the oppression of the poor by the rich and came to the conclusion that life could not go on in this way and that destruction would surely follow. His writings are among the most cutting and bitter of all the prophetical works, revealing him as a vigorous personality. From a reference in Jeremiah (26:18–19) it appears that Micah's preaching might have influenced King Hezekiah to make some reforms.

The text is in poetic form and is arranged in three sections: prophecies of God's judgment on Judah and Israel; denunciations of the nation's leaders; and a call for repentance.

Prophecies of Judgment (Chapters 1–2). Micah preached of judgment to come to both the Northern and the Southern Kingdom. He denounced the exploitation of the poor ceaselessly carried on by greedy landowners, and pictured God's judgment like an army of destruction marching through the country.

Denunciations of Leaders (Chapters 3–5). This section repeats the charges of injustice, specifically mentioning princes, judges, priests, and prophets as those that "abhor judgment, and pervert all equity" (3:9). Because of such grievous sins Zion shall "be plowed as a field," and "Jerusalem shall become heaps, and the mountains of the house as the high places of the forest" (3:12).

Chapter 5, perhaps part of a later addition to the book, contains what has been regarded by some as a prediction that Bethlehem would be the birthplace of Christ, or the Messiah. As it is rendered in poetic form in the Revised Standard Version:

> But you, O Bethlehem Ephrathah,
> who are little to be among the clans of Judah,
> from you shall come forth for me
> one who is to be ruler in Israel,
> whose origin is of old,
> from ancient days. (5:2.)

Call for Repentance (Chapters 6–7). This section includes warnings of the consequences of sin and tells of God's pleading with the people to reform. Here occurs the well-known passage:

> Will the Lord be pleased with thousands of rams, or with ten thousands of rivers of oil? shall I give my firstborn for my transgression, the fruit of my body for the sin of my soul?
> He hath shewed thee, O man, what is good; and what doth the Lord require of thee, but to do justly, and to love mercy, and to walk humbly with thy God? (6:7–8.)

NAHUM

Nahum is the thirty-fourth book of the Bible and is placed seventh among the minor prophetical works. The prophet Nahum was probably active about 650–612 B.C. He is described only as a native of Elkosh, probably a lost site in Southern Judah. Nahum steadfastly fixed his attention on Nineveh (capital of Assyria), the enemy of his people. He seems to have assumed that the destruction of Assyria would deliver Israel, and, unlike other prophets, he was not critical of his own people. The book may have been written just prior to the fall of Nineveh to a coalition of her enemies in 612 B.C.

Nahum's work is in one way like that of Obadiah—it is a succession of oracles directed only to one foreign nation. But with this the resemblance closes, for Nahum is written in beautiful poetic form with fire and power seldom encountered in literature. The sentences are short, colorful, meaningful.

There is a striking difference in style between the section of the book 1:2 to 2:2 and the remainder, leading some scholars to the belief that the first part was composed by a later editor. Its general thought, however, is in harmony with the prophecy that follows. It begins with a solemn warning:

> The Lord is slow to anger, and great in power, and will not at all acquit the wicked: the Lord hath his way in the whirlwind and in the storm, and the clouds are the dust of his feet. . . .
> The mountains quake at him, and the hills melt, and the earth is burned at his presence, yea, the world, and all that dwell therein.
> (1:3,5.)

The prophet now passes to a special denunciation of Nineveh and predicts her day of destruction. He tells Nineveh that her destroyer is already at her gates, that those defending her are in retreat and cannot be reorganized, and that the holocaust is complete (2:3–13). The sin of the city's people "all full of lies and robbery," has brought about this disaster (3:1–7). Nineveh will try to turn the tide of battle but will fail (3:8–19). "There is no healing of thy bruise . . . for upon whom hath not thy wickedness passed continually?" (3:19).

HABAKKUK

Habakkuk is the thirty-fifth book of the Bible and the eighth among the minor prophetical books. About the writer nothing is known except what may be gathered from reading his book—that he was a native of Judah and probably lived in Jerusalem. His main concern was the threat of the Chaldeans (Babylonians) to Judah's national security.

The book was probably put into its first form between 625 and 600 B.C. and added to by later editors. In 612 B.C. the Chaldeans led the coalition that captured Nineveh. A few years earlier they had defeated the army of the Pharaoh of Egypt. It seemed to be only a matter of time before they would dominate or control all of western Asia. The three chapters of Habakkuk, in poetic form, deal realistically with Chaldean power.

The spirit of the writing in some passages is much like that of Nahum; from the religious viewpoint the stress is upon God's justice exemplified in his judgment upon oppressors. The author's style is strikingly original. The book tells of a drama acted between God and the prophet.

Chapter 1 opens with a declaration of the prophet's suffering as he considered the situation. "Spoiling and violence are before me," reads part of 1:3. In 1:6 God is reported to have spoken: "I raise up the Chaldeans, that bitter and hasty nation, which shall march through the breadth of the land, to possess the dwellingplaces that are not theirs." The prophet then replied, understanding that God had raised up the Chaldeans for judgment upon Judah's sins, but questioning why God permits such evils to exist.

Chapter 2 opens with another vision, of God's appearance to the prophet on the watchtower. (The familiar declaration in 2:4, "The just shall live by his faith," is quoted by Paul in Romans 1:17 and Galatians 3:11.) This is followed by a bitter description of the violence of Chaldeans, and a declaration of woes unto them. "Woe to him that buildeth a town with blood, and stablisheth a city by iniquity! . . . Woe to him that giveth his neighbor drink . . . and makest him drunken . . ." (2:12,15). Now comes a vehement preachment against idolatry: "What profiteth the graven image that the maker thereof hath graven it . . . ?" (2:18). The final verse is one often used in services of worship: "The Lord is in his holy temple: let all the earth keep silence before him."

The third chapter, called "a prayer of Habakkuk," is a psalm equal in rhythm and beauty to those in the Psalter. It tells how God appeared to help his people against their wicked enemies. "His glory covered the heavens, and the earth was full of his praise. And his brightness was as the light . . ." (3:3–4). A prayer of great faith in God concludes the chapter and the book:

Although the fig tree shall not blossom, neither shall fruit be in the vines; the labour of the olive shall fail, and the fields shall yield no meat; the flock shall be cut off from the fold, and there shall be no herd in the stalls:
Yet I will rejoice in the Lord, I will joy in the God of my salvation. The Lord God is my strength . . ." (3:17–19.)

ZEPHANIAH

Zephaniah, the thirty-sixth book of the Bible, is the ninth of the minor prophetical books. The author was probably active during the period of King Josiah of Judah, who reigned from 640 to 609 B.C., and, like Jeremiah, he declared principles upon which the Deuteronomic reforms (see p. 16) may have been based.

Zephaniah is recorded as having an ancestor, fourth generation removed, named Hezekiah. In that generation there was a

King Hezekiah of Judah (see p. 34). It is thought probable that because Zephaniah traced his ancestry no further back, he was a descendant of that sovereign. If so, he was in a special position to condemn the sins of princes (1:8). The book also dates the prophet's activity, "in the days of Josiah the son of Amon, king of Judah" (1:1). It seems likely, however, that the writing was done prior to 621 B.C., the date of Josiah's Deuteronomic reforms, which were evidently inspired by prophetical teachings. The book has three chapters and is in poetic form.

First, there is plain pronouncement of God's judgment on Judah for her various sins. "I will utterly consume all things from off the land, saith the Lord. I will consume man and beast . . ." (1:2–3). In the day of judgment God would destroy idolatry and punish the rulers of Judah for their faithlessness. A great and awesome time would follow, "a day of the trumpet and alarm against the fenced cities, and against the high towers." (1:3–16.)

Second, the prophet urged a return to God by repentance. "Seek ye the Lord, all ye meek of the earth, which have wrought his judgment; seek righteousness, seek meekness: it may be ye shall be hid in the day of the Lord's anger" (2:3). Chapter 2 continues with the prophet's declaring God's specific condemnations of the Philistines, Moab, Ammon, the Ethiopians, and Assyria (for example, God "will make Nineveh a desolation, and dry like a wilderness" (2:13).

Third, in Chapter 3 the prophet turns to Jerusalem. "Her princes within her are roaring lions; her judges are evening wolves . . . Her prophets are light and treacherous persons: her priests have polluted the sanctuary . . ." (3:3–4). God's judgment will bring destruction to the evil, but a God-fearing remnant would be saved. "The remnant of Israel shall not do iniquity, nor speak lies; neither shall a deceitful tongue be found in their mouth: . . . and none shall make them afraid" (3:13). Zephaniah described the remnant in the way of other prophets—for example, Isaiah, Ezra, and Zechariah. They made broad predictions of desolation; then they explained that a remnant of the people would survive the severe judgment and begin a new Israel. Some scholars believe that these prophecies were added by postexilic editors at a time when a remnant had actually been restored to Judah.

Finally, a vision of a happy day concludes the book (3:14–20). "Sing, . . . shout, . . . be glad and rejoice" (3:14). All the dispersed people of Judah should return to their own land. "The Lord thy God in the midst of thee is mighty; he will save, he will rejoice over thee with joy; he will rest in his love, he will joy over thee with singing" (3:17).

HAGGAI

Haggai is the thirty-seventh book of the Bible and the tenth of the minor prophetical works. (The name Haggai is probably derived from an adjective meaning "festal." It may also have been a contraction of Haggiyah, a family name.) The main concern of the author of the book was the rebuilding of the Temple as the center of worship at Jerusalem.

Haggai, a contemporary of Zechariah (see p. 89), was active in the second year of King Darius of Persia, about 520 B.C. He may have lived in Babylon during the period of Jewish exile there. It appears that he had seen the Temple before it was destroyed by the Babylonians (about 586 B.C.). Now, as an old man, he devoted himself to its rebuilding. This dominant interest in the restoration of a place of worship makes his book different from other prophetic works. The book has four distinct sections, each being precisely dated.

Chapter 1, the first dated section, begins with an account of how Haggai reproved the people for their indifference to the rebuilding of the Temple. "Is it time for you . . . to dwell in your cieled houses, and this house lie waste? Now therefore thus saith the Lord of hosts; Consider your ways" (1:4–5). He urged the people to begin to build immediately: "Go up to the mountain, and bring wood, and build the house; and I will take pleasure in it, and I will be glorified, saith the Lord" (1:8). Troubles were sent to the people because of their neglect of God's house ("Ye looked for much, and, lo, it came to little" [1:9]).

As a result of his exhortation, two leaders, Zerubbabel and Joshua, "obeyed the voice of the Lord their God" (1:12). "The spirit of all the remnant of the people" heard them and responded; ". . . they came and did work in the house of the Lord of hosts, their God" (1:14).

The second dated section (2:1–9) is a message of encouragement to those who have been building: " . . . be strong, all ye people of the land, saith the Lord, and work: for I am with you, saith the Lord of hosts" (2:4). The rebuilt Temple would be even more glorious than the old. "And I will shake all nations, and the desire of all nations shall come: and I will fill this house with glory, saith the Lord of hosts" (2:7).

The third dated section (2:10–19) deals with practices that have made the people unclean but holds out hope of favor and blessings.

88

The final dated section (2:20–23) tells how the word of God came to Haggai asking him to praise Zerubbabel, governor of Judah, and to say to him that the Lord had chosen him and would make him "as a signet." (The signet was a sort of seal, often used to sign documents.) Scholars regard this passage as referring to the widely expected Messianic kingdom, to be ruled by an ideal king, under whom there would be universal prosperity and peace. (See Isaiah 9:2–7.)

ZECHARIAH

Zechariah is the thirty-eighth book of the Bible and the eleventh of the minor prophetical works. Zechariah, a contemporary of Haggai (see p. 88), was probably a young man when he began his prophetic work, about 520 B.C. He stressed the importance of Temple worship and looked toward a Messianic kingdom with an ideal ruler.

Zechariah probably wrote only Chapters 1–8 of the book that bears his name. His writing is conspicious for its symbolism in the form of visions interpreted by an angel. Like many other Old Testament books, this one emphasizes the teaching of righteousness. Chapters 9–14 differ sharply in subject matter and style from the earlier chapters, and they are probably by a later author. However, no definite date of authorship can be set.

Chapters 1–8 are divided into three sections: a call to repentance; a series of nocturnal visions; and the prophet's reply to questions about fasting. Chapters 9–14 are anonymous and somewhat miscellaneous writings.

Call to Repentance (1:1–6). The prophet told the people that their fathers had not been penitent and had therefore received judgment. Now these ancestors were gone, but the word of God abides.

Visions (1:7–6:15). Zechariah records a series of visions, each of which was explained to him by an angel. The prophet here summarizes his great hopes for the people in the Messianic time. The passage beginning at 6:9 tells that God directed him to use silver and gold brought to Jerusalem by agents of the Babylonian Jews and to have a crown made of them for Zerubbabel (see p. 40). The crown was to be placed in the Temple as a memorial to these men. Joshua, as priest, was to take his place beside the throne of Zerubbabel, and the two authorities were to co-operate peacefully.

Then people would come from far and wide to help build the Temple.

Questions about Fasting (Chapters7–8). The prophet was asked whether or not fasts should still be observed, as they had been during the Exile. In the tradition of the great prophets he replied that God wanted not outward observance but morality: "Execute true judgment, and shew mercy and compassions every man to his brother" (7:9). He pointed to the coming of the Messianic age, when "Jerusalem shall be called a city of truth" (8:3).

Miscellaneous Writings (Chapters 9–14). Chapter 9 announces God's judgment of Damascus, Tyre, Sidon, and the Philistines. Jerusalem was to be the site of a Messianic kingdom ruled by an ideal king, who would ride into the city on an ass, the animal of peace. In Chapter 11 the prophet pictures worthless shepherds failing to care for their sheep. In Chapter 13 the people are assured that God would smite the shepherds and save a remnant of the nation; he would root out the names of the idols and expel prophets (many of whom were at this time corrupt) along with unclean spirits from the land. In Chapter 14 God is portrayed as defending Jerusalem against attack by other nations. The book concludes with a prediction that all those that were left of the enemy peoples would come to Jerusalem to worship God and to keep the Feast of the Tabernacles.

MALACHI

Malachi, the thirty-ninth book of the Bible, is the last book both of the Old Testament and of the minor prophetical works. (Malachi means "messenger"; the name of the author is unknown.) The date of Malachi's activity is difficult to determine; it is thought to have been from about 458 to 432 B.C. when the condition of the people must have been one of great anxiety. They had been disillusioned on returning to their homeland from the Exile and finding life there very different from the ideal prophecies. They had been afflicted by drought and destructive locusts. The priests were careless and sacrifices were neglected. The root of the difficulties, Malachi found, was in the weak religious life and dim spiritual vision.

In contrast to most other prophetic writings, this book emphasizes correct observance of religious ritual. It states that the priests must be purified so that they may properly lead the people. The style of writing is also different from other prophetic literature. The method of presentation, for example, differs considerably from the forthright preachings of Amos, the farmer from Tekoa (see p. 78). Malachi does not seek to develop great principles. He rather applies certain established principles to the practical issues of life. He states his thesis, then gives objections and answers them.

The four chapters are arranged in distinct sections, as follows:

God's Love (1:2–5). When the people asked for evidence of the reality of God's love for their nation, Malachi answered in terms of history, reminding Judah of the sufferings of the neighboring Edom (see p. 80). Judah should recognize the love of God in that her own conditions were far less hard than were those of her old enemy.

Neglect of Religious Observance (1:6–2:9). God expected a return for his love. Instead, the ritual observances had deteriorated. The priests were told that if they did not listen, God would send a curse upon them. God recalled his covenant with Levi, the founder of the priestly tribe, who "walked with me in peace and equity"; but the priests had "departed out of the way."

Deterioration of Marriage (2:10–16). The people had married "the daughter of a strange god" (heathen women); God would "cut off the man that doeth this."

God's Messenger (2:17–3:5). To the question "Where is the God of judgment?" the prophet replied that God's messenger would surely come. But his coming was to be followed by God's judgment "against the sorcerers, . . . the adulterers, . . . false swearers, and . . . those that oppress the hireling in his wages, the widow, and the fatherless, and that turn aside the stranger from his right . . ." (3:5).

Neglect of Offerings (3:6–12). Malachi spoke directly to the people, rebuking them for robbing God and promising that if they would bring in their tithes and offerings God would send the abundance that they lacked and longed for.

Rewards of Obedience (3:13–4:4). The prophet returned to the root of the difficulty—the people thought that God did not care for his servants. He told them not to despair but to obey the Mosaic law. He said that, in the time of sifting, God would remember those who worshipped and obeyed him.

Return of Elijah (4:5–6). Malachi (or, as some scholars believe, a later editor) predicted the return of Elijah to earth. "And he shall turn the heart of the fathers to the children, and the heart of the children to their fathers, lest I come and smite the earth with a curse."

PALESTINE DURING THE PERIOD OF THE DIVIDED KINGDOM

PALESTINE DURING THE TIME OF CHRIST

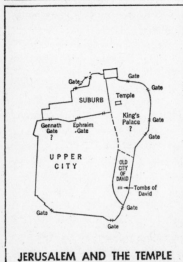

JERUSALEM AND THE TEMPLE DURING OLD TESTAMENT TIMES

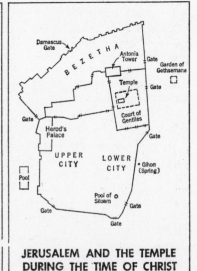

JERUSALEM AND THE TEMPLE DURING THE TIME OF CHRIST

PART II: THE NEW TESTAMENT, BOOK BY BOOK

The first four books of the New Testament are called Gospels, meaning "good news." They tell of the coming of Christ, his teachings, his crucifixion, and his resurrection. The first three Gospels, Matthew, Mark, and Luke, are termed synoptic, because their general viewpoint and arrangement, are similar. The fourth Gospel, John, has a different emphasis and order.

MATTHEW

Matthew, the first book of the New Testament, and the fortieth book of the Bible, is like the other Gospels in that its text does not give a hint of authorship. Thus, information about the supposed writer comes only from study of the text in relation to the traditions of the early Christian Church, which identified him as one of the twelve apostles. Some modern scholars believe that the book is not an eyewitness account but is based upon oral traditions and written sources available to the author. The Gospel, as it has come down to us, may have been composed as early as A.D. 80. There is one theory that Matthew's Gospel was the first; another, more generally accepted one, that the writing of Matthew came considerably after Mark's and was based in part on Mark's. Matthew's narrative, next to Luke's the longest of the Gospels, presents an account of the life of Jesus that emphasizes topics of Jesus' teaching and is relatively unconcerned with stories, descriptions, and theology.

Matthew is named as one of the apostles in the lists of these given in Matthew (10:3), Mark (3:18), Luke (6:15), and Acts (1:13). It is evident that he was a Jew. He was a tax-gatherer, a despised occupation to most Jews during the Roman rule of Palestine. While he was stationed at Capernaum, his "place of toll" on the trade route between the Mediterranean and Damascus, Jesus called him to be one of his disciples. Mention is made of this call in Matthew (9:9), Luke (5:27), and Mark (2:14). (Luke and Mark give his name as Levi.) The calling of Matthew from a class ceremonially outlawed was of special significance, for it showed the people that Jesus' ministry was independent of the organized religion of his time. After Matthew had responded to Jesus' call, he arranged a "great feast" for his Master. The guests, in addition to Jesus and his disciples, included other tax-collectors (publicans) and "sinners," with whom Matthew had been associating. It was upon this occasion that Jesus, when he was criticized for his choice of companions replied, "They that are whole have no need of the physician, but they that are sick" (Mark 2:17).

There are important differences between Matthew and the other three Gospels. Matthew makes more references to Old Testament writings and the Law of Moses than do the others. The book includes (in Chapters 5–7) the most complete text of the Sermon on the Mount. It gives unique detail on the birth of Jesus. Declarations of the nation's impending doom appear only in Matthew, as do most of Jesus' denunciations of the scribes and the Pharisees and his sayings on the "last things" (eschatology). Matthew gives more instructions for the Church including (16:18–19) the charge to Peter, on which the claim of papal authority was based. Matthew alone gives Jesus' command to go into all the world and seek disciples.

Matthew's main purpose seems to have been to write, especially for Jews, the life and message of Jesus as the fulfillment of their religion and the consummation of their history, but not as an answer to the national hope for the ideal Messianic kingdom. In other words, Jesus is presented as the Jewish Messiah but not as the Messiah had been generally expected. Matthew also stressed that the teaching of the kingdom of God was world-wide in its application and scope. Like the other writers of the synoptic Gospels, he tells the story of Jesus' life and ministry in chronological sequence, concluding with an account of his trial, crucifixion, and resurrection.

Jesus' Birth and Childhood (Chapters 1–2). The book opens with a genealogy giving the descent of Jesus through many generations, including among his ancestors Abraham and David. The author then tells of the birth of Jesus as the fulfillment of the prophecy (Isaiah 7:14) that "a virgin shall be with child, and shall bring forth a son." The baby was born to Mary in Bethlehem, and her husband, Joseph, named him Jesus, as an angel of the Lord had commanded in a dream. The angel also told Joseph that the child "shall save his people from their sins" (1:21). "Wise men from the east" came to worship the infant, calling him "King of the Jews." Herod, then the ruler of Judaea, under the Roman Empire (see p. 178), was troubled by reports of this visit and sought the child to have him killed. But an angel again appeared in a dream to Joseph and told him to flee to Egypt with Jesus and Mary. The family remained in

Egypt until Herod's death made it safe for them to return to Judaea. Then they settled in Nazareth, which became Jesus' home.

Jesus' Baptism (Chapter 3). John, who preached repentance in the Judean wilderness, baptized Jesus. Then there came "a voice from heaven, saying, This is my beloved Son, in whom I am well pleased."

Jesus' Temptation (4:1–11). Jesus spent forty days fasting in the wilderness. At the end of this time the devil appeared, tempting him: to make bread from stones to feed himself; to cast himself down from a pinnacle of the Temple as proof that God would not let him be harmed; and to gain possession of all the kingdoms of the world by worshipping Satan. To each of these temptations Jesus replied with a word of God which forbade it. His final rebuke to the devil was: "Thou shalt worship the Lord thy God, and him only shalt thou serve."

The Beginning of Jesus' Work in Galilee (4:12–25). Jesus left Nazareth and went to the coastal city of Capernaum, in Galilee, again fulfilling a prophecy. "From that time Jesus began to preach, and to say, Repent: for the kingdom of heaven is at hand." Walking by the Sea of Galilee, he saw two brothers, "Simon called Peter," and Andrew, both fishermen. "And he saith unto them, Follow me, and I will make you fishers of men. And they straightway left their nets, and followed him." Then he called two other fishermen brothers, James and John, who "left the ship and their father, and followed him." Having gathered his first disciples, "Jesus went about all Galilee, teaching in their synagogues, and preaching the gospel of the kingdom, and healing all manner of sickness . . . among the people." His fame spread even throughout neighboring Syria. Many sick people were brought to him "and he healed them." And from regions round about "there followed him great multitudes of people."

The Galilean Ministry of Jesus (Chapters 5–13). This section includes accounts of sermons, parables, and miracles.

THE SERMON ON THE MOUNT. (Chapters 5–7). Matthew records this sermon as preached on a mountain, where Jesus' disciples came to him. It opens with the well-known Beatitudes:

Blessed are the poor in spirit: for theirs is the kingdom of heaven.
Blessed are they that mourn: for they shall be comforted.
Blessed are the meek: for they shall inherit the earth.
Blessed are they which do hunger and thirst after righteousness: for they shall be filled.
Blessed are the merciful: for they shall obtain mercy.
Blessed are the pure in heart: for they shall see God.
Blessed are the peacemakers: for they shall be called the children of God.

Blessed are they which are persecuted for righteousness' sake: for theirs is the kingdom of heaven.

Blessed are ye, when men shall revile you, and persecute you, and shall say all manner of evil against you falsely, for my sake.

Rejoice, and be exceeding glad: for great is your reward in heaven: for so persecuted they the prophets which were before you. (5:3–12.)

Jesus continued with more teachings.

Think not that I am come to destroy the law, or the prophets: I am come not to destroy, but to fulfil. (5:17.)

Ye have heard that it was said by them of old time, Thou shalt not kill; and whosoever shall kill shall be in danger of the judgment; But I say unto you, That whosoever is angry with his brother without a cause shall be in danger of the judgment . . . (5:21–22.)

Ye have heard that it was said by them of old time, Thou shalt not commit adultery: But I say unto you, That whosoever looketh on a woman to lust after her hath committed adultery with her already in his heart. (5:27–28.)

Ye have heard that it hath been said, Thou shalt love thy neighbour . . . But I say unto you, Love your enemies, bless them that curse you, do good to them that hate you, and pray for them which despitefully use you, and persecute you . . . (5:43–44).

He admonished: "Do not your alms before men" (6:1). Do not, he went on, pray like the hypocrites on public street corners, but go into your room and shut the door. Do not use vain repetitions like the heathen but pray in this way:

Our Father who art in heaven, Hallowed be thy name. Thy kingdom come. Thy will be done on earth, as it is in heaven. Give us this day our daily bread. And forgive us our debts, as we forgive our debtors. And lead us not into temptation, but deliver us from evil: For thine is the kingdom, and the power, and the glory, for ever. Amen. (6:9–15; the above is the form of the Lord's Prayer commonly used in worship services; the King James "which art" is changed to "who art" and the King James "in earth" to "on earth.")

Other sayings central to Christianity follow:

Lay not up for yourselves treasures upon earth, where moth and rust doth corrupt, and where thieves break through and steal: But lay up for yourselves treasures in heaven, where neither moth nor dust doth corrupt, and where thieves do not break through nor steal. (6:19–20).

No man can serve two masters: for either he will hate the one, and love the other; or else he will hold to the one and despise the other. Ye cannot serve God and mammon. (6:24.)

. . . seek ye first the kingdom of God, and his righteousness; and all these things shall be added unto you. (6:33.)

Ask, and it shall be given you; seek, and ye shall find; knock, and it shall be opened unto you. (7:7.)

Therefore all things whatsoever ye would that men should do to you, do ye even so to them: for this is the law and the prophets. (7:12.)

. . . strait is the gate, and narrow is the way, which leadeth unto life, and few there be that find it. (7:14.)

Not every one that saith unto me, Lord, Lord, shall enter into the kingdom of heaven; but he that doeth the will of my Father which is in heaven. (7:21.)

He told a parable comparing those who heard his words and did then to a man who built his house on a rock, so that it was safe from floods and wind, while the houses built upon sand were destroyed.

SERIES OF HEALINGS (8:1–9:34). In this section a number of miraculous healings by Jesus are reported. The cured included a leper, Peter's mother-in-law (sick with a fever), a palsied man, and the daughter of a prominent official, whom Jesus raised from the dead. It was during this time that "as Jesus passed forth . . . he saw a man, named Matthew, sitting at the receipt of custom: and he saith unto him, Follow me. And he arose and followed him" (9:9).

FURTHER TEACHING AND INSTRUCTIONS TO APOSTLES (9:35–13:58). The following twelve disciples were made apostles and instructed by Jesus to go forth preaching and healing: Simon (Peter), Andrew, James, John, Philip, Bartholomew, Thomas, Matthew, James, Lebbaeus (Thaddaeus), Simon the Canaanite, and Judas Iscariot, "who also betrayed him." Jesus told them how to conduct themselves on their journeys and reminded them of the costs and rewards of his service. "He that findeth his life shall lose it: and he that loseth his life for my sake shall find it" (10:39).

This section records events indicating opposition to Jesus, including pointed inquiries from Pharisees. Despite this hostility, he went on teaching his disciples. Familiar parables are included in Chapter 13. One compares the kingdom of heaven to a man who sowed wheat in his field, which grew beside the tares that his enemy had sowed among it. He would not let his servants weed out the tares lest they root out the wheat too, but he commanded that wheat and tares should grow together until the harvest, at which time the tares would be burned while the wheat was gathered into the barn. Another parable likens the kingdom of heaven to a pearl of great price found by a merchant, who thereupon "went and sold all that he had, and bought it."

When Jesus had finished telling the parables, he went to visit his own village of Nazareth, where he taught in the synagogue, astonishing the people with his wisdom. They asked, "Is not this the carpenter's son?" And did they not know his brothers and sisters?

"But Jesus said unto them, A prophet is not without honour, save in his own country, and in his own house. And he did not many mighty works there because of their unbelief." (13:54–58.)

Miracles and Miscellaneous Teachings (Chapters 14–20). This section opens with an account of the execution by Herod of John the Baptist. When Jesus heard of it he went to a desert place, where the multitude followed him and where the miracle of the feeding of the five thousand occurred. Next is told the story of Jesus' walking on the water. Chapter 15 tells how Jesus left Galilee to preach for a while in the Phoenician coastal cities of Tyre and Sidon.

These chapters include a number of varied teachings, some of which relate to the coming Church. In reply to Jesus' question, "Whom say ye that I am," Peter answered, "Thou are the Christ, the Son of the living God." Then Jesus told him, "And I say also unto thee, That thou art Peter, and upon this rock * I will build my church; and the gates of hell shall not prevail against it" (16:18). From that time on, Jesus impressed upon his disciples, "how that he must go unto Jerusalem, and suffer many things . . . and be killed, and be raised again the third day" (16:21).

Chapter 17 tells how Jesus went up on a mountain with Peter, James, and John and was there transfigured so that "his face did shine as the sun, and his raiment was white as the light" (17:2).

Speaking at Capernaum, Jesus told the parable of the lost sheep: The man having a hundred sheep would leave the ninety-nine to seek the one gone astray and rejoice more upon finding it than over the ninety-nine which had not gone astray. "For the Son of man is come to save that which was lost." (18:11–14.) Then Jesus again left Galilee and went beyond the Jordan to the coasts of Judaea, where he continued his teaching and healing.

Journey to Jerusalem and Teachings There (Chapters 21–25). Jesus rode triumphantly into Jerusalem on an ass, as his followers shouted Hosanna! He drove out of the Temple the money-changers and those who bought and sold, afterward performing healing miracles there. He told more parables and answered questions put to him. When someone asked which was the great commandment in the law,

Jesus said unto him, Thou shalt love the Lord thy God with all thy heart, and with all thy soul, and with all thy mind.

This is the first and great commandment.

And the second it like unto it, Thou shalt love thy neighbour as thyself.

---

* The name Peter means stone, and Jesus follows this appellation with a reference to the bedrock that will be the foundation of the Church.

On these two commandments hang all the law and the prophets.
(22:37–40.)

He spoke of his coming rejection, denounced the scribes and
Pharisees for their hypocrisy and their neglect of "judgment, mercy
and faith," and lamented over Jerusalem ("thou that killest the
prophets, and stonest them which are sent unto thee"). Chapters
24–25 tell of his predictions of the destruction of Temple and the
Last Judgment, "when the Son of man shall come in his glory,
and all the holy angels with him." Then those would inherit the
Kingdom who had fed the hungry, clothed the naked, taken in the
stranger, visited the sick and the prisoners; "Inasmuch as ye have
done it unto one of the least of these my brethren, ye have done it
unto me" (25:40).

Trial, Passion, and Resurrection (Chapters 26–28). "The Son
of man is betrayed to be crucified" (26:2). Jesus held a last supper
with his disciples. Afterward he went to Gethsemane and prayed,
"O my Father, if it be possible, let this cup pass from me: nevertheless not as I will, but as thou wilt" (26:39). Then Judas, the
betrayer, came with the priests and elders, who arrested him. All of
the disciples fled. Even Peter, "the rock," denied knowing Jesus.

In the morning he was delivered, bound, to Pilate, the Roman
governor. (Judas repented his betrayal, for thirty pieces of silver,
and hanged himself.) When Pilate asked him if he was King of the
Jews, Jesus answered only, "Thou sayest." "And when he was
accused of the chief priests and elders, he answered nothing."
(27:11–12.) The people cried out "Let him be crucified" (27:22).

Then the soldiers of Pilate took Jesus to Golgotha, outside of the
city, and crucified him between two thieves, while the people
mocked, "He saved others; himself he cannot save" (27:42). One
of Jesus' disciples, Joseph of Arimathaea, who was given his body,
placed it in a new tomb of rock and rolled a great stone to the door
of the sepulchre. On the third day thereafter, an angel appeared to
Mary Magdalene "and the other Mary," who were visiting the
sepulchre, to announce: "He is not here: for he is risen" (28:6).
"And as they went to tell his disciples, behold Jesus met them, saying, All hail. And they came and held him by the feet, and worshipped him" (28:9). Then the eleven remaining apostles went to
a mountain in Galilee, and there Jesus told them: "All power is
given unto me in heaven and in earth. Go ye therefore, and teach
all nations, baptizing them in the name of the Father, and of the
Son, and of the Holy Ghost: Teaching them to observe all things
whatsoever I have commanded you: and, lo, I am with you always,
even unto the end of the world." (28:18–20.)

MARK

Mark is the second Gospel and the forty-first book of the Bible. It is the shortest Gospel, having only 16 chapters, and is one of the synoptic Gospels (see p. 93). It is generally thought to have been the first Gospel written (about A.D. 70) and is traditionally attributed to a Jewish Christian, John, who like many of his day had a Latin surname, Marcus (Mark). The book was written for Gentiles outside of Palestine. It is not only the shortest Gospel but also the most direct and simple. Mark seems in a hurry to record his marvelous tidings. Although he was evidently not a trained writer, his style appeals to many readers.

Mark probably lived in Jerusalem, and his writing reveals much knowledge of Jewish customs. However, he frequently used Latin terms and explained Aramaic ones, evidently as part of his purpose to be understood by the non-Jews to whom his book was addressed. For the same reason, he seldom quoted Old Testament sources.

"John whose surname was Mark" accompanied Paul and Barnabas on several missionary journeys (Acts 12:25). His mother lived in Jerusalem (Acts 12:12), and she was a Christian; how the two became affiliated with the early Church is not known. Mark was also associated with Peter, possibly in Rome, where it is believed that the Apostle was martyred. The book was probably written after Peter's death and toward the end of, or just after, the reign of the Roman Emperor Nero (A.D. 54–68), under whom Christians were persecuted and many were put to death. It is thus addressed to those in danger of being killed for their faith. Details of Mark's later life are lacking, although there is speculation that he may have been the first bishop of Alexandria.

A difference between the style of Mark and that of the other Gospel writers may easily be seen. For example, Mark writes (1:32–33): "And at even, when the sun did set, they brought unto him all that were diseased, and them that were possessed with devils. And all the city was gathered together at the door." Describing the same event, Matthew (8:16) writes, "When the even was come," omitting the poetic but redundant "when the sun did set"; Luke (4:40) says, "Now when the sun was setting." Both Matthew and Luke omit the colorful "all the city." Mark's book is also distinguished for his vivid observations of the settings of events—he notes the "green grass" and uses expressions like "asleep on a pillow."

Like the other synoptic Gospels, Mark gives a sort of chronology of the public life of Jesus. However, unlike Matthew and Luke, Mark includes nothing about his birth and childhood. An introductory statement gives the title of the Gospel, and then the record begins.

Jesus' Baptism and Temptation (1:1–13). The ministry of John the Baptist is described. People were "baptized of him in the river of Jordan, confessing their sins" (1:5). However, John said that one mightier than he would come who would baptize them "with the Holy Ghost" (1:8). "And it came to pass in those days, that Jesus came from Nazareth of Galilee, and was baptized of John in Jordan" (1:9). Then "the heavens opened," and "there came a voice from heaven, saying, Thou art my beloved Son, in whom I am well pleased" (1:10,11).

Immediately after his baptism Jesus went into the wilderness for forty days. There he was tempted by Satan and ministered to by angels. (1:12–13.)

Galilean Ministry (1:14–6:6). Jesus' work among the people is described in much the same way that it is in Matthew and in Luke. He came into Galilee saying: "The time is fulfilled, and the kingdom of God is at hand: repent ye, and believe the gospel" (1:14–15). He called to himself the four fishermen: Simon (Peter); Andrew, his brother; James, the son of Zebedee; and John, his brother (1:16–20). They all went to the city of Capernaum, where Jesus taught in the synagogue, and people "were astonished at his doctrine: for he taught them as one that had authority, and not as the scribes" (1:22).

Miracles of healing followed. Jesus called an "unclean spirit" out of a suffering man. "Simon's wife's mother lay sick of a fever." Jesus "took her by the hand, and lifted her up; and immediately the fever left her . . . And he healed many that were sick of diverse diseases, and cast out many devils" on that first day of work in Capernaum. (1:23–34.)

Then Jesus and the disciples went "into the next towns" of Galilee, where Jesus also taught and healed. There were three tours, in Galilee as follows:

Work in and around Capernaum (1:39–3:19). Jesus healed a leper and "one sick of palsy." He aroused the hostility of the Pharisees by dining with "publicans and sinners," by not observing the customary fasts, and by allowing his disciples to pluck grain to eat on the Sabbath (it was then that he replied, "The sabbath was made for man, and not man for the sabbath"). He broke the Sabbath again by healing a man with a withered hand on that day, asking, "Is is lawful to do good on the sabbath days, or to do evil? to save life or to kill?" (3:4).

After the healings Jesus went to a mountain, and many came there to him at his call.

And he ordained twelve, that they should be with him, and that he might send them forth to preach,
And to have power to heal sicknesses, and to cast out devils:
And Simon he surnamed Peter;
And James the son of Zebedee, and John the brother of James; and he surnamed them Boanerges, which is, The sons of thunder:
And Andrew, and Philip, and Bartholomew, and Matthew, and Thomas, and James the son of Alphaeus, and Thaddaeus, and Simon the Canaanite,
And Judas Iscariot, which also betrayed him . . . (3:14–19.)

MORE EXTENDED MISSION FROM CAPERNAUM (3:20–4:34). During this period, Jesus "taught them many things by parables"— for example, the parable of the sower whose seed fell in various ways, to be destroyed or, if it fell on good ground, to yield fruit. "The sower soweth the word" (4:14). Jesus also compared the growth of the kingdom of God to that of a mustard seed, which "is less than all the seeds that be in the earth: But when it is sown, it groweth up, and becometh greater than all herbs, and shooteth out great branches; so that the fowls of the air may lodge under the shadow of it" (4:31–32). And "without a parable spake he not unto them."

TRIP ACROSS SEA OF GALILEE TO GADARA AND NAZARETH (4:35–6:6). While Jesus and his disciples were crossing the sea, a great storm arose. The disciples were frightened, but Jesus "rebuked the wind, and said unto the sea, Peace, be still. And the wind ceased, and there was a great calm. And he said unto them, Why are ye so fearful? how is it that ye have no faith?" (4:39–40.)

In his own country he said to skeptical inquirers, "A prophet is not without honour, but in his own country, and among his own kin, and in his own house." There he could "do no mighty work, save that he laid his hands upon a few sick folk, and healed them" (6:5).

Ministry outside Galilee (6:7–8:21). Jesus now sent out the the twelve apostles, two by two, to preach and have power over unclean spirits. He instructed them to take only a staff—"no scrip, no bread, no money in their purse." They went forth and "preached that men should repent." Herod, hearing of Jesus' work, was afraid that John the Baptist, whom he had beheaded, had risen from the dead.

Chapter 7 tells how Jesus spoke in defense of his work and against the formalism of the Pharisees: "Full well ye reject the commandment of God, that ye may keep your own tradition"

(7:9). It was not, he said, the things that went into a man that defiled him but "What comes out of a man, is what defiles a man. For from within, out of the heart of man, come evil thoughts, fornication, theft, murder, adultery, coveting, wickedness, deceit, licentiousness, envy, slander, pride, foolishness. All these evil things come from within, and they defile a man." (RSV 7:20–23.)

Jesus then went to the borders of Tyre and Sidon and returned to the Sea of Galilee by way of Decapolis, a region north of Galilee. He performed many miracles on this journey.

Labors and Instruction of Jesus among the Disciples and at Jerusalem (8:22–13:37). In this section Jesus speaks particularly to the disciples, in preparation for the journey to Jerusalem. He confessed that he was Christ, the Messiah, but "charged them that they should tell no man of him" (8:27–30). And "he said unto them, Whosoever will come after me, let him deny himself, and take up his cross, and follow me. For whosoever will save his life shall lose it; but whosoever shall lose his life for my sake and the gospel's, the same shall save it. For what shall it profit a man, if he shall gain the whole world, and lose his own soul?" (8:34–36.)

On a mountain with Peter, James, and John, Jesus was transfigured, "And his raiment became shining, exceeding white as snow." Elijah and Moses appeared, talking to Jesus, and a voice from a cloud said, "This is my beloved Son: hear him." Jesus charged the disciples "that they should tell no man what things they had seen, till the Son of man were risen from the dead." (9:2–10.)

When a dispute arose among the disciples as to which of them was greatest, Jesus said, "If any one would be first, he must be last of all and servant of all" (RSV 9:35). He took a child in his arms, telling the disciples that "Whosoever shall receive one of such children in my name, receiveth me" (9:37). Despite this teaching, the disciples later rebuked those who brought children to Jesus "that he should touch them"; but Jesus said, "Suffer the little children to come unto me, and forbid them not: for of such is the kingdom of God" (10:14).

In Chapter 10 also occurs the account of the rich young man who asked Jesus how he might inherit eternal life; he had, he said, kept the commandments from his youth. Jesus told him, "One thing thou lackest . . . sell whatsoever thou hast, and give to the poor . . . come, take up the cross, and follow me." (10:17–27.)

Mark describes Jesus' triumphal entry into Jerusalem, as people cast their garments and strewed branches in his path, to shouts of Hosanna! In Jerusalem he carried on his Messianic work. He drove the money-changers and those who sold doves out of the Temple.

He went on teaching and answering questions, including those put by Pharisees and Sadducees in an attempt to trap him. When one such question was asked, "Is it lawful to give tribute to Caesar, or not?" Jesus requested that a coin be brought to him and pointing to Caesar's image and inscription on it, said, "Render to Caesar the things that are Caesar's and to God the things that are God's" (12:13–17). He predicted the destruction of the Temple, wars, false prophets, and persecution of his disciples; but he promised that after this tribulation the Son of man would come in glory. "Heaven and earth shall pass away: but my words shall not pass away" (13:31). Then he told a parable comparing the Son of man to a man "taking a far journey," who left his servants with the command to keep constant watch, "for ye know not when the master of the house cometh" (13:32–37).

Passion and Resurrection (Chapters 14–16). At the time of the Passover, Judas Iscariot, one of the twelve apostles of Jesus, "went unto the chief priests, to betray him unto them" (14:10). Jesus observed the Passover, eating with the twelve. He "took bread, and blessed, and brake it, and gave to them, and said, Take, eat: this is my body. And he took the cup, and when he had given thanks, he gave it to them: and they all drank of it. And he said unto them, This is my blood of the new testament, which is shed for many." (14:22–24.)

After the meal Peter, James, and John went with Jesus to Gethsemane on the Mount of Olives, where Jesus prayed in agony that "the hour might pass from him." The apostles slept, and Jesus reproached Peter, "Couldest not thou watch one hour?" Then he was taken prisoner by the "chief priests and the scribes and the elders," as Judas identified him to them by kissing him. "And they all forsook him, and fled" (14:50). Despite his promise to remain faithful, Peter, under questioning, denied his master three times (as Jesus had foreseen "before the cock crow twice").

Brought before Pilate, the Roman governor, for trial, Jesus was accused of "many things: but he answered nothing" (15:3). It was customary at the feast of the Passover for the authorities to release one prisoner, and Pilate asked, "Will ye that I release unto you the King of the Jews?" But, stirred up by the chief priests, the people asked instead for a prisoner named Barabbas. To Pilate's further question concerning Jesus, "What evil hath he done?" they shouted, "Crucify him!" Pilate then ordered the crucifixion. On the Cross, Jesus cried, "My God, my God, why hast thou forsaken me?" (Some scholars believe that he was recalling Psalm 22, which begins with these words but ends with an assurance of salvation.)

Joseph of Arimathea received permission to take the body of Jesus. He wrapped it in fine linen, laid it in a sepulchre, and "rolled a stone unto the door of the sepulchre" (15:46).

On the morning of the day after the following Sabbath, Jesus' followers found that the stone had been rolled away from the sepulchre. A young man appeared and told them that Jesus was not there; he was risen. "Go your way, tell his disciples and Peter that he goeth before you into Galilee: there shall ye see him, as he said unto you" (16:7).

Verses 9–20 of Chapter 16 tell of the appearances of the risen Jesus to his disciples. Some authorities believe that they were not part of the original Gospel of Mark, because their style varies from the rest of the book and because they were not included in early manuscript versions. It is thought that Mark was for some reason prevented from finishing his work and that the conclusion was added from another source.

LUKE

Luke, the third synoptic Gospel and the forty-second book of the Bible, was probably written between A.D. 80 and 90. Luke is also the author of Acts (see p. 118), which was prepared as a sequel to his Gospel. Like the other authors of the synoptic Gospels, Luke portrays God as a sovereign power of absolute goodness and the Divine Father of all; he portrays Jesus Christ as Son of God and Son of Man; and he looks for Christ's second coming to earth. He emphasizes the universal character of the kingdom of God, and with broad human sympathies, he describes the blessings of this Kingdom as close to the poor and humble. His style of writing Greek is regarded as of higher quality than that of the other Gospel authors; and the beauty, grace, and tenderness of his book have made it one of the most beloved in the Bible.

Like the other Gospels, this book contains no information about the author. The introduction, however, does state that it was written specifically for one Theophilius (1:3), undoubtedly a Gentile Christian who was not acquainted with Jewish customs or with the geography of Palestine. There is a tradition accepted by some scholars that Luke himself was a Greek Gentile. We learn from other sources that he was one of Paul's companions and had various contacts with the early Church. He is mentioned in the Epistles (Colossians 4:14, II Timothy 4:11, Philemon 1:24). In

Colossians he is called the "beloved physician." He was undoubtedly a man who knew the science of his time and one who
associated with other educated people. He is recorded as having
been with Paul during his first imprisonment and also toward the
end of his second captivity. His frequent references in Acts to
Antioch may mean that this city was his home, although there is
no indication of where he composed his Gospel.

Luke's writings show that he was not an eyewitness of the events
described in the Gospels but that he probably lived within the
"Gospel generation." Numerous portions of his work are so close
to Matthew as to indicate that they used a common written source.
Luke also seems to have based his narrative on personal investiga-
tion of what was being communicated by word of mouth about
Jesus.

Luke's thought is in some ways much in accord with that of Paul
as revealed in the Epistles. He has a similar breadth of knowledge
and like Paul stresses forgiveness and salvation through repentance
and faith. However, Luke does not demonstrate his doctrine by
theology, as Paul does, but by stories of individuals in their relation
to Christ. It is thought that part of his purpose in writing his Gospel
was to convince the Roman authorities that Christianity was not a
subversive political movement but a world-wide religion that
transcended racial and national barriers.

The sequence of events in Jesus' life as reported by Luke is in
general that of the other synoptic Gospels. Like Matthew, Luke
begins with an account of Jesus' birth; he then describes events in
the public ministry of Jesus; and he concludes with an account of
Jesus' trial, passion, and resurrection.

Introduction 1:1–4. As noted above, Luke begins his Gospel
with a statement that it is addressed to Theophilius. He also says
that many narratives had been composed on the "things which are
most surely believed among us" and that it seemed good to him as
a close student "of all things from the very first" to write an
account of them "in order."

Birth and Childhood of Jesus (Chapters 1–2). Luke's account of
the birth of Jesus is unique among the Gospels in its detail and lyric
quality. He relates first, how an angel of the Lord appeared to the
husband of Mary's cousin Elisabeth, who was "well stricken in
years," and told him that she would bear a son to be named John.
Five months later the angel Gabriel was sent by God to Nazareth,
a city of Galilee, "to a virgin espoused to a man whose name was
Joseph . . . and the virgin's name was Mary."

The angel said, "Fear not, Mary: for thou hast found favour
with God . . . thou shalt conceive in thy womb, and bring forth

a son, and shalt call his name Jesus." To Mary's question, "How shall this be, seeing I know not a man?" the angel replied, "The Holy Ghost shall come upon thee, and the power of the Highest shall overshadow thee: therefore also that holy thing which shall be born of thee shall be called the Son of God" (1:30–35).

Mary sang the great song now called the Magnificat:

My soul doth magnify the Lord,
And my spirit hath rejoiced in God my Saviour.
For he hath regarded the low estate of his handmaiden: for, behold, from henceforth all generations shall call me blessed. . . .
He hath shewed strength with his arm; he hath scattered the proud in the imagination of their hearts. . . .
He hath filled the hungry with good things; and the rich he hath sent empty away. (1:46–53.)

"In those days . . . there went out a decree from Caesar Augustus that all the world should be taxed. . . . And all went to be taxed, every one into his own city" (2:1,3). Because Joesph was of the house of David, he and Mary traveled to Bethlehem, "the city of David." There Jesus was born, in a manger because there was no room in the inn.

And there were in the same country shepherds abiding in the field, keeping watch over their flock by night.
And, lo, the angel of the Lord came upon them, and the glory of the Lord shone round about them: and they were sore afraid.
And the angel said unto them, Fear not: for, behold, I bring you good tidings of great joy, which shall be to all people.
For unto you is born this day in the city of David a Saviour, which is Christ the Lord.
And this shall be a sign unto you; Ye shall find the babe wrapped in swaddling clothes, lying in a manger.
And suddenly there was with the angel a multitude of the heavenly host praising God, and saying,
Glory to God in the highest, and on earth peace, good will toward men. (2:8–14.)

Mary and Joseph took the baby Jesus to Jerusalem "to present him to the Lord." Then they returned to Nazareth, where "the child grew, and waxed strong in spirit, filled with wisdom: and the grace of God was upon him" (2:40).

When Jesus was twelve years old he was taken to Jerusalem again for the Passover feast. There his parents, after a long search for him, found him in the Temple sitting in the midst of learned men, "both hearing them and asking them questions. And all that heard him were astonished at his understanding and answers" (2:46–47).

To his mother's reproach for causing them anxiety, Jesus replied, "How is it that you sought me? Did you not know that I must be in my Father's house?" (RSV 2:49).

Baptism and Temptation (3:1–4:13). The word of God came to John called the Baptist, the "voice of one crying in the wilderness, Prepare ye the way of the Lord, make his paths straight" (3:4). (This was the same John who was the son of Elisabeth, Mary's cousin (see p. 106). As recorded in Matthew and Mark, John baptized Jesus, and a voice from heaven declared, "Thou art my beloved son; in thee I am well pleased" (3:22). Luke then notes that John was imprisoned by Herod for daring to attack "the evils which Herod had done." Luke's account of Jesus' sojourn in the wilderness and his temptation also parallels Matthew and Mark.

Galilean Ministry (4:14–9:50). Jesus taught in the synagogues of Galilee, "being glorified of all." He returned to his own town of Nazareth and in the synagogue there he read from Isaiah: "The Spirit of the Lord is upon me, because he hath anointed me to preach the gospel to the poor; he hath sent me to heal the broken-hearted, to preach deliverance to the captives, and recovering of sight to the blind, to set at liberty them that are bruised, To preach the acceptable year of the Lord." Then he closed the book and said, "This day is this scripture fulfilled in your ears." But because of the doubts expressed by his fellow townsmen, he added, "No prophet is accepted in his own country." (4:14–24.)

On hearing these things, the people in the synagogue were filled with wrath; and Jesus "passing through the midst of them went his way." The healings at Capernaum, described by Matthew and Mark, are reported by Luke in this chapter. The next chapter recounts the calling of the first disciples, also paralleling the earlier Gospels.

"On a certain day, as he was teaching," a man with palsy was brought to Jesus by his friends, who, unable to approach in any other way because of the crowds, let him down on his bed from the roof. When Jesus "saw their faith, he said unto him, Man, thy sins are forgiven thee." This caused a discussion among the scribes and the Pharisees, who asked, "Who can forgive sins, but God alone?" In reply Jesus asked them which was easier, "to say, Thy sins be forgiven thee; or to say, Rise up and walk? But that ye may know that the Son of man hath power upon earth to forgive sins, (he said unto the sick of the palsy,) I say unto thee, Arise, and take up thy couch, and go into thine house." And the man rose up and glorified God. (5:17–26.)

Chapter 6 lists the twelve disciples, whom Jesus "also . . . named apostles": Simon; Andrew; James; John; Philip; Bartholomew; Matthew; Thomas; James, "the son of Alphaeus"; Simon "called Zelotes" (the Zealot); Judas, the brother of James; and Judas Iscariot, "which also was the traitor" (6:13–16).

SERMON ON THE PLAIN. Chapter 6 continues with an account of how Jesus came down from the mountain, where he had chosen the apostles, and stood on a plain, healing the people who came to him. He also spoke. (Luke's version of the Sermon on the Plain has a number of parallels to Matthew's version of the Sermon on the Mount.)

Blessed be ye poor: for yours is the kingdom of God.

Blessed are ye that hunger now: for ye shall be filled. Blessed are ye that weep now: for ye shall laugh.

Blessed are ye, when men shall hate you, and when they shall separate you from their company, and shall reproach you, and cast out your name as evil, for the Son of man's sake.

Rejoice ye in that day, and leap for joy: for, behold, your reward is great in heaven: for in the like manner did their fathers unto the prophets.

But woe unto you that are rich! for ye have received your consolation.

Woe unto you that are full! for ye shall hunger. Woe unto you that laugh now! for ye shall mourn and weep.

Woe unto you, when all men shall speak well of you! for so did their fathers to the false prophets.

But I say unto you which hear, Love your enemies, do good to them which hate you,

Bless them that curse you, and pray for them which despitefully use you.

And unto him that smiteth thee on the one cheek offer also the other; and him that taketh away thy cloke forbid not to take thy coat also. . . .

Be ye therefore merciful, as your Father also is merciful.

Judge not, and ye shall not be judged: condemn not, and ye shall not be condemned: forgive, and ye shall be forgiven. (6:20–30, 36–37.)

FURTHER TEACHINGS AND HEALINGS. Luke next tells the story of a Gentile centurion who sent to Jesus, beseeching him to heal his servant, who was at the point of death. Jesus went toward the house, but he was intercepted by friends of the centurion with a message from him, "Lord, trouble not thyself: for I am not worthy that thou shouldest enter under my roof . . . say in a word, and my servant shall be healed." Jesus "marvelled at him, and turned . . . and said unto the people that followed him, I say unto you, I have not found so great faith, no, not in Israel." When the friends returned to the centurion's house they found his servant healed. (7:1–10.)

Jesus "went throughout every city and village, preaching and shewing the glad tidings of the kingdom of God: and the twelve were with him" (8:1). Luke's accounts of Jesus' sending forth the apostles to preach and heal; his revelation to them that he was the Christ; his promise that those who lost their lives for his sake would ultimately be saved; and his prediction of his suffering, death, and resurrection—are much the same as the reports of these sayings found in Matthew and Mark.

Journey to Jerusalem and Teachings There (9:51–21:38). "And it came to pass, when the time was come that he should be received up, he stedfastly set his face to go to Jerusalem" (9:51). On the way to the city he continued to heal and to teach. He appointed seventy disciples, in addition to the twelve, saying, "I send you forth as lambs among wolves." The seventy returned joyfully from their first mission, reporting, "Lord, even the devils are subject unto us through thy name." (10:1–17.)

MARTHA AND MARY. It was on his way to Jerusalem that Jesus visited the house of the two sisters Martha and Mary. While "Martha was cumbered about much serving," Mary sat at Jesus' feet and listened to his words. To Martha's request that he bid her sister come to help her serve, Jesus answered, "Martha, Martha, thou art careful and troubled about many things: But one thing is needful: and Mary hath chosen that good part, which shall not be taken away from her." (10:38–42.)

PRAYER AND TEACHING. When one of his disciples asked, "Lord, teach us to pray," Jesus answered,

When ye pray, say, Our Father which are in heaven, Hallowed be thy name. Thy kingdom come. Thy will be done, as in heaven, so in earth. Give us day by day our daily bread. And forgive us our sins; for we also forgive every one that is indebted to us. And lead us not into temptation; but deliver us from evil. (11:1–4.)

. . . Ask, and it shall be given you; seek, and ye shall find; knock, and it shall be opened unto you. For every one that asketh receiveth; and he that seeketh findeth; and to him that knocketh it shall be opened. (11:9–10.)

In reply to attacks by the Pharisees, who charged him with failing to observe a ritual, Jesus said that "judgment and the love of God" were more important (11:42).

PARABLES. Luke includes many of Jesus' parables, and he narrates them with such understanding, immediacy, and beauty of expression that some in his book are among the most familiar and acclaimed stories in all literature. A *parable* (the word comes from the Greek, meaning "to throw beside") is a short narrative about a possible human experience told to suggest a moral or spiritual truth. Jesus used parables often in his teaching: to reply to questions and accusations, to illustrate his message from chance circumstances, and to make his spiritual meaning understandable in terms recognizable by all who heard him. Perhaps the most celebrated parables in the Gospel of Luke are the parable of the Good Samaritan and the parable of the Prodigal Son.

The Good Samaritan (10:25–37). A lawyer asked about the commandment to "love thy neighbour as thyself," who his neighbor was to be thus loved. Jesus told a parable about a man on the way from Jerusalem to Jericho who "fell among thieves, which stripped him of his raiment, and wounded him, and departed, leaving him half dead." A priest and a Levite passed him but did not stop. Then a Samaritan "had compassion on him," bound up his wounds and took him to an inn, paying the innkeeper to care for him. Which of these three, Jesus asked, was the man's neighbor? The lawyer replied, "He that shewed mercy on him. Then said Jesus unto him, Go, and do thou likewise."

The Prodigal Son (15:11–32). Jesus told a number of parables to the Pharisees and scribes who attacked him for associating with sinners. One was about a man who had two sons. The younger asked for his inheritance and took it to a far country, where he wasted it in riotous living. Then, poor, hungry, and forced to labor as a swineherd, he decided to return to his father and ask to become one of his hired servants.

And he arose, and came to his father. But when he was yet a great way off, his father saw him, and had compassion, and ran, and fell on his neck, and kissed him.

And the son said unto him, Father, I have sinned against heaven, and in thy sight, and am no more worthy to be called thy son.

But the father said to his servants, Bring forth the best robe, and put it on him; and put a ring on his hand, and shoes on his feet;

And bring hither the fatted calf, and kill it; and let us eat, and be merry:

For this my son was dead, and is alive again; he was lost, and is found. . . .

Now his elder son . . . was angry, and would not go in: therefore came his father out, and intreated him.

And he answering said to his father, Lo, these many years do I serve thee, neither transgressed I at any time thy commandment: and yet thou never gavest me a kid, that I might make merry with my friends . . .

And he said unto him, Son, thou art ever with me, and all that I have is thine.

It was meet that we should make merry, and be glad: for this thy brother was dead, and is alive again; and was lost, and is found.

(15:20–32.)

MINISTRY IN JERUSALEM. Luke's record of Jesus' ministry in

Jerusalem tells of his triumphal entry into the city, his teachings there, and his replies to those in authority who opposed him.

Trial, Passion, Resurrection, and Ascension (Chapters 22–24). After the Last Supper, the agony in Gethsemane, and the betrayal by Judas, Jesus was brought before Pilate, accused of "perverting the nation, and forbidding to give tribute to Caesar, saying that he himself is Christ a King" (23:2). Learning that the prisoner was a Galilean, Pilate turned him over for examination by Herod, who was in Jerusalem at the time. Jesus did not answer Herod's questions, but neither Herod nor Pilate could find any reason for putting him to death. Nevertheless, at the demand of the mob, "Pilate gave sentence that it should be as they required" (23:24).

And when they were come to the place, which is called Calvary, there they crucified him, and the malefactors, one on the right hand, and the other on the left.

Then said Jesus, Father, forgive them; for they know not what they do. And they parted his raiment, and cast lots. (23:33–34.)

One of the criminals hanging beside him "railed on him, saying, If thou be Christ, save thyself and us." But the other one said, "Lord, remember me when thou comest into thy kingdom." To him Jesus replied, "To-day shalt thou be with me in paradise." Jesus' last words were, "Father into thy hands I commend my spirit." (23:39–47.)

Afterward, as recounted in the other Gospels, Joseph of Arimathea "begged the body of Jesus" from Pilate and laid it in a new tomb of stone. On the third day thereafter, those coming to the tomb "found the stone rolled away from the sepulchre. And they entered in, and found not the body of the Lord Jesus." Two men in shining garments appeared before them and asked, "Why seek ye the living among the dead? He is not here, but is risen . . ." Mary Magdalene, Joanna, and Mary the mother of James told the apostles, who were doubtful; Peter went to the sepulchre to see for himself. (23:50–24:12.)

That same day on the road to Emmaus, a village near Jerusalem, two of the disciples met Jesus, who went with them, unrecognized. They told him about the crucifixion and invited him to supper with them. There, "as he sat at meat with them, he took bread, and blessed it, and brake, and gave it to them. And their eyes were opened, and they knew him; and he vanished out of their sight." After appearing to the apostles and blessing them, "he was parted from them, and carried up into heaven. And they worshipped him, and returned to Jerusalem with great joy: And were continually in the temple, praising and blessing God. Amen." (24:13–53.)

JOHN

John, the fourth Gospel and the forty-third book of the Bible, was prepared for adult members of the new churches to confirm and strengthen them in the faith that "Jesus is the Christ the Son of God" and that by believing in him they should "have life through his name." This Gospel appears in its present form as a result of careful planning. John gives a succession of dramatic scenes, all leading to one conclusion, summed up in Thomas' words, "My Lord and my God" (20:28). The book probably dates from about A.D. 85–95.

Although there is no specific indication in the text, the author is traditionally considered to have been the Apostle John because of evidence both in the book itself and external to it. The author was evidently a Jew with a thorough knowledge of Jewish life, opinions, and customs. He knew the Old Testament in Hebrew and could quote it exactly. He seems to have been not only an eyewitness of many of the events that he reports but also an intimate disciple, knowing the ways of the apostles and the thought of Jesus. To many scholars, the one person who qualifies for this situation and character of writing is John, son of Zebedee, who was one of the twelve apostles. John is believed to have spent the later years of his life in the city of Ephesus, where he taught and wrote his Gospel.

John drew somewhat on the tradition that was incorporated in the three synoptic Gospels, but his is a strikingly original work, written to declare the significance of what he had seen and heard "concerning the word of life." He does not record the genealogy or the birth of Jesus, nor does he mention Jesus' childhood, baptism, temptation, transfiguration, or ascension. He does not give the text of parables or of the Sermon on the Mount. John instead emphasizes such spiritual concepts as the bread and the water of life, the good Shepherd, the new birth, the Incarnation, and the existence of the Word from the beginning. When John does go over the same ground as the other Gospel writers (for example, in his accounts of the feeding of the five thousand, the Passion, and the Resurrection), he gives new details, possibly based on personal knowledge. He also quotes more fully the farewell statements of Christ to his disciples before his crucifixion. Moreover, while the others tell the "good news" as relatively simple, often conveyed in stories called parables (see p. 110), John expresses a mystical and theological doctrine, using only a few brief allegories.

Writing perhaps as many as twenty to thirty years after the other

Gospel authors, John was able to see more clearly the significant issues that had developed, particularly those that arose between Judaism and the new religion and those involving heresies that denied either the humanity or the divinity of Christ. Living in a Hellenistic culture, John was also influenced by Greek philosophy. There were thus different audiences and occasions, but the main difference between John's Gospel and the others is found within the writer himself.

Simple in style and intense in meaning, this Gospel has short sentences and a comparatively limited vocabulary. But John has sufficient command of language to make him a writer of power. He frequently repeats, but in ways that impress the mind and heart. There are intangibles in John's style that make it very difficult to analyze. His use of "the Word," or "Logos," for example, is wrought into a sort of prose poem that sums up a theology.

Prologue (1:1–18). The book begins with a declaration that the Word is a divine Person who eternally interprets God the Creator of the universe and the fountain of light and life.

In the beginning was the Word, and the Word was with God, and the Word was God.

The same was in the beginning with God.

All things were made by him; and without him was not any thing made that was made.

In him was life; and the life was the light of men.

And the light shineth in darkness; and the darkness comprehended it not.* (1:1–5.)

And the Word was made flesh, and dwelt among us, (and we beheld his glory, the glory as of the only begotten of the Father,) full of grace and truth. (1:14.)

These sentences sum up much of the insight of John's Gospel.

Narrative Demonstrating the Incarnation (1:19–12:11). The revelation of God the Father by his Incarnate Son comes to the world through words, acts, and symbols.

Recognition by John the Baptist and Disciples. John the Baptist said on seeing Jesus, "Behold the Lamb of God, which taketh away the sin of the world" (1:29). The first disciples, Andrew and Peter, were drawn to Jesus by these words. John records how some disciples sought out others; Philip, for example, brought Nathanael to Jesus. At a marriage feast in Cana of Galilee, Jesus turned water into wine. This miracle "manifested forth his glory; and his disciples believed on him." According to John, it was

---

* The RSV translates, "The darkness has not overcome it." The New English Bible translates, "The darkness has never quenched it."

after this event that Jesus first journeyed to Jerusalem, where he cleansed the Temple. This visit, at the time of the Passover, was evidently undertaken with the motive of reform. Jesus' words on this occasion, "Destroy this temple, and in three days I will raise it up," were later interpreted by the disciples as referring to his resurrection. (Chapters 1–2.)

REPLY TO NICODEMUS. To Nicodemus, a Pharisee who came to question him, Jesus said: "Except a man be born of water and of the Spirit, he cannot enter into the kingdom of God. . . . Ye must be born again. . . . For God so loved the world, that he gave his only begotten Son, that whosoever believeth in him should not perish, but have everlasting life." (3:1–16.)

TESTIMONY OF JOHN THE BAPTIST. From Jerusalem Jesus and his disciples went to the Judean countryside where John the Baptist was working. A question arose among John's disciples about purifying, and they were also puzzled by Jesus, whom they apparently regarded as a rival of their own leader. But John told them: "I am not the Christ, but . . . I am sent before him. He must increase, but I must decrease. . . . He that hath received his testimony hath set to his seal that God is true." (3:23–36.)

THE SAMARITAN WOMAN. Jesus then went through Samaria, on his way to Galilee. Wearied from his journey, he stopped at a well and requested a drink of water from a woman there.

Then saith the woman of Samaria unto him, How is it that thou, being a Jew, askest drink of me, which am a woman of Samaria? for the Jews have no dealings with the Samaritans.

Jesus answered and said unto her, If thou knewest the gift of God, and who it is that saith to thee, Give me to drink; thou wouldest have asked of him, and he would have given thee living water. . . . Whosoever drinketh of this water shall thirst again: But whosoever drinketh of the water that I shall give him shall never thirst; but the water that I shall give him shall be in him a well of water springing up into everlasting life. (4:9–14.)

After amazing the woman by his knowledge of her past life and sins, Jesus went on to tell her, "God is a Spirit: and they that worship him must worship him in spirit and in truth" (4:24). The woman then went back to the city and "saith to the men, Come see a man, which told me all the things that ever I did: is not this the Christ?" (4:28–29).

OTHER SIGNS AND MIRACLES. After spending two more days in Samaria, where many believed in him because of the woman's testimony and "many more believed because of his own word," Jesus returned to Cana in Galilee. There a nobleman whose son lay sick at Capernaum, begged him to go to heal the boy. But

Jesus said to him, "Go thy way; thy son liveth." The man departed and was met on the road by his servants, who told him that his son's fever had left him. (4:39–54.)

Jesus went again to Jerusalem, where he displeased people because of his alleged disregard of Sabbath observance (in performing cures on that day) and because he "said also that God was his Father, making himself equal with God." Jesus rebuked them, saying, "He that honoureth not the Son honoureth not the Father which hath sent him." (Chapter 5.)

THE BREAD OF LIFE. John's account of the feeding of the multitude parallels those of the other Gospels. John, however, adds Jesus' teaching, "Ye seek me, not because ye saw the miracles, but because ye did eat of the loaves, and were filled. Labour not for the meat which perisheth, but for that meat which endureth unto everlasting life, which the Son of man shall give unto you: for him hath God the Father sealed. . . . I am the bread of life: he that cometh to me shall never hunger; and he that believeth on me shall never thirst." (6:26,27,35.) The disciples murmured at such sayings, and many "went back, and walked no more with him." Jesus then asked the twelve, "Will ye also go away?" Peter answered for them, "Lord, to whom shall we go? thou hast the words of eternal life. And we believe and are sure that thou art that Christ, the Son of the living God." (Chapter 6.)

FURTHER SAYINGS. In continuing witness to the Incarnation, the Gospel of John records words that have ever since illuminated Christianity. When a woman in danger of being stoned to death for adultery was brought to him, Jesus said to her accusers, "He that is without sin among you, let him first cast a stone at her" (8:7). To his disciples, he promised that those who continued in his word "shall know the truth, and the truth shall make you free" (8:31–32). A man born blind whose sight Jesus had restored replied to those who attacked his belief that this was the Christ, "Whether he be a sinner or no, I know not: one thing I know, that, whereas I was blind, now I see" (9:25). "I am the good shepherd," Jesus said, "the good shepherd giveth his life for the sheep. . . . And other sheep I have, which are not of this fold: them also I must bring, and they shall hear my voice; and there shall be one fold, and one shepherd" (10:11,16). When Jesus was pressed with demands, "If thou be the Christ, tell us plainly," he answered, "I told you, and ye believed not: the works that I do in my Father's name, they bear witness of me" (10:24–25).

THE RAISING OF LAZARUS (Chapter 11). On his last journey to Jerusalem, Jesus learned that Lazarus, the brother of the Mary and Martha described in Luke (see p. 110), was sick at Bethany. Jesus waited two days and then told the disciples that Lazarus was dead. They went to Bethany and were met by Martha, who said,

Lord, if thou hadst been here, my brother had not died. But I know, that even now, whatsoever thou wilt ask of God, God will give it thee.

Jesus saith unto her, Thy brother shall rise again. . . . I am the resurrection, and the life: he that believeth in me, though he were dead, yet shall he live: And whosoever liveth and believeth in me shall never die. (11:21–26.)

Later Jesus was met by Mary and friends of the family, who had followed her, weeping. Jesus, too, wept. Then he went with them to the grave and commanded them to take away the stone that closed it. Jesus prayed, and then "cried with a loud voice, Lazarus, come forth. And he that was dead came forth, bound hand and foot with graveclothes . . . Jesus said unto them, Loose him, and let him go" (11:43–44).

The Pharisees and chief priests, hearing reports of the miracles, were afraid that Jesus would stir up the people so that the Roman authorities would move in to suppress them; hence they made plans to capture Jesus before trouble occurred.

Mary, the sister of Lazarus, took costly ointment and anointed Jesus' feet. To those disciples who thought that the ointment should instead have been sold and the money given to the poor, Jesus replied, "The poor always ye have with you; but me ye have not always." (12:1–8.)

Trial, Passion, and Resurrection (12:12–21:25). John portrays the triumphal entry into Jerusalem, events and discourses there, the opposition of the Pharisees, and Jesus' awareness of his coming agony: "Now is my soul troubled; and what shall I say? Father, save me from this hour: but for this cause came I unto this hour" (12:27).

At the Last Supper, Jesus washed the disciples' feet, saying, "If I . . . your Lord and Master, have washed your feet; ye also ought to wash one another's feet" (13:14). He told them, "A new commandment I give unto you, That ye love one another; as I have loved you" (13:34); and, "In my Father's house are many mansions: if it were not so, I would have told you. I go to prepare a place for you" (14:2). He promised that he would not leave them comfortless but would come to them. "Peace I leave with you, my peace I give unto you . . . Let not your heart be troubled, neither let it be afraid" (14:27). "I came forth from the Father, and am come into the world: again, I leave the world, and go to the Father" (16:28). After thus consoling them he prayed for them.

In the Garden of Gethsemane, Jesus was betrayed by Judas and captured. He was brought before Pilate, who replied to his words that he had come to bear witness to the truth with the famous question, "What is truth?" At the demand of the mob, Pilate finally ordered Jesus crucified. "And Pilate wrote a title, and put it on the cross. And the writing was, JESUS OF NAZARETH THE KING OF THE JEWS" (19:19).

As recounted in the other Gospels, the body was entombed, but the first day of the following week, the tomb was found empty. John tells of Jesus' appearance to Mary, who stood at the sepulchre weeping, "Because they have taken away my Lord, and I know not where they have laid him." He spoke her name, and she recognized him, "and saith unto him, Rabboni; which is to say, Master" (20:15–16). To Thomas, the doubting apostle, Jesus showed the wounds in his hands and side. "And Thomas answered and said unto him, My Lord and my God." Then Jesus said, "Thomas, because thou hast seen me, thou hast believed: blessed are they that have not seen, and yet have believed." (20:24–29.)

Another appearance of Jesus to his disciples, at the sea of Tiberias, and his charge to Peter, "Feed my sheep," are given in a sort of supplement (Chapter 21), regarded by some scholars as a later addition to John's Gospel. "And there are also many things which Jesus did, the which if they should be written every one, I suppose that even the world itself could not contain the books that should be written. Amen." (21:25.)

THE ACTS OF THE APOSTLES

The Acts of the Apostles, commonly known as Acts, is the forty-fourth book of the Bible and the fifth of the New Testament. It is an extension of the Gospel of Luke (see p. 105). "The former treatise," the Gospel, portrays the Christ through his life, teachings, and resurrection; Acts records effects of the Christ through the Spirit acting on his apostles and others. By relating the labors of Peter among the Jews and of Paul among the other peoples of the Mediterranean world, Acts shows the progress of the new faith from Jerusalem (the center of Judaism) to Rome (the center of paganism and of the civilized world). It is thus a link between the Gospels, as biographies of Jesus Christ, and the Epistles, as commentaries on his life and message. The Gospels, The Acts of the Apostles, and the Epistles together depict in succession: Jesus Christ in the world; the beginnings of his Church in the world; and the establishment of churches in specific places. Acts has been called The "Gospel of the Holy Spirit" because it tells of the coming of this Spirit and mentions it more often than does any other New Testament book.

Few matters pertaining to the New Testament seem more settled among Biblical scholars than their consensus that the author of the third Gospel was also the author of Acts and that this was Luke, who was a companion of Paul. Luke was an educated man, knowing the science of his era. In Colossians he is designated as the "beloved physician." The date of the writing cannot be precisely determined. Estimates vary from A.D. 62 to 100. Evidence favoring A.D. 70–80 is strengthened by the omission in Acts of references to Paul's Epistles or to later events in his life. The place of writing is also uncertain; Rome, Ephesus, and Antioch (thought to have been Luke's home) have been suggested by various scholars.

Like Luke's Gospel, Acts is addressed to one Theophilus, believed to have been a Greek Gentile. Ostensibly for him, Luke sums up much information about the earliest work of those who sought to spread the Gospel in widening circles. Although Luke was evidently not an eyewitness of most of the events that he records, he probably had both oral and written sources. At any rate his memory and notes enabled him to prepare his work, intended for men of faith who were perplexed by opposition to the Gospel from the outside world, as well as by their own questions and doubts. The book is a straightforward and practical apology for the new religion personified and taught by Jesus Christ.

It is an historical book, although selectively so, and contains both unity and progressive development. Christ's words to his apostles reported in the opening chapter (1:8) indicate this progression: the apostles witness first, "in Jerusalem" (1:15–8:3); second, "in all Judaea" and "in Samaria" (8:4–11:18); and, third, "unto the uttermost part of the earth" (11:19–28:31).

The book may be considered in three sections on as many periods of apostolic activities: the period from the ascension of Jesus to the establishment of the Antioch church; the period of the first missionary journey of Paul and other disciples; and the period of the second and third missionary journeys, ending with Paul's arrest and his voyage as a prisoner to Rome.

Period from the Ascension to the Antioch Church (Chapters 1–12). This period, thought to have lasted from about A.D. 30 to 41, begins with the last words and the ascension of Christ and concludes with the establishment of the church among non-Jews in Antioch, where the followers of Jesus were first called Christians.

Following forty days, during which the resurrected Jesus showed "himself alive . . . by many infallible proofs," he assembled the apostles and told them: "Ye shall receive power, after that the Holy Ghost is come upon you: and ye shall be witnesses unto me both in Jerusalem, and in all Judaea, and in Samaria, and unto the uttermost part of the earth." After speaking thus, Jesus "was taken up . . . into heaven." (1:1–11.)

THE HOLY SPIRIT. On the day of Pentecost (a Hebrew feast), the followers of Christ "were all with one accord in one place," when "there came a sound from heaven as of a rushing mighty wind . . . And they were all filled with the Holy Ghost, and began to speak with other tongues, as the Spirit gave them utterance." Reports of this event caused great amazement among the people of Jerusalem. Peter preached to them "that God hath made that same Jesus, whom ye have crucified, both Lord and Christ" and "that whosoever shall call on the name of the Lord shall be saved." As a result, about three thousand were baptized in the new faith. "And all that believed were together, and had all things common . . . And the Lord added to the church daily such as should be saved." (Chapter 2.)

APOSTOLIC WORK. Now the historian reports, among other works, the healing of a lame man who begged alms of Peter and John at a Temple gate. "Silver and gold have I none," said Peter, "but such as I have give I thee: In the name of Jesus Christ of Nazareth rise up and walk." While preaching after this miracle, Peter and John were arrested by the priests and the Sadducees but released with orders "not to speak at all nor teach in the name of Jesus." The apostles replied, "Whether it be right in the sight of God to hearken unto you more than unto God, judge ye. For we cannot but speak the things which we have seen and heard." And they continued speaking "the word of God with boldness." (3:1–4:31.)

"Great grace was upon them all," and those that had lands or houses sold them and laid down the money at the apostles' feet. Two who deceitfully kept back part of the price, Ananias and his wife Sapphira, fell down dead when Peter condemned them. In a second clash with the Sadducees, the apostles were arrested and imprisoned but released by an "angel of the Lord." Continuing to preach of Jesus Christ in defiance of official orders, they were finally tolerated on the sage advice of a Pharisee named Gamaliel: "If this counsel or this work be of men, it will come to nought . . . if it be of God, ye cannot overthrow it." (4:32–5:42.)

PERSECUTION AND THE MARTYRDOM OF STEPHEN. To supervise the care of the poor the apostles appointed the first deacons, of whom Stephen was the most outstanding, "full of faith and power."

But encountering hostility in one of the synagogues, he was accused of blasphemy and brought before the council. (Chapter 6.)

But he, being full of the Holy Ghost, looked up stedfastly into heaven . . . And said, Behold, I see the heavens opened, and the Son of man standing on the right hand of God.

Then they cried out with a loud voice, and stopped their ears, and ran upon him with one accord,

And cast him out of the city, and stoned him: and the witnesses laid down their clothes at a young man's feet, whose name was Saul.

And they stoned Stephen . . . And he kneeled down, and cried with a loud voice, Lord, lay not this sin to their charge. And when he had said this, he fell asleep.

And Saul was consenting unto his death. . . . (7:55–8:1.)

This same Saul (the Hebrew name of Paul) afterward led the persecution of the new church in Jerusalem which forced many Christians to take refuge in other places. Philip went to Samaria, where he preached Christ and performed miracles of healing, with the result that "there was great joy in that city." (Chapter 8.)

PAUL'S CONVERSION. The conversion of Paul, undoubtedly one of the most important events of all time, took place on the road to Damascus; he was traveling to that city to extradite Christians as prisoners to Jerusalem. "Suddenly there shined round about him a light from heaven," and Jesus spoke to him, saying, "Saul, Saul, why persecutest thou me?" When Paul, "trembling and astonished said, Lord, what wilt thou have me to do?" Jesus told him to go on to Damascus, where he would receive word. Paul, blinded by the vision, was led to the city and remained three days without food or drink. Then the Lord sent a disciple named Ananias to tell him that he would receive back his sight and "be filled with the Holy Ghost. And immediately there fell from his eyes as it had been scales: and he received sight forthwith, and arose, and was baptized." From that time forth he preached Christ, "the son of God," despite the enmity of the unconverted Jews and the hesitancy to accept him of many Christians who remembered his former deeds. (Chapter 9.)

BEGINNING OF MISSION TO GENTILES. The mission to the Gentiles, which was to become Paul's lifework, started with a Roman centurion named Cornelius, whom God told in a vision to send for Peter. The next day Peter had a vision in which he was commanded to eat food forbidden by Jewish laws. When Peter protested, "I have never eaten any thing that is common or unclean," the voice replied, "What God hath cleansed, that call thou not common." Going to Cornelius, Peter told him that, although it had been regarded as unlawful for a Jew to associate with those from other nations, "God hath shewed me that I should not call any man common or unclean. . . . God is no respecter of persons . . . in every nation he that feareth him, and worketh righteousness, is accepted with him." (Chapter 10.)

When Peter was criticized by the Jerusalem church for preaching to Gentiles, he told them the story of his vision and said: "Forasmuch then as God gave them the like gift as he did unto us, who believed on the Lord Jesus Christ; what was I, that I could withstand God?" At Antioch Greek converts joined the church, and Paul spent a year there teaching. "And the disciples were called Christians first in Antioch." (Chapter 11.)

PERSECUTION BY HEROD. About this time the Herod who was then ruling began a persecution of the Church. The Apostle James was killed with the sword. Peter was arrested, but an angel of the Lord rescued him from the soldiers guarding the prison.

Period of the First Missionary Journey (13:1–15:35). The Holy Ghost directed the Antioch church to send Paul and Barnabas on a missionary journey. Taking Mark, they went from Seleucia to Salamis and then to Cyprus, where the proconsul Sergius Paulus was converted. Then they sailed to Perga in Pamphylia, where John Mark left them to return to Jerusalem. Paul and Barnabas proceeded to Pisidia. At Pisidian Antioch Paul preached that by Christ, "all that believe are justified from all things, from which ye could not be justified by the law of Moses." The next Sabbath multitudes came to hear him, and the envious Jews began to contradict him. Thereupon Paul and Barnabas boldly announced that they would henceforth "turn to the Gentiles." They went to Iconium and then to Lystra, where Paul was at first welcomed but later, at the instigation of hostile Jews, stoned. Then they made their way to Derbe for rest, teaching, and preaching. From there they returned to Syrian Antioch, reversing their steps by way of Lystra, Iconium, Pisidian Antioch, Perga, and Attalia. Back at their home church, "They rehearsed all that God had done with them, and how he had opened the door of faith unto the Gentiles." The first missionary journey is thought to have taken about four years, A.D. 45–49. (Chapters 13–14.)

Despite the work of Paul and Barnabas among the Gentiles, controversy continued about admitting them to the Church, with some insisting that they practice circumcision and other Mosaic laws. "And the apostles and elders came together for to consider of this matter." At this council a compromise was reached, prescribing less strict regulations for the Gentile converts. (15:1–35.)

Period of the Second and Third Missionary Journeys (15:36– 28:31). This period, thought to have lasted from about A.D. 50 to

63, begins with the second missionary journey and ends with Paul's imprisonment in Rome. Paul and Silas left Antioch and journeyed to Syria, Cilicia, Derbe, and Lystra, where they were joined by the young disciple Timothy, the son of a Jewish mother and a Greek father. (Paul and Barnabas had parted after a sharp dispute over whether John Mark should be taken with them on this journey, Paul distrusting him because he had not completed the first journey; Barnabas took Mark and went to Cyprus.) Paul, Silas, and Timothy established churches in Phrygia and in Galatia but were forbidden by the Holy Ghost to preach in Asia or Bithynia.

PHILIPPI. They passed through Mysia to Troas, where Paul beheld a vision of a man saying, "Come over into Macedonia, and help us." Immediately they set sail for Europe, where they gained the first converts at Philippi in Macedonia. Among them was a slave girl whose soothsaying ability was exploited by her masters. When they saw that as a Christian she would no longer be profitable to them, they charged Paul and Silas with teaching customs unlawful for Romans. The two missionaries were cast into prison, where they "Prayed, and sang praises unto God: and the prisoners heard them." Suddenly an earthquake opened the prison doors, "and every one's bands were loosed." The keeper of the prison, awaking and assuming that the prisoners (for whom he was responsible) had escaped, was about to kill himself, "But Paul cried with a loud voice saying, Do thyself no harm: for we are all here." The jailer fell down before Paul and Silas and asked what he must do to be saved. "And they said, Believe on the Lord Jesus Christ, and thou shalt be saved, and thy house." (Chapter 16.)

ATHENS. After their release from prison, Paul left Philippi and visited other cities, most well-known of which was Athens. There Paul preached on Mars Hill one of the world's most famous sermons. Seeing an altar with the inscription "TO THE UNKNOWN GOD," Paul said, "Whom . . . ye ignorantly worship, him declare I unto you. God that made the world and all things therein . . . And hath made of one blood all nations of men . . . he be not far from every one of us . . . For in him we live, and move, and have our being. . . ." Although Paul made a few converts in Athens with this sermon, some mocked on hearing of the resurrection of the dead and others said merely, "We will hear thee again of this matter." (Chapter 17.)

CORINTH. After leaving Athens, Paul went to Corinth, where he was joined by Silas and Timothy and remained about a year and a half, teaching and baptizing many people. He then went to Jerusalem for the feast of Pentecost and returned from there to Antioch. (18:1–22.)

EPHESUS. On the third missionary journey Paul arrived at Ephesus, where he stayed more than two years, baptizing, speaking in the synagogue, and performing healing miracles. Many magicians burned their books, "So mightily grew the word of God and prevailed." Demetrius, a silversmith, aroused his fellow workers to riot against those who preached "that they be no gods, which are made with hands." Seeing the danger to their craft from this doctrine, they caused an uproar in the city with their cries, "Great is Diana of the Ephesians!" The town clerk restored order by reminding the people that the courts were open for legal charges and that any extralegal actions would make them liable to punishment by the Romans. (Chapter 19.)

JERUSALEM. After leaving Ephesus, Paul made visits to other cities on his way to Jerusalem. Warned of danger to him there, he replied, "I am ready not to be bound only, but also to die at Jerusalem for the name of the Lord Jesus." In Jerusalem he was seized by a mob who accused him of bringing Greeks into the Temple. After being rescued by Roman soldiers, he begged as "a Jew of Tarsus, a city in Cilicia, a citizen of no mean city," to be allowed to speak to the people. He told them of his conversion on the road to Damascus and of his commission to preach to the Gentiles. At this the mob cried out against him, and the chief captain of the soldiers commanded him to be brought up for examination. As he was about to be scourged, Paul claimed his rights as a Roman citizen. The chief captain said of his own citizenship, "With a great sum obtained I this freedom. And Paul said, But I was free born." (Chapters 21–22.)

ROME. Paul appeared before the Sanhedrin, where he caused a dissension between the Sadducees and the Pharisees that enabled him to escape. A conspiracy to assassinate him was revealed to the Roman authorities, who again rescued him by removing him to Caesarea. Appearing before the Roman governor there, Paul made his dramatic plea, "I appeal unto Caesar" (25:11). Very well, then he was told, to Caesar you shall go. After many vicissitudes, including shipwreck at Malta, Paul landed at the Bay of Naples and was taken to Rome, where although still a prisoner, he was allowed to speak and to write. He lived at Rome for "two whole years in his own hired house, and received all that came in unto him . . . teaching those things which concern the Lord Jesus Christ." (Chapters 23–28.)

Here ends the formal history of Acts. From the Epistles, we learn about Paul's later life, including his release and second imprisonment. He was again sent, bound, to Rome, where he is believed to have met a martyr's death by the sword.

ROMANS

The Epistle of Paul to the Romans, the forty-fifth book of the Bible and the sixth of the New Testament, contains the most systematic statement of Paul's beliefs. It is one of four comprehensive documents (together with the two Epistles to the Corinthians and the one to the Galatians) which sum up what he regarded as the essentials of the Christian faith. It was written while the apostle was living in Corinth and eagerly planning his trip to the center of his world. (As noted in the chapter on Acts [see p. 124] when Paul did go to Rome it was as a prisoner.) He sent his Epistle before him so that the group of Christians in Rome would know the facts about his life, the general conditions of his missionary labors, and his future plans. His broader purpose was to deal with the somewhat difficult situation in the Roman church, as well as other churches, which arose from the mixed membership of Jews and Gentiles. Thus the Epistle to the Romans becomes a theological treatise addressed to both groups and stressing their union in Christ.

Of the four Epistles mentioned above, that to the Romans was probably written last and not long after that to the Galatians (see p. 135), which seems to contain a rough sketch of the theses developed in Romans. The date of the writing is placed by some scholars at A.D. 56 to 57 and by others as early as A.D. 53. It was written in Greek, which was the language most likely to be understood by both Jewish and Gentile Christians and also the language in which Paul could write most easily.

The origin of the Roman church is not known, but Christians were continually migrating to Rome from various parts of the Mediterranean world, and in Rome the zealous ones had undoubtedly made new converts. Paul evidently had friends in Rome and had long wished to go there. Moreover, he sensed that the conditions of Christians in the capital of the great empire would be momentous for the whole new Church. When a deaconess named Phebe left Corinth to go to Rome, Paul took advantage of the opportunity to send his Epistle by her.

Parts of the letter (for example, 1:6,13; 11:13) are addressed specifically to Gentiles; others (for example, Chapter 2, 3:19, 7:1) specifically to Jews; and others (for example, Chapters 9–11) to both. Of the individuals mentioned in the Epistle, some are Jews, some Greeks, and two have Latin names. It is to this metropolitan group that Paul addresses a full communication, which is presented deliberately and apparently with no sense of crisis either in the city itself or among the Romans who were Christians.

In this Epistle, as in his others, Paul stresses the doctrine of redemption through acceptance of the gospel of Christ. Salvation comes not through law but through the grace of God in sending Christ into the world to die as an atonement for man's sins. The risen Lord's revelation has become a New Covenant that reconciles his followers with God and frees them from sin and death. All men stand in need of this deliverance. All who believe and submit themselves to the service of Christ, regardless of suffering and persecution, are assured of "the glorious liberty of the children of God."

The Epistle is arranged in four distinct parts: (1) introduction; (2) a long doctrinal statement; (3) practical applications of the teaching in terms of Christian duties; and (4) valedictory.

Introduction (1:1–17). In the introduction Paul expresses his desire to visit the Roman church and his thanks to God that their "faith is spoken of throughout the whole world." In an affirmation which sums up much of the following doctrinal teaching, he says:

. . . I am not ashamed of the gospel of Christ: for it is the power of God unto salvation to every one that believeth; to the Jew first, and also to the Greek. For therein is the righteousness of God revealed from faith to faith: as it is written, The just shall live by faith. (1:16–17.)

Doctrinal Statement (1:18–11:36). Paul begins this argument with a demonstration that the entire human race has been unable to attain a righteousness acceptable to God by works or by law. "There is none righteous, no, not one."

Only justification by faith brings reconciliation with God, who "commendeth his love toward us, in that, while we were yet sinners, Christ died for us" (5:8).

Therefore being justified by faith, we have peace with God through our Lord Jesus Christ:

By whom also we have access by faith into this grace wherein we stand, and rejoice in hope of the glory of God.

And not only so, but we glory in tribulations also: knowing that tribulation worketh patience;

And patience, experience; and experience, hope . . . because the love of God is shed abroad in our hearts by the Holy Ghost which is given unto us. (5:1–5.)

Paul emphasizes the futility of man's own efforts to obey the law.

For I know that in me (that is, in my flesh,) dwelleth no good thing: for to will is present with me; but how to perform that which is good I find not.

For the good that I would I do not: but the evil which I would not, that I do. . . . I see another law in my members, warring against the law of my mind, and bringing me into captivity to the law of sin . . .
O wretched man that I am! who shall deliver me from the body of this death? (7:18–19, 23–24.)

But God in Christ has given man a new spirit and those led by this Spirit are his sons.

For ye have not received the spirit of bondage again to fear; but ye have received the Spirit of adoption, whereby we cry, Abba, Father. . . .
And if children, then heirs; heirs of God, and joint-heirs with Christ; if so be that we suffer with him, that we may be also glorified together.
For I am persuaded, that neither death, nor life, nor angels, nor principalities, nor powers, nor things present, nor things to come,
Nor height, nor depth, nor any other creature, shall be able to separate us from the love of God, which is in Christ Jesus our Lord. (8:15, 17, 38–39.)

Chapters 9–11 specifically concern Israel. Paul laments because his people have sought righteousness by law rather than by faith. However, he says that God has not cast them away; a remnant has been saved by grace even now, and all would eventually be saved.

For I would not, brethren, that ye should be ignorant of this mystery, lest ye should be wise in your own conceits; that blindness in part is happened to Israel, until the fulness of the Gentiles be come in.
And so all Israel shall be saved: as it is written. There shall come out of Sion the Deliverer, and shall turn away the ungodliness from Jacob. (11:25–26.)

Christian Duties (12:1–15:13). The Apostle next outlines ethical Christian requirements in the light of the foregoing doctrine. Duties to God, to one's neighbor, to the Church, to the state, to society, and to the poor are mentioned.

. . . be not conformed to this world: but be ye transformed by the renewing of your mind, that ye may prove what is that good, and acceptable, and perfect, will of God. (12:2.)
Recompense to no man evil for evil . . . if thine enemy hunger, feed him; if he thirst, give him drink . . . (12:17,20.)
Let every soul be subject unto the higher powers. For there is no power but of God: the powers that be are ordained of God. (13:1.)
Love worketh no ill to his neighbour: therefore love is the fulfilling of the law. (13:10.)
. . . whether we live, we live unto the Lord; and whether we die, we die unto the Lord: whether we live therefore, or die, we are the Lord's. (14:8.)
We then that are strong ought to bear the infirmities of the weak, and not to please ourselves. (15:1.)

Valedictory (15:14–16:27). In his conclusion to the Epistle Paul promises to go to Rome.

> And I am sure that, when I come unto you, I shall come in the fulness of the blessing of the gospel of Christ.
> Now I beseech you, brethren, for the Lord Jesus Christ's sake, and for the love of the Spirit, that ye strive together with me in your prayers to God for me. (15:29–30.)

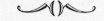

I CORINTHIANS

Paul's first Epistle to the Corinthians, the forty-sixth book of the Bible and the seventh of the New Testament, was written at or near Ephesus, probably between A.D. 54 and 57, while Paul was on his second and long sojourn there (see p. 124) and before he made his second visit to Greece. The planting of the Gospel and Church in Corinth had been the work of Paul, who was probably the first Christian to set foot in the city (see p. 123). About five years later he had written to the members of the Corinthian church advising them not to keep company with evil persons. The reply he had received was evidently not satisfactory. Moreover, immorality within the church had been reported; factions had developed among its members; and they had sent Paul a letter inquiring about various problems. Paul's Epistle in response to this situation has been called a "tract for the times."

Corinth, which had been destroyed by the Roman general Mummius in 146 B.C. but restored by Julius Caesar in 46 B.C., had succeeded in becoming the commercial and political center of Greece under the Roman Empire. (Paul's appearance before Gallio, then Roman proconsul in Corinth, is reported in Acts 18:12–16.) Noted for its luxury and its worship of Aphrodite, the Greek goddess of love and beauty, the city had become a symbol of licentiousness. Though the Corinthians who became Christians were believed to have been rescued from the evils of their environment, its influence was always present.

Paul's style of writing was never better illustrated than by his First Epistle to the Corinthians. He dictated most of his letters and thus often seems to be speaking rather than writing to the recipients. The result is a marked informality and directness. His Epistles are a mixture of talk, composition, and oratory, unlike any other well-known correspondence in the world.

The fact that I Corinthians was quoted at an early date under its author's name is considered proof of its authenticity. It contains much information about practices in the early Church with respect to such matters as baptism, the ministry, public worship, a creed, belief in a future life, and Sunday observance. This information does not pertain to the earliest stage of ecclesiastical development, because the Jerusalem and Antioch churches were older than the one in Corinth. However, we have no such direct source of knowledge about these churches as is found in Paul's Epistles.

The contents of I Corinthians are more varied than those of any other Epistle, comprising: (1) introduction; (2) advice on factions; (3) advice on morality; (4) advice on marriage; (5) advice on dietary regulations; (6) advice on public worship and spiritual gifts, including the famous passage (the thirteenth chapter) on Christian love; (7) teaching on the resurrection; and (8) conclusion.

Introduction (1:1–9). Paul starts with a salutation and a thanksgiving for the young church. "I thank my God always on your behalf, for the grace of God which is given you by Jesus Christ."

On Factions (1:10–4:21). Paul had heard of contentions among various groups of church members. The main body of his Epistle begins with a strong plea against such disputes.

Now I beseech you, brethren, by the name of our Lord Jesus Christ, that ye speak the same thing, and that there be no divisions among you; but that ye be perfectly joined together in the same mind and in the same judgment. (1:10.)

He warns against the worldly wisdom which forestalls belief in the gospel of the Cross.

For after that in the wisdom of God the world by wisdom knew not God, it pleased God by the foolishness of preaching to save them that believe.

For the Jews require a sign, and the Greeks seek after wisdom:

But we preach Christ crucified, unto the Jews a stumblingblock, and unto the Greeks foolishness;

But unto them which are called, both Jews and Greeks, Christ the power of God, and the wisdom of God. (1:21–24.)

Paul goes on to say that a factional spirit is contrary to the purpose of the church that he has established among them and that of his earlier ministry to them. It is, moreover, contrary to the purpose of God, "for the temple of God is holy, which temple ye are" (3:17).

He concludes his blunt address more gently: "I write not these things to shame you, but as my beloved sons I warn you . . . .

for in Christ Jesus I have begotten you through the gospel"
(4:14–15). For this cause also he tells them that he has sent
Timothy to them and he himself will soon come. "What will ye?
shall I come unto you with a rod, or in love, and in the spirit of
meekness?" (4:21).

On Morality (Chapters 5–6). Paul had received reports of im-
purity of life among church members, including a case of incest
(of a man with his stepmother). He rebukes them for their in-
sensitivity to such conduct, their arrogance, and their boasting.
They were not to associate any more than necessary with those
who were immoral, idolaters, drunkards, or extortioners; particularly they were not to eat with them. Controversies between
Christians were not to be brought before civil authorities but
settled within their own fellowship. Was there no one among them
wise enough "to judge between his brethren? . . . ye do wrong,
and defraud . . . Know ye not that the unrighteous shall not
inherit the kingdom of God?" (6:5,8,9.)

On Marriage (Chapter 7). Here, in answer to questions put to
him in a letter from the Corinthians, Paul declares absolute standards. Marriage, he says, even to an unbeliever, is a bond never to
be dissolved by a Christian. He himself prefers the unmarried state
and considers it more desirable for Christians so that they will not
be distracted from their religion by family considerations. However,
he realizes that marriage is often a preventive of immorality and
hence should be esteemed. (Paul's views on this subject were in
part a result of his belief that the Last Judgment was imminent.)

On Dietary Regulations (8:1–11:1). A problem had arisen at
Corinth, as elsewhere, concerning whether or not Christians were
allowed to eat food that had been offered to idols. Paul says that
although an idol "is nothing," there are some who feel it to be real
and therefore defile their consciences by eating food that they regard as polluted. He advises the principle of self-denial, influenced
by consideration for the feelings of others. If meat should offend
a brother, then take no meat, lest "through thy knowledge . . .
the weak brother perish, for whom Christ died" (8:11). In
Chapter 9 Paul cites his own renunciations and discipline in the
service of Christ.

For though I be free from all men, yet have I made myself servant
unto all . . .
And unto the Jews I became as a Jew, that I might gain the Jews;
to them that are under the law, as under the law, that I might gain
them that are under the law;
To them that are without the law, as without law, (being not without
law to God, but under the law to Christ,) that I might gain them that
are without law;

To the weak became I as weak, that I might gain the weak: I am made all things to all men, that I might by all means save some. . . . . . . I keep under my body, and bring it into subjection: lest that by any means, when I have preached to others, I myself should be a castaway. (9:19–22,27.)

In Chapter 10 Paul cites the consequences to sinners of Israel as a warning against idolatry, immorality, and other temptations. He speaks of the Lord's Supper as the communion of the body and the blood of Christ. "For we being many are one bread, and one body: for we are all partakers of that one bread" (10:17). Returning to the problem of meat offered to idols, he advises that those invited to eat with nonbelievers should not ask questions about where the food comes from, nor should they inquire the source of meat that they buy, but if someone points out to them that it has been offered to idols, they should refrain from eating it. In summation, the principle to be remembered is, "Whether therefore ye eat, or drink, or whatsoever ye do, do all to the glory of God" (10:31).

On Public Worship and Spiritual Gifts (11:2–14:40). Paul prescribes regulations for worship services. A man should have his head uncovered; a woman should have hers covered. Conduct at the observance of the Lord's Supper should be orderly. Before taking the bread or the cup, "let a man examine himself."

As for spiritual gifts of the church members, "there are diversities of gifts, but the same Spirit" (12:4). "Just as the body is one and has many members, and all the members of the body, though many, are one body, so it is with Christ" (RSV 12:12). "Now you are the body of Christ and individually members of it" (RSV 12:27).

Next, in the celebrated Chapter 13, Paul leads his hearers to a consideration of the greatest gift—love.

If I speak in the tongues of men and of angels, but have not love, I am a noisy going or a clanging cymbal. . . .
Love is patient and kind; love is not jealous or boastful; it is not arrogant or rude. Love does not insist on its own way; it is not irritable or resentful; it does not rejoice at wrong, but rejoices in the right.
Love bears all things, believes all things, hopes all things, endures all things. . . .
So faith, hope, love abide, these three; but the greatest of these is love. (RSV 13:1,4–7,13.)

In Chapter 14 the value of prophecy, which is understandable to other men, is placed above that of "speaking with tongues," understandable only to God. Paul says that such utterances should not be forbidden but that "all things should be done decently and in order" (RSV 14:40).

On Resurrection (Chapter 15). The resurrection of Christ, the first teaching of Paul, was witnessed by many, including Paul himself. This shows that resurrection from the dead is possible.

For if the dead rise not, then is not Christ raised:
And if Christ be not raised, your faith is vain . . .
For as in Adam all die, even so in Christ shall all be made alive. . . .
So also is the resurrection of the dead. It is sown in corruption; it is raised in incorruption:
It is sown in dishonour; it is raised in glory: it is sown in weakness; it is raised in power:
It is sown a natural body; it is raised a spiritual body. . . .
So when this corruptible shall have put on incorruption, and this mortal shall have put on immortality, then shall be brought to pass the saying that is written, Death is swallowed up in victory.
O death, where is thy sting? O grave, where is thy victory? (15:16–17, 22,42–44,54–55.)

Conclusion (Chapter 16). In concluding, Paul refers to specific Corinthian matters; gives instructions for a special collection to help needy Jerusalem Christians; and asks for regular weekly Sunday collections. He sends the Corinthian church the salutations of fellow Christians: "All the brethren greet you. Greet ye one another with an holy kiss" (16:20); and he ends with his own benediction: "The grace of our Lord Jesus Christ be with you. My love be with you all in Christ Jesus. Amen" (16:23–24).

II CORINTHIANS

Paul's Second Epistle to the Corinthians is the forty-seventh book of the Bible and the eighth of the New Testament. It was written over a period of time (probably between A.D. 55 and 57) from various places in Macedonia. It tells of Paul's gratification because of news brought to him by Titus of the way in which his first letter (see p. 128) had been received and of his concern about opposition that had been developing in Corinth and elsewhere to his apostolic authority. This Epistle contains the first piece of autobiography in the early Christian Church. Since this information is unrecorded elsewhere, it is the only source for many details of Paul's career.

Less eloquent than the first Epistle, this one is more intense and personal. Love and thankfulness pervade the first half of the letter;

severity and indignation, the second. Paul reveals his wisdom as a pastor and the strength of his apostolic zeal. He tells the Corinthians of his happiness because of evidences of their loyalty and his suffering because of their delinquencies. He reminds them that throughout their trials Christian brotherhood must be at the heart and center of their religion. He speaks of other joys and sorrows of his office, including the burden of a recurring physical ailment, his "thorn in the flesh," the nature of which scholars have never been able to determine, although various hypotheses have been suggested.

This very personal letter to a group that had special significance for the Apostle was taken to Corinth by Paul's close associate Titus and two other unnamed "brethren." It may be divided into the following parts: (1) introduction; (2) a discussion of the news brought to him from Corinth by Titus; (3) an appeal for a collection for Jerusalem churches; (4) a discussion of Paul's apostolic authority; and (5) a warning and a blessing.

Introduction (1:1–11). The introduction includes the salutation and thanksgiving with which Paul's Epistles usually begin. It also tells of the Apostle's recent dangers: "We were pressed out of measure, above strength, insomuch that we despaired even of life."

Discussion of News from Corinth (1:12–7:16). Paul explains why he has postponed his visit to Corinth. He speaks of his thankfulness for the Corinthians' change of heart after receiving his previous letter of admonition. But he beseeches them to forgive the leader of the opposition to his authority, "lest perhaps such a one should be swallowed up with overmuch sorrow." He goes on to a great defense of the apostolic ministry.

. . . God . . . hath made us . . . ministers of the new testament; not of the letter, but of the spirit: for the letter killeth, but the spirit giveth life. (3:5–6.)

For we preach not ourselves, but Christ Jesus the Lord; and ourselves your servants for Jesus' sake.

For God, who commanded the light to shine out of darkness, hath shined in our hearts, to give the light of the knowledge of the glory of God in the face of Jesus Christ. . . .

We are troubled on every side, yet not distressed; we are perplexed, but not in despair;

Persecuted, but not forsaken; cast down, but not destroyed . . .

While we look not at the things which are seen, but at the things which are not seen: for the things which are seen are temporal; but the things which are not seen are eternal. (4:5–6,8–9,18.)

For we walk by faith, not by sight . . .

Therefore if any man be in Christ, he is a new creature: old things are passed away; behold, all things are become new.

And all things are of God, who hath reconciled us to himself by Jesus Christ, and hath given to us the ministry of reconciliation;

To wit, that God was in Christ reconciling the world unto himself . . . and hath committed unto us the word of reconciliation.

Now then we are ambassadors for Christ . . . (5:7;17–20.)

Collection for Jerusalem Churches (Chapters 8–9). Paul urges the Corinthians to complete their collection for the poor Christians of Jerusalem.

. . . this I say, He which soweth sparingly shall reap also sparingly; and he which soweth bountifully shall reap also bountifully.

Every man according as he purposeth in his heart, so let him give; not grudgingly, or of necessity: for God loveth a cheerful giver. (9:6–7.)

Paul's Apostolic Authority (10:1–12:13).* In this passage Paul speaks from the depth of his own experience and in his own defense.

Now I Paul myself beseech you by the meekness and gentleness of Christ . . . (10:1.)

. . . Howbeit whereinsoever any is bold . . . I am bold also.

Are they Hebrews? so am I. Are they Israelites? so am I. Are they the seed of Abraham? so am I.

Are they ministers of Christ? . . . I am more; in labours more abundant, in stripes above measure, in prisons more frequent . . .

Of the Jews five times received I forty stripes save one.

Thrice was I beaten with rods, once was I stoned, thrice I suffered shipwreck, a night and a day I have been in the deep;

In journeyings often, in perils of waters, in perils of robbers, in perils by mine own countrymen, in perils by the heathen, in perils in the city, in perils in the wilderness, in perils in the sea, in perils among false brethren;

In weariness and painfulness, in watchings often, in hunger and thirst, in fastings often, in cold and nakedness.

Beside those things that are without, that which cometh upon me daily, the care of all the churches. (11:21–28.)

. . . I take pleasure in infirmities, in reproaches, in necessities, in persecutions, in distresses for Christ's sake: for when I am weak, then am I strong.

I am become a fool in glorying; ye have compelled me . . .

Truly the signs of an apostle were wrought among you in all patience, in signs, and wonders, and mighty deeds. (12:10–12.)

Warning and Blessing (12:14–13:13). This passage is for the bitterness of spirit and heaviness of heart that it expresses probably

---

* Some scholars believe that Chapters 10–13 were originally part of the first, "stern" letter, rather than of the second, "thankful" one.

unique among the writings of Paul. Yet his love for the torn and errant church shines through it. He tells the Corinthians that he expects to come for a third visit, "and I will not be burdensome to you: for I seek not yours, but you." He speaks of his anxiety about what conditions he would find on his arrival and warns them: "Examine yourselves, whether ye be in the faith; prove your own selves" (13:5). But he concludes with words of hope and comfort and a benediction (13:14): "The grace of the Lord Jesus Christ, and the love of God, and the communion of the Holy Ghost, be with you all. Amen."

GALATIANS

Paul's Epistle to the Galatians is the forty-eighth book of the Bible and the ninth of the New Testament. It was written to the church, or churches, in Galatia, following reports that some of the members were attempting to "Judaize" Christianity and also that Paul's apostolic authority was being questioned. In this Epistle Paul proclaims the supremacy, sufficiency, freedom, and universality of the gospel of Christ. He makes it clear that he regards the Mosaic law as of divine origin, but he insists that it is not binding on Christians because their redemption in Christ has superseded it. The letter was evidently composed rapidly under pressure, and with strong feeling. It contains material that was enlarged and more carefully composed in the longer Epistle to the Romans (see p. 125), apparently prepared when the writer was less under the influence of emotion; and it has autobiographical passages similar to, though not as long as, those in II Corinthians (see p. 132). The date has been a subject of argument among scholars; it may have been between A.D. 49 and 52.

The inhabitants of the Roman province of Galatia were a mixed people with some Celtic elements among them. It is not certain whether Paul was writing to the several churches of this province or only to one in the northern part, Galatia proper. However, the specific nature of the Epistle probably indicates the latter.

In Galatia, as in other places, the earliest churches were composed predominantly of Jews, who of course had been accustomed to Jewish thought, worship, and practices. Many of those who accepted the gospel of Christ and formed a new religious body considered this new religion to be essentially a fulfillment of Judaism. But the reception of new members who were not Jews raised great issues among the older adherents. Although they accepted in theory the doctrine of salvation by faith, in practice some of the early churches were influenced by their Jewish background to subordinate this belief to observance of the Mosaic law. To this issue Paul wrote burning words that became so important in the development of the Church that Galatians has been called the declaration of Christian independence.

The order of this Epistle is relatively simple; it has the following parts: (1) introduction; (2) a defense of Paul's apostolic authority and an account of the Jerusalem dispute about Gentile converts; (3) the central teaching on the gospel of Christ as superseding the law; (4) a discussion of the practical application of this teaching; and (5) personal conclusion.

Introduction (1:1–10). The salutation, "Grace be to you and peace from God the Father, and from our Lord Jesus Christ. . . ," is followed immediately by a stern rebuke, "I marvel that ye are so soon removed from him that called you into the grace of Christ unto another gospel" (1:6). (This Epistle is notable for its omission of Paul's customary thanksgiving for the quality of the spiritual life of those to whom it is addressed.)

Paul's Apostolic Authority and the Jerusalem Dispute (1:11–2:21). The gospel that Paul had preached to the Galatians was taught him by "the revelation of Jesus Christ." Paul acknowledges that before his conversion he had "persecuted the church of God." He had been advanced in Judaism beyond many of his contemporaries and had been "more exceedingly zealous" in observing the traditions of his fathers. But it pleased God "to reveal his Son in me, that I might preach him among the heathen. . . ." Three years after his conversion he went to Jerusalem, where he stayed for fifteen days with Peter and also saw James, Jesus' brother. (It is on this occasion that Paul is believed to have learned much about the historical life of Jesus.) Meanwhile, the news had spread among Christians, "That he which persecuted us in times past now preacheth the faith which once he destroyed" (1:23).

Paul then tells of his second visit to Jerusalem, fourteen years later, when the dispute occurred about the extent to which Gentile converts should submit to Jewish law. Paul convinced the other leaders of the Church, including Peter (who despite his great vision [see p. 121] was now on the side of the Judaizers), to allow him to preach freely to the Gentiles. The only condition was that he should have collections taken for the poor of Jerusalem, which condition he faithfully observed (see pp. 132 and 134).

However, the conflict did not end. Paul had to emphasize repeatedly "that a man is not justified by the works of the law, but by the faith of Jesus Christ" (2:16).

For I through the law am dead to the law, that I might live unto God.

I am crucified with Christ: nevertheless I live; yet not I, but Christ liveth in me: and the life which I now live in the flesh I live by the faith of the Son of God, who loved me, and gave himself for me. (2:19–20.)

The Supremacy of the Gospel of Christ (Chapters 3–4). It is this doctrine that the Galatians have lost sight of. "O foolish Galatians," Chapter 3 begins, "who hath bewitched you. . . ?" Paul proceeds to expound what he regards as the true meaning and purpose of the law.

. . . It was added because of transgressions, till the seed should come to whom the promise was made; . . .

Is the law then against the promises of God? God forbid: for if there had been a law given which could have given life, verily righteousness should have been by the law.

But the scripture hath concluded all under sin, that the promise by faith of Jesus Christ might be given to them that believe.

But before faith came, we were kept under the law, shut up unto the faith which should afterwards be revealed.

Wherefore the law was our schoolmaster to bring us unto Christ, that we might be justified by faith. . . .

There is neither Jew nor Greek, there is neither bond nor free, there is neither male nor female: for ye are all one in Christ Jesus. (3:19, 21–24,28.)

In Chapter 4 Paul portrays Christians as children coming of age to be heirs of a loving father and thus having their status changed from bondage to freedom.

. . . when the fulness of the time was come, God sent forth his Son, made of a woman, made under the law,

To redeem them that were under the law, that we might receive the adoption of sons.

And because ye are sons, God hath sent forth the Spirit of his Son into your hearts, crying, Abba, Father.

Wherefore thou art no more a servant, but a son; and if a son, then an heir of God through Christ. (4:4–7.)

Ethical Applications (5:1–6:10). Paul then reminds his hearers of their responsibility under this freedom.

Stand fast therefore in the liberty wherewith Christ hath made us free . . . (5:1.)

For all the law is fulfilled in one word, even in this; Thou shalt love thy neighbour as thyself. (5:14.)

. . . the fruit of the Spirit is love, joy, peace, longsuffering, gentleness, goodness, faith . . . (5:22.)

If we live in the Spirit, let us also walk in the Spirit. (5:25.)

Bear ye one another's burdens, and so fulfil the law of Christ. (6:2.)

Personal Conclusion (6:11–18). Paul records that he has written to them with his own hand (as noted previously he usually dictated his letters); he tells them that he glories only in the cross of Christ, "by whom the world is crucified unto me, and I unto the world"; and he concludes:

For in Christ Jesus neither circumcision availeth any thing, nor uncircumcision, but a new creature.

And as many as walk according to this rule, peace be on them, and mercy, and upon the Israel of God.

From henceforth let no man trouble me: for I bear in my body the marks of the Lord Jesus.

Brethren, the grace of our Lord Jesus Christ be with your spirit. Amen. (6:15–18.)

EPHESIANS

The Epistle to the Ephesians is the forty-ninth book of the Bible and the tenth of the New Testament. There has been a question about authorship, with some scholars maintaining that the author was not Paul himself but a disciple who after Paul's death wrote in his honor and memory. The Epistle is thought by others to have been written during Paul's imprisonment in Rome, probably between A.D. 58 and 60. It may have been a sort of "circular letter" which went to a number of churches. In this book Paul's concept of the ideal Church and the practical conclusions that he draws from this concept are expounded. The fullness of the Godhead is in Christ, and the fullness of Christ is in his Church. Though the actual Church has many defects and delinquencies, the ideal Church is continually in process of being realized, and it is the duty of every member to labor in this process. To this end Paul emphasizes unity, mutual aid, and a holy family life among Christians.

The Epistle to the Ephesians was apparently written about the same time as the Epistle to the Colossians (see p. 143), and there are many resemblances between them. Of the 155 verses in the six chapters of Ephesians, 78 contain expressions also found in Colossians. Despite these similarities, however, the central themes of the two Epistles are different. In Ephesians Paul stresses the authenticity and the universality of Christ's Church and the work of the Spirit that manifests Christ's power and presence in the Church. In Colossians he emphasizes the glory of Christ as head of the Church and Lord of the universe.

There do not seem to have been any special developments in the churches of Asia Minor to call forth this communication. It was apparently occasioned by the imminent departure of Tychicus for Colossae and was sent with him. It thus resembles the Epistle to the Romans (see p. 125) in that it was not composed under pressure of a crisis or of unfavorable reports.

The style of Ephesians is grand and overflowing compared with Paul's other writings. Indeed it is marked, especially in Chapter 1, by some prolonged and complex constructions. It is as if the broad resources of the Greek language were not sufficient for the writer to convey the splendor of the spiritual truth that flows from his mind.

The content of the Epistle is arranged in this sequence: (1) introduction; (2) a passage on the differences between the converted and the unconverted; (3) a proclamation on the unity of the Church and the duties of its members; (4) personal conclusion.

Introduction (1:1–2:10). The Epistle begins with Paul's customary salutation and thanksgiving, followed by a prayer of intercession. Here Paul says: "By grace are ye saved through faith; and that not of yourselves: it is the gift of God . . . For we are his workmanship, created in Christ Jesus unto good works" (2:8,10).

Differences between Converted and Unconverted (2:11–22). The converted Gentiles and Jews have been united in Christ, "For he is our peace, who hath made both one, and hath broken down the middle wall of partition between us . . . to make in himself of twain one new man . . ." (2:14–15).

Now therefore ye [Gentiles] are no more strangers and foreigners, but fellow citizens with the saints, and of the household of God;
And are built upon the foundation of the apostles and prophets, Jesus Christ himself being the chief corner stone (2:19–20).

The Unity of the Church and the Duties of Its Members (3:1–6:20). The revelation to Paul has led him to "preach among the Gentiles the unsearchable riches of Christ" (3:8).

For this cause I bow my knees unto the Father of our Lord Jesus Christ,
Of whom the whole family in heaven and earth is named . . .
That Christ may dwell in your hearts by faith; that ye, being rooted and grounded in love,

May be able to comprehend with all saints what is the breadth, and length, and depth, and height;

And to know the love of Christ, which passeth knowledge, that ye might be filled with all the fulness of God. (3:14–15,17–19.)

In Chapter 4 Paul exhorts the members of the Church to unity.

There is one body, and one Spirit, even as ye are called in one hope of your calling;

One Lord, one faith, one baptism,

One God and Father of all, who is above all, and through all, and in you all. (4:4–6.)

He speaks of the Church as the body of Christ, edified by the various gifts of its members. Next he admonishes the members on their duties as Christians, "for we are members one of another."

. . . be renewed in the spirit of your mind . . . put on the new man . . . sin not . . . let not the sun go down upon your wrath. (4:23–24,26.)

And be ye kind one to another, tenderhearted, forgiving one another, even as God for Christ's sake hath forgiven you. (4:32.)

And walk in love, as Christ also hath loved us . . . (5:2.)

Paul compares marriage to the relationship between Christ and his Church and speaks of Christian obligations in family life.

Wives, submit yourselves unto your own husbands . . . Husbands, love your wives . . . (5:22,25.)

For this cause shall a man leave his father and mother, and shall be joined unto his wife, and they two shall be one flesh.

This is a great mystery: but I speak concerning Christ and the church. (5:31–32.)

Children, obey your parents in the Lord . . . And ye fathers, provoke not your children to wrath: but bring them up in the nurture and admonition of the Lord.

Servants, be obedient to them that are your masters according to the flesh * . . . With good will doing service, as to the Lord, and not to men . . . masters, do the same things unto them, forbearing threatening: knowing that your Master also is in heaven; neither is there respect of persons with him. (6:1,4,5,7,9.)

Finally, my brethren, be strong in the Lord . . . Put on the whole armour of God . . . Praying always with all prayer and supplication in the Spirit . . . (6:10,11,18.)

Personal Conclusion (6:21–24). Tychicus, a faithful friend who carries the letter, will tell the recipients about Paul's own affairs and will comfort their hearts. "Grace be with all them that love our Lord Jesus Christ in sincerity. Amen." (6:24.)

* The RSV translates "earthly masters."

PHILIPPIANS

Paul's Epistle to the Philippians is the fiftieth book of the Bible and the eleventh of the New Testament. One of a series of letters sent by Paul from prison, it is thought to have been written during his first imprisonment in Rome, about A.D. 60–62. This Epistle reveals the Apostle at his tenderest and noblest. Though written when he was facing martyrdom, it is almost wholly an expression of joy, with doctrine mentioned only incidentally.

The church at Philippi, a Macedonian city founded by Philip II (father of Alexander the Great) was the crown and joy of the Apostle Paul. In spite of intense opposition, he apparently won many loyal converts there, and to no other local group does he seem to have been so deeply attached.

Luke tells in Acts 16:11–40 (see p. 123) of Paul's first visit to Philippi, which occurred on his second missionary journey. He made two later visits, the last while on his final journey to Jerusalem, when he kept Easter with his devoted Philippian followers. In addition to their loyalty to Paul the group at Philippi were distinguished for one other talent—they contributed money for the relief of poor Judean Christians, a cause dear to the Apostle's heart.

The Epistle is plainly a spontaneous statement of love and gratitude for the evidence that Paul had received of the Philippians' generosity and affection. It was sent by Epaphroditus, who had come from Philippi to Rome to bring help to his imprisoned leader at great cost to himself; he was stricken by a severe illness which was almost fatal. When he had recovered, he naturally wished to hurry home. Paul encouraged him and sent him with this letter.

The Epistle, a reflection of the author's courage and faith, overflows with cheerfulness and contains not one word of disappointment or reproach. "Rejoice" is its characteristic word. Because it was an impulsive personal letter, there was no attempt at systematic arrangement of its brief contents. The sequence is as follows: (1) introduction; (2) personal witness; (3) exhortation to follow Christ; (4) personal message; (5) warning; and (6) conclusion.

Introduction (1:1–11). The Epistle begins with a salutation and thanksgiving "upon every remembrance of you . . . For your fellowship in the gospel from the first day until now" (1:3,5).

Personal Witness (1:12–26). Paul reassures his followers that "the things which happened unto me have fallen out rather unto the furtherance of the gospel" (1:12). Admitting the opposition to him within the Church, he boldly says,

141

What then? notwithstanding, every way, whether in pretence, or in truth, Christ is preached; and I therein do rejoice, yea, and will rejoice.

For I know that this shall turn to my salvation through your prayer, and the supply of the Spirit of Jesus Christ,

According to my earnest expectation and my hope, that in nothing I shall be ashamed, but that with all boldness, as always, so now also Christ shall be magnified in my body, whether it be by life, or by death.

For to me to live is Christ, and to die is gain. (1:18–21.)

Exhortation to Follow Christ (1:27–2:18). After speaking of his hope to visit the Philippians again, Paul exhorts them a way of life worthy of Christians.

Let nothing be done through strife or vainglory; but in lowliness of mind let each esteem other better than themselves. (2:3.)

Let this mind be in you, which was also in Christ Jesus . . . Who . . . made himself of no reputation, and took upon him the form of a servant, and was made in the likeness of men:

And being found in fashion as a man, he humbled himself, and became obedient unto death, even the death of the cross.

Wherefore God also hath highly exalted him, and given him a name which is above every name:

That at the name of Jesus every knee should bow, of things in heaven, and things in earth, and things under the earth;

And that every tongue should confess that Jesus Christ is Lord, to the glory of God the Father. (2:5–11.)

Personal Message (2:19–30). Paul tells the Philippians that he will soon send Timothy to them to inform him of their conditions and that he is now sending Epaphroditus back to them, mercifully recovered from his dangerous illness.

Warning (Chapter 3). Paul warns against the Judaizers (see p. 136), reminding his hearers that he also had once been a proud inheritor of Judaism, "But what things were gain to me, those I counted loss for Christ" (3:7).

Conclusion (Chapter 4). In farewell Paul pleads for concord in the Philippian church, beseeching in particular two women, Euodias and Syntyche, to be "of the same mind in the Lord" (4:2).

Rejoice in the Lord, alway: and again I say, Rejoice. . . .

. . . in every thing by prayer and supplication with thanksgiving let your requests be made known unto God.

And the peace of God, which passeth all understanding, shall keep your hearts and minds through Christ Jesus.

Finally, brethren whatsoever things are true, whatsoever things are honest, whatsoever things are just, whatsoever things are pure, whatsoever things are lovely, whatsoever things are of good report; if there be any virtue, and if there be any praise, think on these things. (4:4–8.)

COLOSSIANS

Paul's Epistle to the Colossians is the fifty-first book of the Bible and the twelfth of the New Testament. It was occasioned by a report that had reached Paul concerning a dangerous heresy that was spreading in Colossae. In it Paul warns the Colossian church against ideas that were leading some of its members away from the gospel of Christ. Though this Epistle is written in a much less finished style than most of Paul's letters, it retains his familiar forcefulness and doctrines. Purification of the heart is the essential, and not formal observances. Christ is the one mediator between God and man, uniting the Creator and the creature. In him alone can holiness of life be attained and the evils of the world be overcome. "Christ is all, and in all."

The church at Colossae, a city in Asia Minor, was not well known in the early Christian era and was probably the least important of the congregations to whom an Epistle was addressed. Paul had never visited it; he simply tells its members that he has "heard of their faith."

It was Epaphras, a native of the city, who brought Paul the news of the situation there that moved him to write. However, he kept the dedicated Epaphras with him (or he may have been a fellow prisoner) and sent his message by Tychichus and Onesimus. The letter was apparently sent just before the Apostle's release from his first imprisonment in Rome (about A.D. 61–62), although some scholars regard the date and place of writing as uncertain. As noted previously (see p. 138), it has a number of resemblances to Ephesians.

The threatening heresy is not defined, but some scholars believe it to have been a mystery cult resulting from the infiltration of Oriental beliefs. Its spread does not seem to have been limited to the Colossians who were church members. There is a reference in Colossians 2:18 to "worshipping of angels," which was apparently carried on in another religious group.

The brief contents of the Epistle are arranged in this sequence: (1) introduction; (2) warning against error; (3) comment on specific duties of individuals; and (4) conclusion.

Introduction (Chapter 1). The Epistle begins with a salutation, thanksgiving, and expression of interest in the Colossians.

We give thanks to God . . . praying always for you . . . Since we heard of your faith in Christ Jesus . . .

Paul then declares, in a passage frequently quoted, the exalted nature and the absolute supremacy of Christ.

[God] hath delivered us from the power of darkness, and hath translated us into the kingdom of his dear Son:

In whom we have redemption through his blood, even the forgiveness of sins:

Who is the image of the invisible God, the firstborn of every creature:

For by him were all things created, that are in heaven, and that are in earth, visible and invisible, whether they be thrones, or dominions, or principalities, or powers: all things were created by him, and for him:

And he is before all things, and by him all things consist.

And he is the head of the body, the church: who is the beginning, the firstborn from the dead; that in all things he might have the preeminence.

For it pleased the Father that in him should all fulness dwell. . . (1:13–19.)

This is "the mystery which hath been hid from ages and from generations" (1:26) but is now manifested to the disciples of Christ.

Warning against Error (2:1–3:4). Paul next warns the Colossians directly against "enticing words," "philosophy," and "vain deceit." Telling them that he is present with them in spirit, he urges them: "As ye have therefore received Christ Jesus the Lord, so walk ye in him . . ." (2:6). Finding their complete being in Christ, they shall not be spoiled by the teachings of the world. "For in him dwelleth all the fulness of the Godhead bodily" (2:9). Attacking the ascetic regulations of the heresy, which evidently shared with a number of other heresies the belief that matter is evil, Paul says:

Wherefore if ye be dead with Christ from the rudiments of the world, why, as though living in the world, are ye subject to ordinances,

(Touch not; taste not; handle not;

Which all are to perish with the using;) after the commandments and doctrines of men? (2:20–22.)

Specific Christian Duties (3:5–4:6). The ethical requirements of Christianity are not prohibitive but affirmative.

. . . put on the new man, which is renewed in knowledge after the image of him that created him:

Where there is neither Greek nor Jew, circumcision nor uncircumcision, Barbarian, Scythian, bond nor free: but Christ is all, and in all. (3:10–11.)

And whatsoever ye do in word or deed, do all in the name of the Lord Jesus, giving thanks to God . . . by him. (3:17.)

Conclusion (4:7–18). Paul ends the letter with personal explanations and greetings. He says that his messengers, Tychichus and Onesimus, will explain his situation where he is imprisoned. (As noted previously, the place is thought to have been Rome.) Among those with him who send greetings is "Luke, the beloved physician." "Remember my bonds," says Paul in conclusion. "Grace be with you. Amen." (4:18.)

I THESSALONIANS

Paul's First Epistle to the Thessalonians is the fifty-second book of the Bible and the thirteenth of the New Testament. The Apostle wrote it to one of the earliest churches that he had established, and he wrote in response to a troublesome situation that had arisen in that church. The Thessalonians, who had profound interest in the expected return of Jesus Christ to earth, were anxious about the meaning of this Second Coming. Paul wrote to reassure and advise them. One of the least dogmatic of Paul's writings, this Epistle nevertheless urgently states his central doctrines: that Christ is one with God the Father; that Christ is Redeemer and Savior; that he is Lord of the universe; and that he will come again to earth.

Thessalonica was a large and bustling seaport in Macedonia, where many Jews lived. Paul went there on his second missionary journey (as recounted in Acts 17). At first he preached in the synagogue and made some converts; and then, apparently driven out of the synagogue by opposition, he won more followers among the Gentiles. Although the enthusiasm of the converts was great, the vehement hostility of the Jewish population forced Paul to leave just when he felt that the new Christians were most in need of his pastoral guidance. Later, finding it impossible to return, Paul sent Timothy from Athens to Thessalonica to assure the young church of his continuing devotion and to obtain information about it. The report Timothy brought back contained a mixture of satisfying news along with details about serious difficulties. Then Paul wrote the Epistle to express his joy because of the good news and to give advice about the problems.

The Apostle wrote in the name of himself, Silas, and Timothy. The letter bears the marks of a relatively early date, between A.D. 49 and 52, but the dating depends upon the view that one accepts of the over-all chronology of Paul's activities, concerning which there are differing opinions.

There was current at the time a belief that Jesus Christ would soon return to earth and indeed that most Christians would live to see his Second Coming. This belief is said to have led in some cases to idleness and much fruitless discussion. Further, there was speculation that those who had died before the Second Coming might not obtain some of its blessings. Paul rejects this idea, but he writes definitely in support of the possible imminent return of Christ to earth.

The brief document is arranged in this sequence: (1) introduction; (2) declarations of affection and satisfaction; (3) comfort and advice because of the Resurrection; (4) conclusion.

Introduction (Chapter 1). Paul begins as usual with salutations and thanksgiving. He says that he gives thanks to God for all in the Thessalonian church, making mention of them in his prayers, remembering their work of faith and their labor of love. He recalls that they had become followers of himself and of Christ, "in much affliction, with joy of the Holy Ghost," and had been examples to their fellow Christians in Macedonia and elsewhere. They had "sounded out the word of the Lord" and served "the living and true God," waiting "for his Son from heaven, whom he raised from the dead."

Declarations of Affection and Satisfaction (Chapters 2–3). Paul reminds his hearers that even after he had suffered at Philippi, he felt called of God to preach also at Thessalonica. He had exhorted and comforted the Thessalonians "as a father doth his children," and, like him, they had encountered persecution for their faith. Regretting his forced departure from them, he says that he had wished to come to them again, "but Satan hindered us."

. . . what is our hope, or joy, or crown of rejoicing? Are not even ye in the presence of our Lord Jesus Christ at his coming?
For ye are our glory and joy. (2:19–20.)

Paul goes on to tell the Thessalonians how he had sent his brother minister Timothy from Athens to establish and comfort them in their faith. Timothy has returned and "brought us good tidings of your faith and charity, and that ye have good remembrance of us always, desiring greatly to see us, as we also to see you" (3:6). "For now we live, if ye stand fast in the Lord" (3:8).

Comfort and Advice (4:1–5:22). The Apostle urges the faithful to go on in holiness, remembering that they have been taught of God to love one another. "And that ye study to be quiet, and to do your own business, and to work with your own hands . . ." (4:11). As for those of their number who have died, they should not sorrow over them.

For if we believe that Jesus died and rose again, even so them also which sleep in Jesus will God bring with him. . . .
For the Lord himself shall descend from heaven with a shout, with the voice of the archangel, and with the trump of God: and the dead in Christ shall rise first. (4:14,16.)

As for the "times and the seasons" of the day of the coming of the Lord—such things they do not need to know. It will come unexpectedly "as a thief in the night." But they, being children of light, whether they wake or sleep will live together with Christ. Therefore he tells them to "Rejoice evermore. Pray without ceasing. . . . Prove all things; hold fast that which is good" (5:16–17,21).

Conclusion (5:23–28). Paul's final prayer is: "The very God of peace sanctify you wholly; and I pray God your whole spirit and soul and body be preserved blameless unto the coming of our Lord Jesus Christ" (5:23).

II THESSALONIANS

Paul's Second Epistle to the Thessalonians is the fifty-third book of the Bible and the fourteenth of the New Testament. It was evidently sent shortly after his first Epistle to that church (see p. 145). Paul does not refer directly to the results of his previous letter, but he praises the Thessalonians' zeal and attainments with even more depth of feeling. He also deals again with agitation over the belief in Christ's Second Coming, which some in Thessalonica apparently now believed had actually occurred.

This Epistle, like the first, is not a fine literary document but rather an authentic human communication, revealing much of the character of Paul. Written in a conversational style, it has the local and personal references of a communication between friends. Again Paul writes in the names of Silas and Timothy, as well himself. He strongly asserts his affection for his Thessalonian disciples and his indignation at those who are hindering Christ's work in the world.

The Epistle contains valuable information about the struggles of a young church whose eager converts were filled with love for the Gospel but were hindered by their previous culture, from which they had not been separated. It is arranged in the following order: (1) introduction; (2) warning against errors concerning the Second Coming; (3) exhortation to prayer and work; and (4) conclusion.

Introduction (Chapter 1). Paul greets the Thessalonians and praises them. "Your faith groweth exceedingly, and the charity of every one of you all toward each other aboundeth" (1:3).

Warning (Chapter 2). "Be not soon shaken," the Apostle says, concerning the return of Christ. It will come after a "falling away," a great apostasy. (This chapter contains references to events preceding the Second Coming that are difficult for modern readers to understand.) But Paul is thankful for the Thessalonians because God has chosen them "through sanctification of the Spirit and belief of the truth" (2:13).

Now our Lord Jesus Christ himself, and God, even our Father, which hath loved us, and hath given us everlasting consolation and good hope through grace,
Comfort your hearts, and stablish you in every good word and work. (2:16–17.)

Exhortation to Prayer and Work (3:1–15). Then Paul directs the attention of his hearers away from anxiety about the future and toward their daily responsibilities as Christians. Reminding them of his own and his fellow missionaries' orderly and industrious conduct when they visited Thessalonica, he appeals to the Thessalonians to follow this example. They should "with quietness . . . work, and eat their own bread," and "be not weary in well doing" (3:12–13).

Conclusion (3:16–18). Paul's final benediction to the distracted church is: "Now the Lord of peace himself give you peace always by all means. The Lord be with you all."

I TIMOTHY

The First Epistle to Timothy is the fifty-fourth book of the Bible and the fifteenth of the New Testament. It is one of three so-called Pastoral Epistles (the others being II Timothy and Titus), which are directed to the clergy and church officers rather than to the whole people and discuss church government, practices, and teaching. Some scholars believe that the author was Paul and the date of writing about A.D. 60–62; others maintain that the Pastoral Epistles were not written by Paul and came at a much later date, during the second century. A middle view is that they combine fragments of Pauline writings with material added by later editors.
The Timothy to whom the Epistles is addressed was Paul's be-

loved young fellow worker, who first joined him at Lystra, where he lived. He was the son of a Greek father and a Jewish mother (his mother was also a convert to Christianity). He accompanied Paul on his second missionary journey. There are numerous references to him in Acts and the Epistles, as he carried out the assignments given him by Paul, some of which were very difficult.

The many and varied topics of the letter are probably taken up just as they occurred to the writer, in an informal arrangement, as follows: (1) introduction; (2) advice on public worship; (3) criteria for church officers; (4) principles to guide Timothy as a minister; (5) specific rules for relationships within the church; (6) miscellaneous advice and conclusion.

Introduction (Chapter 1). The Epistle begins with a salutation and thanksgiving. Paul calls Timothy "my own son in the faith" and asks for him "grace, mercy, and peace, from God our Father and Jesus Christ our Lord" (1:2). Paul admits having been "a blasphemer, and a persecutor, and injurious" but says that he has obtained mercy. "Christ Jesus came into the world to save sinners; of whom I am chief" (1:15).

Advice on Public Worship (Chapter 2). "Supplications, prayers, intercession, and giving of thanks" are "good and acceptable in the sight of God our Saviour. . . For there is one God, and one mediator between God and men, the man Christ Jesus" (2:1,3,5). Men should "pray every where, lifting up holy hands, without wrath and doubting" (2:8). Women should wear "modest apparel," should do "good works," and "learn in silence with all subjection" (2:9–11). "But I suffer not a woman to teach" (2:12). (It has been pointed out by scholars that these teachings represent a very conservative tradition, even in early New Testament churches, most of which did allow women an active part.)

Criteria for Church Officers (Chapter 3). Here Paul sets forth standards for clerical and lay church leaders. Bishops "must be blameless, the husband of one wife, vigilant, sober, of good behaviour, given to hospitality, apt to teach. . . ." Deacons must be "grave, not doubletongued, not given to much wine, not guilty of filthy lucre; Holding the mystery of the faith in a pure conscience." Their wives must be "grave, not slanderers, sober, faithful in all things."

Principles for a Minister (Chapter 4). Timothy is enjoined to beware of false teachers and those who preached extreme ascetic doctrines, "For every creature of God is good, and nothing to be refused, if it be received with thanksgiving" (4:4). He should train himself in godliness and "be . . . an example . . . in word, in conversation, in charity, in spirit, in faith, in purity" (4:7,12).

Special Church Relationships (Chapter 5). Timothy is advised to entreat rather than to rebuke an elder and to regard the younger men as brothers, the elder women as mothers, and the younger women as sisters. He was to act "without preferring one before another, doing nothing in partiality," and to keep himself pure.

Miscellaneous Advice and Conclusion (Chapter 6). Servants should honor their masters and should not take advantage of "believing masters" but serve them all the better. The Christian is advised to beware of teachers who promote strife and envy by departing from the "wholesome words" of Jesus Christ. He should not seek worldly goods, "For the love of money is the root of all evil . . ." (6:10). The concluding exhortation to Timothy is: "Fight the good fight of faith, lay hold on eternal life . . . O Timothy, keep that which is committed to thy trust . . . Grace be with thee. Amen." (6:12,20–21.)

II TIMOTHY

The Second Epistle to Timothy is the fifty-fifth book of the Bible and the sixteenth of the New Testament. Like I Timothy and Titus, it is a Pastoral Epistle (see p. 148), addressed to brethren in the ministry. It is much more personal than the First Epistle to Timothy. Those who believe that the author was Paul, or that the Epistle incorporates some of Paul's writings, think that it came toward the end of Paul's career, when he was imprisoned and facing martyrdom. The strong leader and organizer was about to turn over to others the tasks into which he had poured his energy. This was a process of great concern to the Apostle because he realized that Timothy as one of the group would be faced with great hostility and would have to endure much suffering. He also knew Timothy well and wondered whether his personality could stand the stress in the positions that he must hold. Therefore, he felt called upon to express his fullest witness to the power of the gospel of Christ.

The contents of the Epistle are a mixture of sorrow and joy. In it the Apostle reveals his faith that death will bring him to Christ and states his own readiness to die. Yet he is aware that the young churches face dark days and need his leadership.

The contents are arranged in the following somewhat unsystematic sequence: (1) introduction; (2) personal appeal to Timothy; (3) instruction on the condition of the churches; and

(4) a solemn charge to Timothy, with reference to the Apostle's own condition.

Introduction (1:1–5). Paul begins with a salutation and thanksgiving, calling Timothy "my dearly beloved son" and saying that he remembers him daily in his prayers.

Personal Appeal (1:6–2:15). Paul exhorts Timothy to be firm and courageous.

. . . God hath not given us the spirit of fear; but of power, and of love, and of a sound mind. (1:7.)

. . . be strong in the grace that is in Christ Jesus . . . endure hardness, as a good soldier of Jesus Christ. (2:1,3.)

If we suffer, we shall also reign with him: if we deny him, he also will deny us: If we believe not, yet he abideth faithful: he cannot deny himself. . . .

Study to shew thyself approved unto God, a workman that needeth not to be ashamed, rightly dividing * the word of truth. (2:12,13,15.)

Instructions on the Condition of the Churches (2:16–3:17). The minister as servant of the Lord must be "gentle unto all men, apt to teach, patient, In meekness instructing those that oppose . . ." (2:24–25). There will be great wickedness in the "last days." "Men shall be lovers of their own selves" (3:2), and "all that will live godly in Christ Jesus shall suffer persecution" (3:12).

Solemn Charge (Chapter 4). In his final charge to Timothy, Paul speaks calmly and confidently of his own approaching martyrdom.

For I am now ready to be offered, and the time of my departure is at hand.

I have fought a good fight, I have finished my course, I have kept the faith:

Henceforth there is laid up for me a crown of righteousness . . .

The Lord Jesus Christ be with thy spirit. Grace be with you. Amen. (4:6–8,22.)

TITUS

The Epistle to Titus is the fifty-sixth book of the Bible and the seventeenth of the New Testament. Like I and II Timothy, it is a Pastoral Epistle (see p. 148) from an experienced leader to an associate. Some scholars believe that it was written by Paul; others

---

* The RSV translates, "handling."

attribute it to a later author. It contains advice about the organization of the churches in Crete, which had been left in charge of
Titus. If the writer was Paul, then undoubtedly his purpose in
writing was to instruct Titus in ways to carry on this work, which he
himself had evidently left uncompleted. The advice is most specific
on the establishment of a regular church government and ministry
and on methods of dealing with false teachers. In this respect the
letter resembles I Timothy (see p. 148); the two Epistles were
probably written at about the same time.

Titus, a Greek Gentile, was probably converted by Paul and
then became one of his most trusted co-workers. He was evidently
a man endowed with great strength of character who worked somewhat independently. He was not one of the Apostle's constant
companions but was sent by him to carry out his plans in various
places. Paul seems to have shown toward Titus none of the anxiety
concerning moral character revealed in his letters to Timothy.

More definite knowledge about Titus is found in the Pastoral
Epistles. The Epistle to Titus states that Titus had been left in
Crete as Paul's deputy. In Titus 3:12 Paul writes of an intention to
meet his brother minister in Nicopolis, but it is not known whether
the meeting ever took place. In II Timothy, thought to have been
written after Titus, Paul reports that Titus has been with him
(probably in Rome during his second imprisonment) but has left
to go to Dalmatia. With this note the historical information on
Titus ends.

The arrangement of the Epistle to Titus, like that of I and II
Timothy, is unsystematic, the subjects evidently being discussed
just as they came to the writer's mind. In general the sequence of
topics is as follows: a salutation, a discussion of the needs of the
Cretan church, and personal details and conclusion.

Salutation (1:1–4). Paul, a servant "according to the commandment of God our Saviour," writes to Titus, "mine own son
after the common faith: Grace, mercy, and peace, from God the
Father and the Lord Jesus Christ our Saviour."

Needs of the Cretan Church (1:5–3:11). Titus is instructed to set
things in order and "ordain elders in every city." A man thus chosen
should

. . . be . . . not self-willed, not soon angry, not given to wine, no
striker, not given to filthy lucre;

But a lover of hospitality, a lover of good men, sober, just, holy,
temperate;

Holding fast the faithful word as he hath been taught, that he may
be able by sound doctrine both to exhort and to convince the gain-
sayers. (1:7–9.)

Titus is to speak "the things which become sound doctrine" (2:1). Directions are given for the teachings to various groups within the church, "For the grace of God that bringeth salvation hath appeared to all men" (2:11).

Not by works of righteousness which we have done, but according to his mercy he saved us, by the washing of regeneration, and renewing of the Holy Ghost;
Which he shed on us abundantly through Jesus Christ our Saviour;
That being justified by his grace, we should be made heirs according to the hope of eternal life. (3:5–7.)

Personal Details and Conclusion (3:12–15). Paul urges Titus to "be diligent to come unto me to Nicopolis" and concludes: "All that are with me salute thee. Greet them that love us in the faith. Grace be with you all. Amen."

PHILEMON

Paul's Epistle to Philemon is the fifty-seventh book of the Bible and the eighteenth of the New Testament. The letter is an urgent and tender communication, pleading with Paul's friend Philemon to take back in Christian love a runaway slave named Onesimus, who had been with Paul in Rome. (Some scholars feel that the implicit purpose of the letter was to persuade Philemon to free Onesimus so that he might return to Paul.) The document has been called an exquisite relic. Wholly a private letter and consisting of only one chapter, it is unique among Biblical books. It reveals much of the character of the writer, particularly his courtesy; and because of its expressed love and fellowship for a slave, it became important in the Christian anti-slavery crusade.

The letter may have been written, from the Roman prison, at about the same time as the Epistles to the Colossians and the Ephesians. Concerning Philemon, the only available information is in this Epistle: He was a prominent and prosperous citizen of Colossae, owned slaves, had been converted to Christianity, and was an active member of the Colossian church. He was the head of a household, two of whose members (Apphia and Archippus, who may have been his wife and son) are included in Paul's greeting at the beginning of the Epistle.

Onesimus was but one of a large number of runaway slaves and thieves who made their way to Rome during the Empire. While there he came under the influence of Paul, who persuaded him to become a Christian and became deeply attached to him.

The name Onesimus means "profitable." Paul plays on the word, in Verse 11, referring to Onesimus as once unprofitable (he had apparently robbed his master) but now profitable to both Philemon and Paul.

Paul beseeches Philemon to welcome the slave and thief as "a brother beloved."

If thou count me therefore a partner, receive him as myself.

If he hath wronged thee, or oweth thee ought, put that on mine account. . .

Having confidence in thy obedience I wrote unto thee, knowing that thou wilt also do more than I say. . . .

The grace of our Lord Jesus Christ be with your spirit. Amen.
(1:17–18,21,25.)

HEBREWS

The Epistle to the Hebrews is the fifty-eighth book of the Bible and the nineteenth of the New Testament. This anonymous and lengthy Epistle has a well worked-out thesis, more in the form of an essay than a letter. In style it is rhetorical and hortatory, so much so that the examples cited seem at times to overshadow the argument. The Epistle is evidently addressed to persons under pressure of persecution or ostracism to give up the new religion of Christ, possibly for a return to Judaism. While this Epistle belongs with other writings that interpret the Christian gospel to Jewish converts, it is also a distinctive document in itself because of its reasoned exposition of Christology. It stresses the supremacy and finality of the revelation of Christ.

The Epistle may have been composed between A.D. 68 and 96. The place of writing is unknown, as is the destination. The reference, "they of Italy salute you" (13:24) could mean either people in Italy or people from Italy. It may be a transcription of an oral address.

"God alone knows" who wrote the manuscript was said more than 1600 years ago. One tradition supports Barnabas as author; another, Luke; a third, Apollos. An older theory crediting Paul now seems to have been abandoned by scholars. The writer apparently knew Paul and Timothy and was aware of Jewish thought in Alexandria as well as in Jerusalem. He frequently used Hebrew scripture and traditions in the development of his thesis. He was familiar with the great personalities of the Old Testament and the religious significance of their characters. It thus seems established that the author was a Jewish Christian and that he wrote for a specific group of Jewish Christians, possibly in Jerusalem, in Rome, or around Ephesus. However, the book became of great significance for all Christians; and because of the power and inspiration of its thought, it has been called the most important anonymous Epistle of the New Testament.

With no salutation or thanksgiving of the Pauline type, the author plunges directly into his thesis, which is arranged in the following order: (1) the finality of the revelation made by Jesus Christ the Son of God; (2) the new dispensation of Christ; (3) the absolute and universal high priesthood of Christ; (4) the excellence of Christ's ministry; (5) applications of this doctrine for Christian witness; and (6) personal instructions and conclusion.

Revelation of Christ (Chapters 1–2). God, who in the past spoke through the prophets, has now spoken to us through his Son, to whom is given dominion of the world. But this Christ, to whom all things are subject, "took not on him the nature of angels . . . he took on him the seed of Abraham" (2:16).

Wherefore in all things it behoved him to be made like unto his brethren, that he might be a merciful and faithful high priest in things pertaining to God, to make reconciliation for the sins of the people.

For in that he himself hath suffered being tempted, he is able to succour them that are tempted. (2:17–18.)

New Dispensation (Chapters 3–4). Christ, "the Apostle and High Priest of our profession," is superior to Moses, as a son is above a servant. God's "rest," lost by the Hebrews who departed from him in the wilderness, is promised again through Christ.

For we have not an high priest which cannot be touched with the feeling of our infirmities; but was in all points tempted like as we are, yet without sin.

Let us therefore come boldly unto the throne of grace, that we may obtain mercy, and find grace to help in time of need. (4:15–16.)

Christ's High Priesthood (Chapters 5–7). This section begins with a description of the requirements for a high priest. He must have compassion for the ignorant and wayward; he must sacrifice for sin; he must be called by God. Christ is the supreme and universal High Priest because he perfectly fills these requirements.

. . . Christ glorified not himself to be made an high priest; but he that said unto him, Thou art my Son, to-day have I begotten thee. . . .

Though he were a Son, yet learned he obedience by the things which he suffered;

And being made perfect, he became the author of eternal salvation unto all them that obey him . . . (5:5,8–9.)

Christ is not bound by the limitations of all earthly priests.

But this man, because he continueth ever, hath an unchangeable priesthood.

Wherefore he is able also to save them to the uttermost that come unto God by him, seeing he ever liveth to make intercession for them.

For such an high priest became us, who is holy, harmless, undefiled, separate from sinners, and made higher than the heavens.

Who needeth not daily, as those high priests, to offer up sacrifice, first for his own sins, and then for the people's: for this he did once, when he offered up himself. (7:24–27.)

Excellence of Christ's Ministry (8:1–10:18). The author summarizes his preceding argument: "Now of the things which we have spoken this is the sum: We have such an high priest, who is set on the right hand of the throne of the Majesty in the heavens" (8:1). He quotes the Old Testament to prove that the New Covenant, prophesied by Jeremiah, supplants the old. "But now hath he obtained a more excellent ministry [than that of Moses], by how much also he is the mediator of a better covenant, which was established upon better promises" (8:6).

. . . Christ being come an high priest of good things to come, by a greater and more perfect tabernacle, not made with hands . . .

Neither by the blood of goats and calves, but by his own blood he entered in once into the holy place, having obtained eternal redemption for us. (9:11–12.)

For the law having a shadow of good things to come, and not the very image of the things, can never with those sacrifices which they offered year by year continually make the comers thereunto perfect. (10:1.)

[But] we are sanctified through the offering of the body of Jesus Christ once for all. (10:10.)

Applications for Christian Witness (10:19–12:17). In the light of this revelation, Christians should have

boldness to enter into the holiest by the blood of Jesus,

By a new and living way, which he hath consecrated for us . . .

And having an high priest over the house of God;

Let us draw near with a true heart in full assurance of faith . . .

And let us consider one another to provoke unto love and to good works . . . (10:19–22,24.)

Reminding his hearers of the courage with which they have endured their afflictions in the past, the author, in a sublime and often quoted passage, exhorts them to persevere.

Now faith is the substance of things hoped for, the evidence of things not seen. . . .

By faith Abel offered unto God a more excellent sacrifice than Cain . . . By faith Enoch was translated that he should not see death . . . By faith Noah, being warned of God of things not seen as yet . . . prepared an ark to the saving of his house . . . By faith Abraham . . . went out, not knowing whither he went. . . .

These all died in faith, not having received the promises, but having seen them afar off, and were persuaded of them, and embraced them, and confessed that they were strangers and pilgrims on the earth. . . .

God having provided some better thing for us, that they without us should not be made perfect. (11:1,4–8,13,40.)

Wherefore seeing we also are compassed about with so great a cloud of witnesses, let us lay aside every weight, and the sin which doth so easily beset us, and let us run with patience the race that is set before us,

Looking unto Jesus the author and finisher of our faith; who for the joy that was set before him endured the cross, despising the shame, and is set down at the right hand of the throne of God. (12:1–2.)

Instructions and Conclusion (12:12–13:25). The author ends with a warning, ethical injunctions, and further encouragement.

Wherefore we receiving a kingdom which cannot be moved, let us have grace, whereby we may serve God acceptably with reverence and godly fear:

For our God is a consuming fire. (12:28–29.)

Let brotherly love continue.

Be not forgetful to entertain strangers: for thereby some have entertained angels unawares. (13:1–2.)

Jesus Christ the same yesterday, and to-day, and for ever.

Be not carried about with divers and strange doctrines. . . . (13:8–9.)

Now the God of peace, that brought again from the dead our Lord Jesus, that great shepherd of the sheep, through the blood of the everlasting covenant,

Make you perfect in every good work to do his will . . .

Grace be with you all. Amen. (13:20–21,25.)

JAMES

The Epistle of James is the fifty-ninth book of the Bible and the twentieth of the New Testament. It is one of the "general"

Epistles, which are so called because they are not addressed to a particular group but to a wide circle of Christian readers. The prevailing situations with which the letter is concerned were probably common for many churches in the Apostolic age: the strains and sufferings of a small group in hostile surroundings; the elementary duties of individuals in such conditions; the temptations from customs of the outside world; the oppression of the poor by the rich; and the comfort and help available from the Gospel. The Epistle of James is distinguished, however, for its consideration of the true relationship between faith and works. Apparently there were many ready talkers in the new faith, and there seemed to be a danger of the multiplication of those who were mere teachers. Against such abuses in the church, James emphasizes the necessity of Christian deeds: "Be ye doers of the word, and not hearers only."

Some scholars believe that James the brother of Jesus was the author of the Epistle. Others hold that it was by a later writer.

James the brother of Jesus, called "the just," was the first overseer, or supervisor, of the church in Jerusalem. Although not a disciple during Jesus' earthly ministry, James seems to have been converted as a result of his appearance after the Resurrection. He was afterward thought of as having apostolic rank and was an influential leader in the early Church, particularly revered by the Eastern groups.

Since James was stoned to death about A.D. 62 or 63, if it is assumed that the Epistle was written by him its date must be fixed as prior to this time, making it one of the earliest New Testament books. Parts of the book resemble Romans (see p. 125) and I Peter (see p. 159), but one cannot be certain which of the three documents was first. Some scholars, however, believe that James was arguing against a distortion of the Pauline teaching of salvation by faith alone and hence that he wrote after Paul.

The letter is addressed to Jewish Christians of the dispersion, i.e., those who were living outside of Palestine, particularly in Egypt and Syria. Sometimes the writer appears to be speaking to Jews who have not accepted Christ, but usually he addresses the humble and suffering members of the early Church.

The writing is repetitious and plainly unplanned; the work is thus one of the most difficult books in the Bible to sum up. It opens and closes with advice on patience and holiness (1:2–27; 5:7–20). The major central portion (2:1–5:6) consist of warnings and rebukes, mingled with moral exhortation and words of Christian comfort.

James warns against barren orthodoxy, covetousness, strife, worldliness, evil tongues, and fraud.

But the wisdom that is from above is first pure, then peaceable, gentle, and easy to be intreated, full of mercy and good fruits, without partiality, and without hypocrisy.

And the fruit of righteousness is sown in peace of them that make peace. (3:17–18.)

Draw nigh to God, and he will draw nigh to you. Cleanse your hands, ye sinners; and purify your hearts, ye double-minded. (4:8.)

James writes of spiritual healing.

Is any sick among you? let him call for the elders of the church; and let them pray over him, anointing him with oil in the name of the Lord:

And the prayer of faith shall save the sick, and the Lord shall raise him up; and if he have committed sins, they shall be forgiven him. (5:14–15.)

The concise yet comprehensive statement on the true relationship between faith and works is found in Chapter 2.

What doth it profit, my brethren, though a man say he hath faith, and have not works? can faith save him?

If a brother or sister be naked, and destitute of daily food,

And one of you say unto them, Depart in peace, be ye warmed and filled; notwithstanding ye give them not those things which are needful to the body; what doth it profit?

Even so faith, if it hath not works, is dead, being alone. (2:14–17.)

I PETER

The First Epistle of Peter is the sixtieth book of the Bible and the twenty-first of the New Testament. The traditional view that the author was the Apostle Peter is still widely held by scholars today, though some have questioned it. This Epistle reveals Peter as a practical adviser of the humble followers of Christ rather than as a learned or systematic theologian. Speaking to Christians who have encountered hostility and persecution for their faith, he reminds them that their Master was rejected and wronged but that the result of his suffering was ultimate glory and victory. He brings them the message of hope that if they courageously follow Christ's example, they will share the blessings of his glorious triumph.

Peter was one of the first small band of fisherman called by Jesus and became one of his most intimate disciples. Jesus chose him as one of the twelve apostles, who were to carry on his work and declare his message. It was Peter who first confessed Jesus as the Messiah, the Christ. To him Jesus said: "Thou are Peter, and upon this rock I will build my church; and the gates of hell shall not prevail against it" (Matthew 16:18). Peter was with Jesus in Jerusalem during the crises that led to the Crucifixion. Although at the time of Jesus' arrest he three times denied knowing him, he immediately repented, and he was present at most of the appearances of Jesus reported by the disciples after the Resurrection. From that time forward, he seems to have regarded it as his special mission to feed the flock of Christ with the spiritual food that they needed for sustenance and refreshment.

Peter had a leading role in the organization of disciples and apostles that became the nucleus of the early Church. His preeminence in the Jerusalem church and his part in the beginning of the mission to the Gentiles are discussed in Acts (see p. 120). Details of his later career are lacking, but he is thought to have suffered martyrdom in Rome. His First Epistle seems to have been written from that city, called "Babylon" by many Christians, at a time when Christians were being persecuted there, possibly between A.D. 64 and 67.

Peter, "an apostle of Jesus Christ," addresses this letter "to the strangers scattered throughout Pontus, Galatia, Cappadocia, Asia, and Bithynia" (names of provinces in Asia Minor). In these provinces there were undoubtedly Christians of varied heritages—Jewish, Greek, and other nationalities. Thus the Epistle is addressed to a broad group of Christ's followers. It is arranged in the following sequence: (1) advice to persevere under affliction; (2) counsel on Christian duties; (3) exhortation to patience and holiness; and (4) instruction of church officers and members and conclusion.

Perseverance (1:1–2:10). Peter knows that his hearers are "in heaviness through manifold temptations" and the trial of their faith. But he reminds them that the sufferings of Christ ended in glory, as the prophets had foretold.

Wherefore gird up the loins of your mind, be sober, and hope to the end for the grace that is to be brought unto you at the revelation of Jesus Christ . . . (1:13.)

Forasmuch as you know that ye were not redeemed with corruptible things, as silver and gold . . . But with the precious blood of Christ, as of a lamb, without blemish and without spot . . . (1:18–19.)

Being born again, not of corruptible seed, but of incorruptible, by the word of God, which liveth and abideth for ever. (1:23.)

Christian Duties (2:11–3:12). Peter tells Christians how they must live, "as strangers and pilgrims," in the world. They should "abstain from fleshly lusts, which war against the soul" (2:11). They should obey the ordinances of government. ("Honour all men. Love the brotherhood. Fear God. Honour the king." [2:17.] Above all, they should follow in the steps of Christ.

Who, when he was reviled, reviled not again; when he suffered, he threatened not; but committed himself to him that judgeth righteously:

Who his own self bare our sins in his own body on the tree, that we, being dead to sins, should live unto righteousness: by whose stripes ye were healed.* (2:23–24.)

Reminding them of their obligations to each other, he concludes:

Finally, be ye all of one mind, having compassion one of another, love as brethren, be pitiful, be courteous:

Not rendering evil for evil, or railing for railing: but contrariwise blessing; knowing that ye are thereunto called, that ye should inherit a blessing. (3:8–9.)

Patience and Holiness (3:13–4:19). Peter goes on with words of comfort (recalling the Beatitudes): Happy are they who suffer for righteousness' sake; "be not afraid of their terror, neither be troubled" (3:14). They should "sanctify the Lord God" in their hearts and willingly tell others the reason for their hope.

For . . . this cause was the gospel preached also to them that are dead, that they might be judged according to men in the flesh, but live according to God in the spirit.

But the end of all things is at hand: be ye therefore sober, and watch unto prayer.

And above all things have fervent charity among yourselves: for charity shall cover the multitude of sins. (4:6–8.)

Beloved, think it not strange concerning the fiery trial which is to try you, as though some strange thing happen unto you:

But rejoice, inasmuch as ye are partakers of Christ's sufferings; that when his glory shall be revealed, ye may be glad also with exceeding joy. (4:12–13.)

Instruction and Conclusion (Chapter 5). Peter exhorts the elders to "feed the flock of God," willingly. All should humble themselves before God, "Casting all your care upon him; for he careth for you."

. . . the God of all grace, who hath called us unto his eternal glory by Christ Jesus, after that ye have suffered a while, make you perfect, stablish, strengthen, settle you. (5:10.)

---

* An identification with the Suffering Servant of Isaiah (see p. 62).

II PETER

The Second Epistle of Peter, one of the general Epistles (see p. 157), is the sixty-first book of the Bible and the twenty-second of the New Testament. Written apparently during a time of threatening heresies, it urges Christians to hold firmly to the truth that they know and to make their "calling and election sure."

This is a very short letter with some passages similar to I Peter and others markedly different from it. The style of writing is different from that of I Peter, leading to the supposition that if Peter was the author, he had a different interpreter, or secretary, for the Second Epistle. This document is somewhat awkwardly composed, with uncommon words being used at times when ordinary ones would seem better.

There have been various arguments for and against Petrine authorship, difficult to prove either way. On the one hand, it is said that there are analogies between the speeches of Peter as reported in Acts and the language of II Peter. Moreover, many unusual words in II Peter are also found in I Peter, the authorship of which is not generally in dispute. On the other hand, no book in the New Testament was more adversely criticized in the process of its selection for inclusion in the Scripture than this one. Again, there were various uses of Peter's name on documents of the early Church, which were considered legitimate for those writing in his tradition. Possibly the letter was written by Peter, but the weight of scholarly evidence is not in favor of this conclusion.

The assigning of place and date is dependent upon the attribution of authorship. If the author was not Peter, a relatively late date is usually suggested, after A.D. 100 and possibly as late as A.D. 150. If the author was Peter, the date may have been about A.D. 68 and the place of writing, Rome.

The Epistle contains material markedly similar to that in the Epistle of Jude (see p. 167), thus indicating either that the authors used a common source or that one borrowed from the other.

The letter begins and ends with exhortation to growth in grace and knowledge (Chapter 1 and 3:14–18). The author tells his hearers of the divine power that "hath given unto us all things that pertain unto life and godliness, through the knowledge of him that hath called us to glory and virtue: Whereby are given unto us exceeding great and precious promises: that by these ye might be partakers of the divine nature . . ." (1:3–4). To their faith should be added virtue, knowledge, temperance, patience, godliness,

162

brotherly kindness, and love. He is reminding them of "these things," though as Christians they know them.

The central part of the Epistle (2:1–3:13) contains warnings against false teachings and a defense of orthodox tenets, including a belief in the Second Coming. The author predicts "damnable heresies," which many will follow. But God has shown by his previous judgments the punishment that will come upon the wicked.

The Lord knoweth how to deliver the godly out of temptations, and to reserve the unjust unto the day of judgment to be punished. (2:9.)

In Chapter 3 the author says that the Epistle has been written in order that the readers "may be mindful of the words which were spoken before by the holy prophets, and of the commandment of us the apostles of the Lord and Saviour" (3:2). Scoffers who say "Where is the promise of his coming?" ignore such portentous past events as the destruction of the world by flood.

But the heavens and the earth, which are now, by the same word are kept in store, reserved unto fire against the day of judgment and perdition of ungodly men.

But, beloved, be not ignorant of this one thing, that one day is with the Lord as a thousand years, and a thousand years as one day. . . .

. . . the day of the Lord will come as a thief in the night; in the which the heavens shall pass away with a great noise, and the elements shall melt with fervent heat, the earth also and the works that are therein shall be burned up.

Seeing then that all these things shall be dissolved, what manner of persons ought ye to be in all holy conversation and godliness,

Looking for and hasting unto the coming of the day of God, wherein the heavens being on fire shall be dissolved, and the elements shall melt with fervent heat?

Nevertheless we, according to his promise, look for new heavens and a new earth, wherein dwelleth righteousness. (3:7–8,10–13.)

I JOHN

The First Epistle of John, the sixty-second book of the Bible and the twenty-third of the New Testament, is one of the general Epistles (see p. 157). The author is considered by some scholars to have been the Apostle John; others think that he was a later, unknown, writer. Some believe that he was also the author of the

Gospel of John (see p. 113). This Epistle discusses the personal spiritual life of Christians. The author wrote in a time of various heresies, some of which, based on the dualistic concept that matter is evil, denied the human life and death of Christ. John emphasizes the Christian doctrine that God has sent his Son into the world and that his followers must live in the world as he has taught them. Starting from the premise that "God is love," he tells them that they must love one another as God in Christ has loved them.

Though the Epistle is addressed to the Church at large, the author may have had particularly in mind Christians in various places in Asia Minor, where Eastern beliefs were prevalent. The book is in some respects more like a sermon than a letter. It frequently employs the same thoughts and words as John's Gospel; but, whereas the Gospel is spiritual and philosophical in outlook, the Epistle is moral and ethical. The Gospel portrays Christ and his message; the Epistle sets forth the duties of his followers.

John was one of the great apostles. He belonged to the first small band of fishermen called by Jesus to be his disciples, and throughout the Gospels he is always described as among the closest of the group around Jesus. Paul includes him with Peter and James as one of the "pillars" of Christendom. He seems to have exerted his influence among the early giants, not as an aggressive organizer but as a thoughtful mystic. Tradition has it that he spent his later life in and around Ephesus and died during the reign of Emperor Trajan.

In tone and style this letter soars above most of the Epistles. It seems indeed to be a statement from the glorious company of the apostles of Christ to the congregations of Christendom. Minor matters are brushed aside; central issues are discussed and resolved. The writing is lofty, poetic, and unified, proceeding in the following order: (1) introduction; (2) the thought that "God is light"; (3) the thought that "God is love"; and (4) conclusion.

Introduction (1:1–4). John declares that he witnesses to "the Word of life" that he has experienced, "For the life was manifested, and we have seen it . . . And these things write we unto you, that your joy may be full."

God as Light (1:5–2:29). Next comes a discourse on the true nature of God as revealed in Christ.

This then is the message which we have heard of him, and declare unto you, that God is light, and in him is no darkness at all.

If we say that we have fellowship with him, and walk in darkness, we lie, and do not the truth *:

But if we walk in the light, as he is in the light, we have fellow-

---

* The RSV translates, "do not live according to the truth."

ship one with another, and the blood of Jesus Christ his Son cleanseth us from all sin. (1:5–7.)

In Chapter 2 the author goes on to tell how Christians witness to this light by keeping Christ's commandments and by walking in his way.

. . . a new commandment I write unto you, which thing is true in him and in you: because the darkness is past, and the true light now shineth.

He that saith he is in the light, and hateth his brother, is in the darkness even until now.

He that loveth his brother abideth in the light, and there is none occasion of stumbling in him. (2:8–10.)

God as Love (3:1–5:12). As children of God, Christians must exemplify the love that Christ has shown as his incarnate Son.

We know that we have passed from death unto life, because we love the brethren. He that loveth not his brother abideth in death. (3:14.)

Hereby know ye the Spirit of God: Every spirit that confesseth that Jesus Christ is come in the flesh is of God . . . (4:2.)

Beloved, let us love one another: for love is of God; and every one that loveth is born of God, and knoweth God.

He that loveth not knoweth not God; for God is love.

In this was manifested the love of God toward us, because that God sent his only begotten Son into the world, that we might live through him.

Herein is love, not that we loved God, but that he loved us, and sent his Son to be the propitiation for our sins. . . .

No man hath seen God at any time. If we love one another, God dwelleth in us, and his love is perfected in us. (4:7–10,12.)

There is no fear in love; but perfect love casteth out fear . . . (4:18.)

If a man say, I love God, and hateth his brother, he is a liar: for he that loveth not his brother whom he hath seen, how can he love God whom he hath not seen? (4:20.)

There are on earth three witnesses to the Incarnation: "the spirit, and the water, and the blood" (signifying events of Christ's earthly mission and the continuing sacraments of the Church).

And this is the record, that God hath given to us eternal life, and this life is in his Son. (5:11.)

Conclusion (5:13–21). In summation the author states his central purpose: "These things have I written unto you that believe on the name of the Son of God; that ye may know that ye have eternal life . . ." (5:13.)

II JOHN

*The Second Epistle of John is the sixty-third book of the Bible
and the twenty-fourth of the New Testament. It is thought by some
to have been written by the Apostle John and by others it has been
attributed to a later author. (See pp. 163–164 for further discussion
of Johannine authorship.) This brief Epistle is addressed to an un-
identified woman who was head of a household and who had
Christian children. (It is believed by some scholars that she is the
personification of a church.)*

The specific words, situations, and quality of writing resemble
those of I John. The tone of communication suggests that the writer
is a person of authority and experience; for example, he begins,
"The elder unto the elect lady and her children."

Three matters are considered in short space: (1) obedience to
the commandment already known, "that we love one another,"
and "walk after" this rule (Verses 5–6); (2) preservation of the
faith already possessed, the doctrine of the incarnate Christ (Verses
8–9); and (3) warning against reception in the home of false
teachers (Verses 10–11).

The author closes graciously by saying that "Having many things
to write unto you . . . I trust to come unto you, and speak face
to face, that our joy may be full" (Verse 13).

III JOHN

*The Third Epistle of John is the sixty-fourth book of the Bible
and the twenty-fifth of the New Testament. It is addressed to one
Gaius, evidently an officer or member of a local church, commend-
ing him for his past deeds and encouraging him to continue in
Christian witness. The Epistle's content and tone point to a responsible supervisor of local churches as author. It is, however,
attributed to John by some scholars on the ground that the content
and style resemble those of the First Epistle. (The whole question
of Johannine authorship is still widely debated.)*

The writer commends Gaius because of reports "of the truth that
is in thee, even as thou walkest in the truth" (Verses 1–4). He
praises Gaius' hospitality toward both brethren and strangers, par-

ticularly to a group of journeying missionaries. He contrasts this attitude with that of one Diotrephes, who has not only been inhospitable himself but has tried to cast out of the church those who wanted to "receive the brethren." John, if he comes, will remember his deeds and malicious words. (Verses 8–10.) Demetrius, on the contrary, "hath good report of all men," and John knows that this report is true. He urges Gaius to follow "that which is good," for "He that doeth good is of God." (Verses 11–12.) He expects to see Gaius soon and talk with him face to face (Verses 13–14).

JUDE

The Epistle of Jude is the sixty-fifth book of the Bible and the twenty-sixth of the New Testament. It is a brief general Epistle, evidently written at a time when heresies had developed. Some scholars believe that the author was the Jude who was a brother of Jesus and of James; others think that he was a later, unknown, writer. As noted previously (see p. 162), the letter has marked resemblances to passages in II Peter. It is an urgent appeal for the preservation of the true apostolic faith.

The text begins, "Jude, the servant of Jesus Christ, and brother of James, to them that are sanctified by God the Father, and preserved in Jesus Christ, and called." The author thus does not identify himself as Jude (or Judas), the brother of Jesus, who was one of the younger sons of Joseph and Mary. Like James, this brother did not follow Jesus until after the Resurrection; he then became a disciple and was one of Paul's associates.

There is no mention in the Epistle of a specific church or group of churches, although the author may have had one in mind. At any rate, the message is of general interest, since he deals with a crisis situation then occurring in a number of churches. It was apparently caused by intrusive or recalcitrant members, who defied the authority of the local leaders or supervisors, under whom church government was being established. There were thus actually within the churches subversive elements of heresy, immorality, and dissension.

Warning against such agents, Jude does not develop a distinct teaching of his own but calls for remembrance of and adherence to the orthodox Christian faith. The sequence is as follows:

Salutation and Explanation of Purpose (Verses 1–4). The author begins with a salutation, identifying himself as noted above, and states his reason for writing: to "exhort you that ye should earnestly contend for the faith which was once delivered unto the saints."

Historical Argument (Verses 5–10). As examples of God's judgment on the wicked, the author cites the destruction of Sodom and Gomorrha as well as other sinful cities.

Characterization of Evildoers and Application of Prophecy (Verses 11–19). Jude says that the heretical and ungodly men are in the midst of the church, "spots in your feasts of charity . . . Raging waves of the sea, foaming out their own shame." But, as the prophets have foretold, God will come to execute judgment.

Exhortation to Good Conduct and Holy Life (Verses 20–23). Jude urges his hearers to stand fast in the true faith and to bring back to it those who have been led astray.

But ye, beloved, building up yourselves on your most holy faith, praying in the Holy Ghost,

Keep yourselves in the love of God, looking for the mercy of our Lord Jesus Christ unto eternal life. (Verses 20–21.)

Benediction (Verses 24–25). He concludes with one of the most beautiful Biblical benedictions.

Now unto him that is able to keep you from falling, and to present you faultless before the presence of his glory with exceeding joy,

To the only wise God our Saviour, be glory and majesty, dominion and power, both now and ever. Amen.

REVELATION

The book of Revelation is the sixty-sixth and last in the Bible, and the twenty-seventh of the New Testament. It is unique because it is the only prophetic book in the New Testament and because of its special form of presentation. The heart of the book is a series of visions, the meaning of which has long puzzled scholars. The writer gathers up previous prophecies relating to the Messiah and the establishment of God's kingdom on earth. He describes in apocalyptic terms a new coming of Christ, a new heaven, and a new earth. The emphasis is on the words, "I come quickly."

The book begins with the statement that it is "the Revelation of Jesus Christ," given "by his angel unto his servant John." It is not explicity stated that John is the author. There has been much discussion among scholars as to whether the John referred to was the Apostle John or a later Church leader. There are sections of

Revelation which are similar to the Gospel attributed to John, but there are also striking differences between the two books.

If an early date (e.g., A.D. 68–70) is assigned, the authorship of the Apostle seems more likely, and the prophecy in the book may refer to the destruction of Jerusalem by the Roman Emperor Titus, which occurred in A.D. 70. If a later date, toward the end of the first century (which scholars considered more probable), is assumed, then the Apostle John would have been a very old man. (He is thought to have died about A.D. 98–100, during the reign of the Roman Emperor Trajan.) A number of scholars who accept the later date think that the book was occasioned by the persecution of Christians during the reign of Emperor Domitian, when under the threat of martyrdom, many are thought to have deserted the faith.

The writer aims to provide encouragement during these dark days, which brought anguish to Christians. He tells them that, although they will experience terrible testing, they should take heart because their trials are known to God, who will eventually triumph over his enemies. The book includes a warning to the wavering and those of little faith and a clear statement of the glory to come for true believers, intended to deepen their fidelity and feeling of security.

The work of Jesus is portrayed as both past and future. He came once to earth for the redemption of man. In the future he will come again to take part in the judgment of man and the renovation of the world with rewards to the faithful and vengeance upon their enemies. The concepts of the Second Coming of Christ, of immortality, and of redemption and restoration to God for those who hold to Christ in faith are elaborated throughout the book.

The author uses much esoteric language, evidently in order to reveal certain ideas to one group of readers, while concealing them from others, especially from those in sympathy with the dark forces vividly portrayed in the book. Part of the symbolism is taken directly or indirectly from the Old Testament books Ezekiel (see p. 69) and Daniel (see p. 72). The presentation is in the following order: (1) prologue; (2) messages to specific churches; (3) a series of visions; and (4) epilogue.

Prologue (1:1–19). The author begins, as noted above, with the statement that his revelation has come to him from an angel of the Lord. He says that they are blessed who read and hear this prophecy. Addressing himself specifically to "the seven churches which are in Asia," he calls himself their brother and "companion in tribulation," and he says that he received the revelation while on the island of Patmos (where he may have been in prison or banishment). He heard

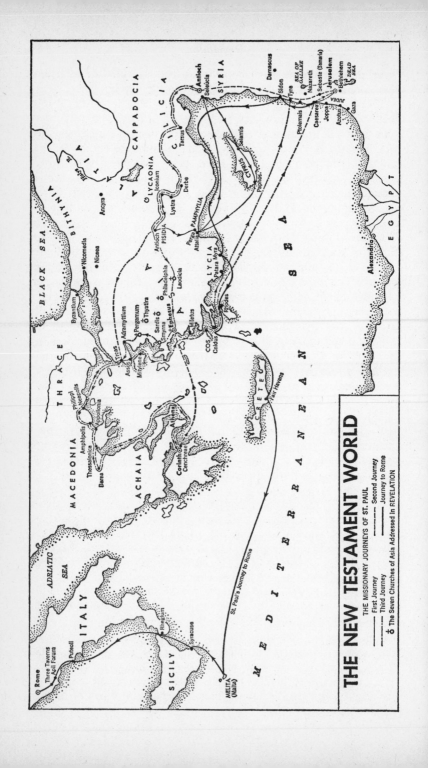

THE NEW TESTAMENT WORLD

THE MISSIONARY JOURNEYS OF ST. PAUL

First Journey
Second Journey
Third Journey
Journey to Rome
ᵭ The Seven Churches of Asia Addressed in REVELATION

a great voice, as of a trumpet,
Saying, I am Alpha and Omega, the first and the last: . . .
Write the things which thou hast seen, and the things which **are,**
and the things which shall be hereafter . . . (1:10–11,19.)

Messages to the Seven Churches (1:20–3:22). John addresses
separately the churches of Ephesus, Smyrna, Pergamos, Thyatira,
Sardis, Philadelphia, and Laodicea, praising their strong points, rebuking their weaknesses, and exhorting them to continue in the faith.

Visions (4:1–22:5). These majestic and dramatic visions have
been variously interpreted. Some hold that they refer to definite
historical events; some, that they describe continuous processes of
world history through which the forces of good and evil struggle;
some, that they are prophecies of Christ's Second Coming. These
approaches are not mutually exclusive; it is possible that the author
intended to combine them. In these visions frequent mention is
made of symbolical numbers: three, four, seven, and twelve.

The visions are arranged in the following sequences: (*a*) a vision
of the throne of God and the adoration of the Lamb (Chapters
4–5); (*b*) a vision of the book with seven seals, each of which
when opened reveals another vision (6:1–8:6); (*c*) a vision of the
seven trumpets, each of which when sounded reveals another vision
(Chapters 8–11); (*d*) visions of the woman and her enemies, the
deadly beasts (Chapters 12–13); (*e*) visions of the enthroned
Lamb and the angels of judgment (Chapter 14); (*f*) visions of
the seven vials of wrath, each of which produces a plague (Chapters
15–16); and (*g*) a vision of the final triumph of the forces of
God (17:1–22:5). The final vision is described in shining words,
which have inspired many artists, writers, and composers.

And I saw a new heaven and a new earth: for the first heaven and
the first earth were passed away; and there was no more sea.
And I John saw the holy city, new Jerusalem, coming down from God
out of heaven, prepared as a bride adorned for her husband.
And I heard a great voice out of heaven saying, Behold the tabernacle
of God is with men, and he will dwell with them, and they shall be
his people, and God himself shall be with them, and be their God.
And God shall wipe away all tears from their eyes; and there shall
be no more death, neither sorrow, nor crying, neither shall there be
any more pain: for the former things are passed away. (21:1–4.)

Epilogue (22:6–21). The author concludes with an assurance that
his sayings are true, that he has seen and heard the things that he
describes, and that the victorious Christ has promised to return:
"He which testifieth these things saith, Surely I come quickly.
Amen. Even so, come, Lord Jesus" (22:20).

NOTES ON THE APOCRYPHA

The precise meaning of the term Apocrypha is a matter of debate. It has at various times been defined as works that are "hidden," "in dispute," "esoteric," "secret," and "mysterious." (The word comes from the Greek *apo,* from + *kryptein,* to hide.) In general Protestant usage, the Apocryphal books of the Old Testament alone are called the Apocrypha. They were usually included in Latin and Greek translations of the Bible but were omitted from the Hebrew canon and, later, from the Protestant versions. They are now sometimes appended to writings considered authoritative; sometimes printed between the Old and the New Testament; and sometimes separately published. For example, the scholars who produced the Revised Standard Version published the Apocrypha in 1957 as an independent text. The Roman Catholic Bible includes in its canon some books that the Protestant Bible places in the Apocrypha.

The Old Testament Apocryphal books consist of both those books that are complete in themselves and those that are additions to earlier Biblical books. Study of this Apocrypha is important to scholars and others because it throws light on the history and thought of the Jewish people during the years between writings of the Old Testament and those of the New. The books are all thought to have been written between about 200 B.C. and A.D. 100.

One grouping of these books is: *History*—I and II Maccabees and I Esdras; *Reflection*—the Wisdom of Solomon and Ecclesiasticus (or the Wisdom of Jesus the Son of Sirach); *Legends*—Tobit, Judith, the Rest of Esther, the Song of the Three Children, Susanna, and Bel and the Dragon; *Prophecy*—Baruch, including the Epistle of Jeremiah (sometimes printed separately) and II Esdras; *Prayer*—the Prayer of Manasses.

The New Testament Apocryphal books have had less general attention and are considered less authentic than those of the Old. They also consist of writings of a different nature, being largely amplifications of accounts of the life of Jesus and the early Christian Church, including gospels, acts, epistles, and prophecy. One classification of these works is: *Gospels*—the Gospel According to the Hebrews, the Gospel According to the Egyptians, the Gospel According to Peter, the Protevangelium of James, the Gospel of Thomas, and others; *Acts*—the Acts of Paul, the Acts of Thecla, and numerous others; *Epistles*—the Epistle of Barnabas, the Epistles of Clement, the Shepherd of Hermas, the Teaching of the Twelve Apostles, and others; *Apocalypses*—the Apocalypse of James, the Apocalypse of Paul, the Apocalypse of Peter, and others.

SOME VERSIONS OF THE
BIBLE IN ENGLISH

The King James Version, as it is known in the United States, or the Authorized Version, as it is called in Britain, is the translation usually quoted in this book. First published in 1611, it became the main Bible of the English-speaking world. Forty-seven scholars were appointed to prepare it, following a conference called by James I of England in 1604 to hear complaints about then existing translations. These scholars consulted a number of prior versions, but it is generally agreed that the one of William Tyndale (see below) pervaded their work. The King James Version, called "the noblest monument of English prose," had an immeasurable influence on later English writing, speech, and general culture.

The Revised Standard Version (RSV), occasionally quoted in this book, is a revision in the King James tradition but one that takes account of recent knowledge of Hebrew and Greek texts, as well as of present English usage. More directly, it is a revision of the 1901 American Standard Version (see p. 175). It was the work of the Standard Bible Committee, appointed in 1929 by the International Council of Religious Education and continued after 1950 by the National Council of Churches of Christ in the U.S.A. The RSV New Testament was first published in 1946; the Old Testament and the complete Bible appeared in 1952.

Other significant versions of the Bible in English, described briefly below, are: the Wycliffe Bible, the Tyndale Bible, the Coverdale Bible, the Great Bible, the Geneva Bible, the Bishops' Bible, the Rheims-Douay Bible and its revisions, the Revised Version and the American Standard Version, the New English Bible, and the Hebrew Scriptures and their revisions.

John Wycliffe, aided by Nicholas of Hereford and John Purvey, prepared the first version of the Bible in English, which appeared between 1382 and 1388. This was a translation, not from the Greek and Hebrew texts but from the Latin Vulgate. Since printing had not yet been invented, it appeared only in manuscript form.

More than a century later William Tyndale produced an English version of the Scriptures by translating from the Hebrew and Greek texts. Printing of the New Testament was begun in Cologne in 1525. Portions of the Old Testament (the Pentateuch and Jonah) were published in 1527. Tyndale was burned at the stake as a heretic in 1536 without completing his Old Testament version, but after his death (his last words were "Lord, open the King of England's eyes"), translations thought to have been made by him of Joshua through Chronicles were published. The work of Tyndale occupies a high place in Biblical scholarship because it became the basis of later English versions, especially, as noted above, the King James Version and particularly the New Testament of the King James.

In 1535 Miles Coverdale published the first complete Bible printed in English; it was based upon German and Latin translations and upon Tyndale's work. Coverdale was a gifted writer, and many of his passages were incorporated in the King James Version. Thomas Matthew (probably a pseudonym for John Rogers) brought out another complete Bible in 1537, based largely upon Tyndale's. Both the Coverdale and the Matthew Bible were claimed to have been licensed by Henry VIII; there is some doubt as to whether the former actually was licensed.

A "Great Bible," so named because of its size, appeared in 1539, prepared under the direction of Coverdale, at the request of Thomas Cromwell, then Henry VIII's vicar general. As the first English authorized Bible, it was used throughout the country.

During the reign of Mary Tudor, Protestant reformers who had taken refuge in Geneva prepared a new translation of the Bible, which was the first one divided into numbered verses. The New Testament translation was based largely upon Tyndale's work, and the Old upon a careful revision of the Great Bible translation from Hebrew and Latin texts. The New Testament was published in 1557 and the complete Bible in 1560.

A revision of the Great Bible was prepared under state auspices during the reign of Elizabeth I. Known as the Bishops' Bible because a number of the revisers held that rank, it was published in 1568. Elizabeth's religious policy was in general one of toleration; hence both the Geneva Bible and the Bishops' Bible were widely used until they were supplanted by the King James.

Meanwhile, Roman Catholic scholars who migrated to the Continent as refugees from English Protestant dominance published an English version (translated from the Latin Vulgate) of the New Testament, at Rheims in 1582, and of the Old Testament, at Douai in 1609–10. The Rheims-Douai text was revised in 1749–50 by Bishop Richard Challoner of London. This revision was for many years the most widely used among American Roman Catholics. However, in 1941 the Confraternity of Christian Doctrine, through its Episcopal Committee, brought out a revised translation of the New Testament. Since that date portions of the Old Testament of the Confraternity Edition have been published from time to time and others are in preparation. In England Ronald Knox prepared an authorized new translation published in 1944–1950. A Catholic edition of the Revised Standard Version, with a few changes requested by Catholic scholars and assented to by the Protestant translators, was published in 1966, with the approval of Archbishop Gordon Gray of Scotland. The same year Cardinal Richard Cushing of Boston approved publication of the complete RSV Bible, with a number of Catholic preferences printed in footnotes only.

The King James Version remained in use among American and English Protestants with no official revisions until the late nineteenth century, when discoveries in linguistics, archeology, and related fields made possible more accurate translation. The English Revised Version was originated in 1870 by the Convocation of Canterbury of the Anglican Church and prepared by a group of scholars, including representatives from other denominations. It was published in 1881–85 with the note that it was "the version set forth A.D. 1611 compared with the most ancient authorities and revised. . . ." It included a number of revisions for accuracy and clarity and printed the text not in verse form but in prose paragraphs and poetry lines. The American Standard Version, published in 1901, was a variant of the English Revised Version, prepared by United States scholars who had co-operated in the work of the British group but thought further changes desirable for American readers.

The New English Bible, a translation directly from the earliest known Greek and Hebrew texts into contemporary idiom, is the work of a Joint Committee on the New Translation of the Bible, made up of scholars from the leading Protestant denominations in the British Isles. The New Testament was published in 1961; the Old Testament and the Apocrypha are in progress.

The Hebrew Scriptures have been revised by Jewish scholars at various times during the past two centuries.* The first complete translation into English was made by Abraham Benisch and published in England, 1851–56. In the United States Isaac Leeser published a translation in 1853 which was widely used. These versions were followed by one published by the Jewish Publication Society of America in 1917 after twenty-five years of preparation by a committee of scholars. In 1961 the Jewish Publication Society announced that work had begun on another version, and the translation of the Pentateuch in this version was published early in 1963.

---

* At an early date these Scriptures were divided into 24 books, classified in three groups: (1) *The Law,* or Torah (Genesis, Exodus, Leviticus, Numbers, Deuteronomy); (2) *The Prophets* in two sections—·Earlier Prophets (Joshua, Judges, Samuel, Kings) and Latter Prophets (Isaiah, Jeremiah, Ezekiel)—and the Twelve (so-called minor prophets grouped in one book); and (3) the Writings, comprising 11 books (Psalms, Proverbs, Job, the Song of Songs, Ruth, Lamentations, Ecclesiastes, Esther, Daniel, Ezra [including also Nehemiah], and one book of Chronicles). In the sixteenth century Samuel, Kings, Ezra-Nehemiah, and Chronicles were subdivided, making a total of 28 books.

A CHRONOLOGY

The following list of dates is provided as an aid to the study and understanding of the Bible. It refers to *events* prior to and during the period when the Bible was written and compiled. For dates of the composition and arrangement of each book of the Bible, see the chapter on that book.

The main sources for this chronology are the dates and related information appearing in *The Interpreter's Bible*, a most comprehensive reference work in twelve volumes (New York and Nashville, Abingdon Press, 1952–1957). Other works consulted are Harold H. Watts, *The Modern Reader's Guide to the Bible* (rev. ed.; New York: Harper and Brothers, 1959); Stewart C. Easton, *The Heritage of the Ancient World* (rev. ed.; New York: Rinehart and Co., 1960); and Kathleen Kenyon, *Archaeology of the Holy Land* (New York: Frederick A. Praeger, Inc., 1960).

Authorities differ with respect to a number of important dates. In some instances all that can be done, even by scholars, is to give approximations. For example, the birth of Jesus is placed between 7 B.C. and A.D. 6. The date selected below, before the spring of 4 B.C., is that given by *The Interpreter's Bible*.

Early History	B.C. Dates
Beginning of Hebrew History	c. 1800
Abraham	Prior to 16th century
Migration into Egypt	16th century
Enslavement in Egypt	To c. 1300
Exodus from Egypt under Moses	After 1300
Entry into Palestine (Canaan) and conquest under Joshua	After 1250
Period of the Judges	c. 1300–1030
United Kingdom	
Saul	c. 1030–1002
David	1002–962
Solomon	962–922
Temple Built	959–952

Divided Kingdom

Judah (Southern Kingdom)		Israel (Northern Kingdom)	
Rehoboam	922–915	Jeroboam I	922–901
Abijam	915–913	Nadab	901–900
Asa	913–873	Baasha	900–877
Jehoshaphat	873–849	Elah	877–876
Jehoram	849–842	Zimri	876
Ahaziah	842	Omri	876–869
Athaliah (queen)	842–837	Ahab	869–850
Jehoash (Joash)	837–800	Ahaziah	850–849

176

Divided Kingdom (Continued)   *B.C. Dates*

(Judah Southern Kingdom)	*Israel (Northern Kingdom)*
Amaziah 800–783	Joram 849–842
Azariah (Uzziah) .. 783–742	Jehu 842–815
Jotham 750–735	Jehoahaz 815–801
Ahaz 735–715	Joash 801–786
	Jeroboam II 786–746
	Zechariah 746–745
	Shallum 745
	Menahem 745–738
	Pekahiah 738–737
	Pekah 737–732
	Hoshea 732–724
	End of Northern Kingdom (conquered by Assyria) .... 722 or 721

Judah (Continued)

Hezekiah 715–687

Manasseh 687–642

Amon 642–640

Josiah 640–609
     (Deuteronomic Reform, 622)

Jehoahaz (taken captive by Egypt after three months' reign) 609

Jehoiakim (enthroned by Egypt) 609–598

Jerusalem captured by Babylon; Jehoiachin (son of Jehoiakim) taken to Babylon as captive with many other Jews after three months' reign ....*c.* 598

Zedekiah (enthroned by Babylon) 598–587

Jerusalem destroyed; many more Jews deported to Babylon . 588

Zedekiah deposed ....*c.* 587

End of Southern Kingdom; third deportation to Babylon ..*c.* 583

Exile and Return (Babylonian and Persian Rule)

Jehoiachin released by Babylon 562

Cyrus, king of Persia, conquers Babylon ....*c.* 538

Group of exiles under Sheshbazzar returns to Jerusalem ...*c.* 538

Rebuilding of the Temple 520–516

Return of exiles under Ezra ....*c.* 458

Nehemiah authorized to rebuild walls of Jerusalem ....*c.* 445–433

Hellenistic Rule and Maccabean Revolt

Alexander the Great conquers Palestine 331

Death of Alexander and division of his empire 323

Rule of Palestine from Egypt by Ptolemies 323–198

Conquest of Palestine by Syria 198

Rule from Syria by Seleucids 198–164

Revolt of Jews led by Judas Maccabaeus 166–160

Hellenistic Rule and Maccabean Revolt (Continued)   *B.C. Dates*

Political independence won by rebels under Simon
    Maccabaeus   142
Rule of John Hyrcanus, son of Simon   134–104
Period of internal conflicts   104–63

Roman Rule

Conquest of Jerusalem by Pompey; beginning of Roman
    rule   63
Herod the Great (nominated king by Rome, 40 B.C.)
    begins to rule   37
Birth of Jesus ....Before spring of 4 B.C.

A.D. Dates

Death of Herod; division of kingdom into three parts;
    Roman Judea (Palestine) ruled by Roman procurators .   6
Pilate, procurator   26–36
Baptism of Jesus ....*c.*   28–29
Crucifixion of Jesus ....*c.*   30–33
Conversion of Paul ....*c.*   34–40
Missionary journeys of Paul ....*c.*   39–58
Paul in Rome ....*c.*   58–60
Christians persecuted by Roman Emperor Nero; Peter and
    Paul believed to have been martyred ....*c.*   64
Revolt of Jews against Rome   66
Fall of Jerusalem to Roman Emperor Titus   70
Renewed and large-scale persecution of Christians under
    Roman Emperor Domitian ....*c.*   93

GLOSSARY

This Glossary defines selected terms deemed essential to an under-standing of Biblical writing. It also includes a few terms that are outgrowths of use of the Bible in the later development of religious bodies. Both standard Bible dictionaries and modern Biblical reference works have been consulted for determining phraseology.

Adventist: a believer, or a member of a religious body which believes, in the imminent Second Coming of Christ to earth.

Allegory: the extended description of one thing under the form of another.

Anoint: to apply oil to a person for consecration or healing.

Apocalyptic: pertaining to or in the nature of a revelation; referring to a belief in the struggle between the forces of God and evil, which will eventually result in the triumph of God and the establishment of his kingdom forever.

Apocrypha: a group of books excluded from the Bible as not sufficiently authoritative, yet considered worthy of study for their religious and historical information. Sometimes printed between the Old and New Testaments.

Apostle: in the New Testament one of the twelve disciples appointed by Jesus to carry out his mission in preaching, teaching, and healing. After the Crucifixion, Matthias was chosen to take the place of Judas. Later Paul, Barnabas, and other leaders of the early Church were considered among the apostles.

Ark of the Covenant: the cask containing the stone tables on which the Ten Commandments were engraved. It was carried in front of the Hebrews during the Exodus and eventually placed in the most sacred part of the Temple.

Atonement: in Christian theology, Christ's redemption of man and reconciliation of man to God.

Baalism: worship of local nature gods; idolatry.

Baptism: the application of water to a person as a symbol of cleansing from sin and admission to a corporate fellowship, especially the Christian Church.

Bible: *Jewish*—a collection of 28 books which are the Scriptures of Judaism, corresponding to the Protestant and Roman Catholic Old Testament; *Protestant*—a collection of 66 books, the Old Testament with 39 and the New Testament with 27; *Roman Catholic*—a collection of 73 books, the Old Testament with 46 (including some placed by Protestants in the Apocrypha) and the New Testament with 27.

Canon: the collection of books admitted to the Bible by standards of authenticity and authority; hence considered by religious bodies to contain the word of God, the source of faith, and the rule for life.

Christ: the Messiah, or "anointed one," expected by the Jews; in Christian theology Jesus is believed to be the fulfillment of this prophecy and also the Son of God and Son of man. The Second Person (Logos) of the Trinity. The Redeemer and Savior of mankind.

Christian: name for the followers of Jesus Christ, first used in Antioch and recorded in Acts; it is derived from the Greek word for Messiah, Christos.

Church: the universal community of Christian believers; it is organized as individual churches, first recorded in Acts as groups that met for prayer, teaching, fellowship, and breaking bread in commemoration of Christ.

Conversion: the act of accepting a religion or of changing from one religion to another; it may be instantaneous or gradual.

Covenant: an expression of God's love and grace toward man. In the Old Testament it is regarded as a sacred contract and bond between man and man or between man and God, especially God's promise to Israel first given through Abraham; in the New Testament it is used to express God's relation to man in terms of communion in Christ and the indwelling of the Holy Spirit.

Decalogue (Ten Commandments): a summary of God's requirements for man as given to Moses on Mount Sinai.

Disciples: in the New Testament all followers of Jesus; in later usage sometimes synonymous with apostles.

Ecumenical: world-wide, referring to the movement toward unity of Christian churches.

Epistle: in the New Testament one of 21 books in the form of apostolic letters, containing in a broad sense commentaries on the gospel of Christ.

Eschatology: doctrine regarding last things, or the ultimate condition of man, the world, and history in relation to God.

Esoteric: intended for and understood only by an inner group; often referring to language used to reveal a message to this group, while concealing it from outsiders.

Eucharist. *See* Lord's Supper.

Fall of man: in Christian terminology mankind's estrangement from God through sin, occasioned or symbolized by Adam's and Eve's disobedience.

God: the object of true worship; the fundamental subject and emphasis of the Bible, which refers to him as One, Most High, Almighty, Creator, Holy One, Father, and Redeemer. The revelation of his nature is given in such Biblical terms as Grace, Mercy, Justice, Holiness, Love. In the New Testament he is revealed through the life, death, and resurrection of Jesus Christ and the activity of the Holy Spirit. The First Person of the Trinity.

Gospel: "good news"; the broad New Testament term for the message of Jesus Christ. Also one of the first four books of the New Testament, which tell of Christ's life, death, and resurrection. Mark's Gospel is the briefest and was probably the first. Matthew and Luke give more lengthy accounts but in much the same sequence as Mark; hence these three are called synoptic Gospels. John's Gospel differs in being more philosophical and making more use of spiritual concepts.

Grace: God's freely given redemptive love for man; in the New Testament regarded as made manifest in Jesus Christ.

Healing, Gifts of: in the Bible, spiritual powers, over disease and infirmity regarded as given by God to prophets, to Jesus, and to the apostles.

Herod: the name of a dynasty established by Rome which ruled Palestine from about 37 B.C. to A.D. 70.

Holy Spirit (Holy Ghost): a term applied in the Old Testament to some of the actions of God, revealed in his Creation, inspiration of rulers and prophets, and the covenant relationship with Israel; in the New Testament, applied to the inner, personal workings of God in the Church and in the human heart, coming from the incarnation, death, and resurrection of Jesus Christ. The Third Person of the Trinity.

Idol: a false god; an image or other object worshipped as a god.

Immanent: indwelling; referring to the presence within the world and man of God's power and spirit.

Incarnation: in Christian theology, God's becoming man in Jesus Christ.

Israel: the name (meaning "contender with God") given to Jacob after his wrestling with an angel; hence the name of his descendants, the Hebrews (Jews) and their nation. After the division of the kingdom, about 922 B.C., Israel was the name of the Northern Kingdom. A new republic of Israel in Palestine was established in 1948.

Jehovah. *See* Yahweh.

Jesus Christ. *See* Christ.

Judaism: the religion of the Jewish people, recorded and interpreted in the Old Testament.

Justification: being brought into a right relationship with God, in Christian theology, being saved through faith in Jesus Christ as Lord and Savior.

Kingdom of God: God's reign. In the Old Testament it was prophesied by apocalyptic writers; in the New Testament it was regarded both as manifested in Christ and as still to come, in the final triumph of God.

Law: divine commandments and rules formulated by Moses and his successors, recorded and interpreted in the Bible. The Torah. The term is also used to designate the first five books of the Bible, the Pentateuch.

Logos: in Christian theology, Christ as the Word, eternally generated from the substance of God the Father. The Second Person of the Trinity.

Lord's Supper: the sacrament of the Eucharist; the common partaking of consecrated bread and wine, as begun by Christ at the Last Supper with his disciples, signifying communion with him.

Manna: food miraculously provided the Hebrews wandering in the wilderness.

Messiah: a term of Hebrew origin, meaning "the anointed one." In the Bible regarded at (1) the human hero, the ideal deliverer, and king expected by the Jews; (2) in Christian theology, the fulfillment of this expectation in Jesus Christ, the Son of God and Son of man, the Savior of the world. *See also* Christ.

Miracle: in the Bible, an event as the work of God, either independent of, or contrary to, the known course or laws of the natural world.

Mysticism: a term used to describe direct knowledge of God, or truth, through spiritual insight, independent of or transcending reason.

Oracle: in the Bible, an utterance of God through priest or prophet, usually the latter, concerning issues or events.

Parable: a short narrative about possible occurrences, told to convey a spiritual or moral teaching.

Passover: a yearly feast of the Jews, celebrating their being spared in Egypt from God's smiting of the first-born and their subsequent escape from Egypt.

Pentecost: an annual Jewish feast of the harvest; it is celebrated by Christians as the day of the Holy Spirit's descent on the disciples.

Pharisee: a member of a Jewish sect noted for strict adherence to rites and to codes of the law, both written and oral.

Priest: a religious leader of the people; in the Old Testament, a member of a hereditary group, descended from Aaron, who had charge of worship and sacred rites and who instructed the people in divine rules and commandments.

Prophet: in the Old Testament, a spokesman for God; a relatively independent leader of the Jews who proclaimed religious ideals, expressed ethical concern, and interpreted historical events in terms of God's will, often criticizing the social order and advocating justice and reform on behalf of its victims.

Publican: a tax collector of ancient Rome and its dependencies.

Purim: an annual feast of the Jews commemorating their deliverance, as recounted in the book of Esther, from the plot of Haman (a favorite of King Xerxes of Persia) to destroy them.

Redemption: in theology, God's deliverance of man; in the New Testament, deliverance from sin and death into a new life, through the atonement of Jesus Christ.

Resurrection: rising from the dead. In Christian theology, the rising of Christ from the dead, evidenced by his empty tomb and his appearances to his disciples after the Crucifixion; hence the rising from the dead of all believers in him.

Revelation: the communication of spiritual truth by removal of barriers, especially through divine action.

Ritual: the form prescribed for conducting a religious ceremony.

Sacrament: a religious ceremony observed by Christians and regarded as having been instituted by Christ. The number varies with different denominations.

Sadducee: a member of a Jewish sect that opposed the Pharisees in observing only the written law (Torah) and denying the resurrection of the dead. Sadducees held many important religious offices in the time of Jesus.

Saint: in the New Testament, a term sometimes applied to any faithful member of the early Church; in later usage, an exceptionally holy person canonized by a religious body.

Salvation: a state of spiritual health; the rescue of a person (by God's power) from sin and other evils so that he may attain blessedness; in Christian theology, it is accomplished through Jesus Christ.

Sanhedrin: the supreme council and chief court of the Jews, presided over by the high priest.

Scribe: a member of a Jewish professional class who copied, taught, and interpreted the law.

Synagogue: the local organization of, and place for, worship among the Jews.

Synoptic Gospels. *See* Gospels.

Tabernacle: the portable sanctuary established by Moses under God's direction, which the Hebrews carried in the wilderness and in Canaan until it was replaced by the Temple; it housed the Ark of the Covenant.

Temple: the center of Jewish worship in Jerusalem, first built by Solomon; in design it was an enlargement of the Tabernacle.

Ten Commandments. *See* Decalogue.

Testament: a term in relation to the Bible meaning not "will" but "covenant."

Torah. *See* Law.

Transcendent: a term applied to God meaning that he is prior to, above, and supreme in relation to the universe that he created and rules.

Trinity: in Christian theology, the union in one divine nature of God the Father, God the Son, and God the Holy Spirit; it is regarded as a revelation that cannot be adequately explained in words.

Unitarianism: a doctrine denying the Trinity; the teaching that God is one Person and hence that Jesus was wholly human.

Yahweh: the Hebrew name for God from the time of Moses, also translated Jehovah.

Zion: originally a hill in Jerusalem on which the Temple and the royal palace were built; the term was later extended to mean the people of Israel; the church of God; the heavenly city.

INDEX

This selective index consists of a listing of Biblical books, principal characters, and certain events and places. The page references are usually to the most comprehensive and significant mentions of these topics. The frequent cross references in the text and the information in the Appendix (pp. 172–82) should also aid the user of this book.